Serving Two Masters?

Serving Two Masters?

Catholic School Governors at Work

Christopher Storr

GRACEWING

First published in 2011

Gracewing
2 Southern Avenue, Leominster
Herefordshire HR6 0QF

UK ISBN 978 085244 742 0

Typeset by
Action Publishing Technology Ltd, Gloucester GL1 5SR

Contents

Acknowledgements

Many people have been generous with their time, expertise and encouragement in the creation of this book. First, Paul Black and Richard Pring, who inspired me to write it, along with Gerald Grace, who has been steadfast in his support throughout the long process of its construction.

Several members of staff of the Institute of Education have been helpful throughout the process of writing, principally David Halpin, and also Peter Earley, Tony Green, Jane Hurry, Alex Moore, Stephen Pickles and Fiona Steele (now at the University of Bristol).

The staff of the Durham County Archives, The Lancashire Record Office, the London Metropolitan Archive and The National Archive, Paul Barber, Director of Schools for the Westminster Archdiocese, Lynn Birchard, Clerk to the Governors of St Gregory's School, Tunbridge Wells, and Greg Pope, Deputy Director of The Catholic Education Service have put me right on a number of significant details with kindness and exemplary efficiency.

As will be clear from the text, the input of many governors and diocesan directors provided the essential building blocks from which the edifice was constructed. I am especially indebted to them for tolerating with good grace the impertinent questions I put to them. But it was a delight to me, at any rate, to have the opportunity to spend time with them in reflecting on issues of concern. It was a particular pleasure to be able to give a voice to the diocesan directors – the unsung heroes of Catholic education – whose enormous contribution to education in general in this country is so often overlooked or taken for granted.

Finally, I thank my daughter, Ann Eve, for her expert proof-reading and helpful comments on the draft text, which have forced me to elucidate many obscurities, and, I hope, thereby make the book more accessible; and my wife, Jo, for her support and great practical help. I take responsibility for any errors in the text.

Introduction

During the last twenty years, a good deal of attention has been paid by official bodies and researchers to the work of school governors, but almost none of this has extended to those who govern Catholic schools. This is surprising, as the schools are popular with parents, and, by the state's criteria, limited though these may be, successful, appearing at or near the top of local authority (LA) league tables, except in those authorities where selective secondary schools continue to exist.

This book is important because it reports the results of a survey of almost one hundred governors of Catholic maintained primary and secondary schools located in four English Catholic dioceses, and publishes previously unknown data about them. Eight of these governors were subsequently interviewed. Further interviews were carried out with six officers working at diocesan level. These officials are, again, largely unknown to researchers, yet their knowledge of the education system and experience are formidable.

The interviews examined relationships between governors and the trustees of the schools (another unknown partner), and explored the tensions that might arise when governors have to balance their obligations to the Catholic Church with those they have to the state. They also examined the extent to which the schools can now be perceived, religious education and worship apart, to be different from other schools.

In summary, the book shows that changes in social attitudes in the developed world, and a decline in religious observance, have combined to produce a situation where, although there is a manifest continuity of philosophy and practice in relation to Catholic schools overall, the details are diffuse and ill-defined. What has emerged is an education system which is locally configured but not church dominated. Since this has arisen, as it were, by accident, it presents challenges to both governing bodies and bishops, if conflicts of the type I review, involving the trustees of the Archdiocese of Westminster and the governors of Cardinal Vaughan school, and the trustees of the Archdiocese of Southwark and the governors of St Osmund's school, Barnes, are to be avoided in the future.

The work is in three parts. The first places contemporary Catholic governing bodies in a historical perspective, tracing their emergence, in penal times, up to 2011. The second offers an examination of the literature relevant to the study, both that which pertains to Catholic schools, as seen through the eyes of the Catholic Church, centrally in Rome, and locally by the Catholic Bishops' Conference of England and Wales; and that which emanates from a number of social theorists who describe changes in contemporary society that have affected the way Western Europeans think and construct their lives. The third gives a detailed account of the governors, shows them at work, and provides fascinating commentaries on the issues by diocesan schools commissioners.

Those who are familiar with Catholic education in England will know that there are three types of people in charge of diocesan education offices: lay women, lay men, and priests.

In order to ensure confidentiality, and because the number of female diocesan directors is small, I refer to all diocesan directors in this book as 'he'. One of those I interviewed was, in fact, a deputy director, but I do not reveal in the text which one this was, because not all dioceses have deputy directors.

For the same reason, I do not reveal whether any of the dioceses are metropolitan, so I do not differentiate between archbishops and bishops in the text, referring to them all as bishops.

It was necessary to conceal the names of the schools and dioceses from which I collected data. None of the schools whose governors gave evidence to me is given its real name. For dioceses, I chose, at random, names from the Great Western Railway's (1925) wonderful book entitled simply *Abbeys*: Athelney, Glastonbury, Lacock, Much Wenlock, Tewkesbury, and Tintern.

Abbreviations

AEN   Alternative Educational Needs
ACC   Associated Catholic Charities of the Metropolis
DES   Department of Education and Science
DESk   Department for Education and Skills
DFE   Department for Education
DFEE   Department for Education and Employment
GCE   General Certificate of Education
GCSE   General Certificate of Secondary Education
HMI   Her/His Majesty's Inspector
ILEA   Inner London Education Authority
LA   Local Authority
LEA   Local Education Authority
NCC   National Curriculum Council
NFER   National Foundation for Educational Research
RE   Religious Education
SATs   Standard Attainment Tests

Chapter 1

How we Came to be Where we Are

Foreword

The purpose of this chapter is to put the work of Catholic maintained schools and their governing bodies into a firm historical context. It describes very briefly their emergence from the obscurity of the penal times, and shows that, at the beginning of the nineteenth century, the Catholic bishops were willing to see Catholic children educated alongside those of other denominations, provided there was no attempt at proselytization on the part of the latter. When it became clear that this was a forlorn hope, the policy of providing a place in a Catholic school for every Catholic child soon developed. This has been pursued ever since.

The review then traces the development of school managing and governing bodies in general, and Catholic ones in particular, through the long period of the twentieth century when they were dominated by local education authorities (LEAs), and the revolution that began with the Education Act 1980.[1] The account is set in the context of the Second Vatican Council (1962–5), which had by then created an even more far-reaching revolution in the Catholic Church. The Council continues to this day to influence profoundly how Catholics think of themselves, and their roles in the Church and in society at large, and, as a consequence, the developing relationship between lay governors and the clergy at all levels.

Two principal themes emerge. The first is that, from 1833 to 2010, there has been continuous tension between the Catholic

[1] LEA is the acronym for local education authority, a local government organization with the responsibility for providing, amongst other things, a network of publicly funded schools in its area. LEAs were first established by the 1902 Education Act and were superseded by similar bodies, but with wider powers, under the terms of the Children Act 2004.

Church in England and successive governments about the provision of Catholic maintained schools, and how they are run, and the nature and purpose of education. The reason for this has remained constant: the fear throughout has been that the state would interfere too much in what went on in Catholic schools, thus bringing about an unacceptable degree of secularization. The second theme is that, within the Catholic community itself, there has frequently been disagreement about some of these issues.

As the story unfolds, the opportunity is taken to provide some account of Catholic managers at work. This has been a neglected aspect of educational history.

Introduction

Consider these statements:-

- The clergy should never stop in their exertions where a school is not established till they effect that desirable object.
- The first necessity ... is a sufficient provision of education, adequate to the wants of our poor. It must become universal ... to ... prefer the establishment of good schools to every other work. Indeed, wherever there may seem to be an opening for a new mission, we should prefer the erection of a school, so arranged as to serve temporarily for a chapel, to that of a church without one.[2]
- The managers of Catholic public schools, acting under central orders, alone refused to give me any information or to admit me to their schools.

The first statement is a resolution of the vicars apostolic,[3] passed in 1846, four years before the restoration of the hierarchy,[4] and the second an extract from the proceedings of the first synod of the archbishop and bishops of the province of Westminster held in 1852. They set out, unequivocally, the Church's conviction about the centrality of the provision of schools in its overall work. This conviction remains unchanged. As recently as 1982, the Jesuit priest appointed to establish a new parish in the community being

[2.] Catholic parishes were not restored till 1918. Till then, sub-divisions of dioceses were referred to as missions.

[3.] Vicars Apostolic were Catholic priests given oversight of the Catholic community in Britain during penal times, when the Catholic Church was outlawed.

[4.] The appointment of Catholic bishops to supervise the Church in Britain for the first time since the Reformation.

constructed on the ruins of the former Surrey docks in Bermondsey, south London, told the me he could not discharge his duties without the provision of a school at the earliest opportunity. Thus began a series of negotiations with the former Inner London Education Authority (ILEA) that eventually led to the establishment of St John's Catholic Primary School, Surrey Quays (London Borough of Southwark) arranged, just as envisaged in 1852, to serve temporarily as a chapel until a church could be built.

The third quotation comes from evidence given by Mr J. S. Winder, one of the Assistant Commissioners appointed by the Newcastle Commission (see p. 13), who surveyed schools in Rochdale and Bradford. This affords an early indication of tensions between the Church and the government arising from fundamental differences with regard to matters relating to educational philosophy. Like the first quotation, and as already noted, it describes an issue that runs through the whole of the period from 1833 to the present.

The Beginnings of School Management and Government

Schools, along with other charitable institutions and foundations, emerged in the early Middle Ages. They were guaranteed by small groups of individuals whose duty it was to safeguard the wealth that was necessary to ensure their continued existence. Then, from the middle of the seventeenth century, the growth of banking led to subscriptions and fees becoming the standard means of financing schools, and with this, the need for a new category of person to take responsibility for regulating the use of the resources generated in this way. Thus, we have, from early times, embryonic trustees and managers.

Early Post-Reformation Catholic Schools

The Elizabethan Religious Settlements of 1558–63 made life difficult for Catholic schools in England and Wales, as a result of which they had a shadowy and transitory existence from then until the end of the eighteenth century at least. But Catholic schools for the poor were in existence by 1760. In London they developed from the Embassy chapels of Bavaria, Portugal, Sardinia and Spain. Public chapels were also important, both in London and elsewhere, in developing educational provision for the poor. The

Charitable Society for the Relief of Poor Children, established in 1764, set up a school in Cockpit Alley, Drury Lane, and by 1807, at the latest, it had a committee.[5]

The first Relief Act of 1778 enabled English Catholics to provide for the religious education of their children. The Laudable Association, established in 1796/7, required subscribers to pay one penny a week towards the education of destitute Catholic orphans. In 1811, these two societies merged with a third, the Benevolent Society (whose objective was the apprenticing of Catholic boys), to form the Associated Catholic Charities of the Metropolis (ACC). The new Association set up a General Committee and sub committees for each separate school that dealt with apprenticing out, orphans, fund raising, and finance. The Association secured premises for schools. Schools were also set up for Catholic children outside the umbrella of the ACC: in Westminster, Soho, Southwark and Wapping.[6]

From the start of the nineteenth century the Catholic population of England increased rapidly in size. Bossy puts it, in 1770, at 80,000, and by 1850 at about three quarters of a million.[7] This increase was largely brought about by two factors: Catholic immigration from Ireland, which was already significant by the end of the eighteenth century; and the Industrial Revolution, which led to a general increase in the population of England and Wales. Many Irish settlers made homes in and around ports, particularly Liverpool and London. Favourite areas of settlement for indigenous Catholics were the new industrial areas of south Lancashire, west Yorkshire, Durham and Northumberland, the Midlands and south Wales, many of which had been barren of Catholics since the Reformation. Bossy examines Catholic congregations in four Lancashire towns: Preston, Wigan, Liverpool and Manchester, and calculates a rise from 4,431 in 1767 to about 120,000 in 1851.

Kitching substantially concurs: he quotes the Manchester Catholic population rising from 'scarcely 600' in 1790 to 10,000 in 1804; and that of Liverpool from 6,600 in 1790 to 80,000 by 1838.[8]

Bossy describes the growth of Catholicism in London as not much less rapid than in Lancashire: there were eight or nine chapels in 1800 serving a community of about 10,000 Catholics.[9] By 1851 there were thirty-five catering for about 100,000. Kitching is

---

[5] Murphy, *The Associated Catholic Charities of the Metropolis*, pp. 5–8.
[6] Ibid., pp. 15ff.
[7] Bossy, *The English Catholic Community 1570–1850*, p. 298.
[8] Kitching, *The Catholic Poor Schools 1800–1845*.
[9] Bossy, *The English Catholic Community 1570–1850*.

again in agreement, quoting bishop Poynter's 1814 estimate of 49,800 Catholics in London and a little over 146,000 in 1837.[10]

White provides a useful reminder that Ireland was far from the only source of migration in the nineteenth century.[11] From the very beginning, Catholics were in flight from the French Revolution, and others were to follow in 1830, 1848 and 1870. War and economic pressures at various times led Germans, Italians, Spanish, Hungarians, Poles and Russians to seek refuge in England throughout the period.

In 1816, the ACC claimed to have five schools. In that year it set up a Commission to investigate their management. The Commission was charged with establishing a system of rewards, uniformity of instruction, hours, Holydays, prayers, religious education and exercises, and with examining Lancaster's and Bell's and other similar monitorial systems of providing cheap instruction in religion and the three Rs. It was then asked to produce a system suitable for Catholic schools, and to find some way of checking attendance.[12]

From time to time the ACC expressed concern about the poor attendance of members of school committees at their meetings. Indeed, when abuses occurred at Lincoln's Inn Fields and Moorfields schools, it rebuked the committees, asking them to carry out their duties properly. In 1817 a committee was set up, which included members from each school committee, to examine the actual state of the schools. Teachers were from time to time reprimanded or dismissed for misconduct, and in 1842, Lord Clifford referred to expenses he had incurred in bringing the Lincoln's Inn Fields school up to a standard that would enable it to apply for grant (the ACC's third attempt to secure state funding).[13]

Overall, however, at this time, the provision of schools for Roman Catholics was inadequate, chiefly because of the small numbers of middle-class subscribers, but compounded by the constant influx of miserably poor immigrants from Ireland.

1833: The First State Grants

The 1830s and 1840s were a time of turbulence in England. There were two interlocking causes. The first was economic. At this time,

[10.] Kitching, *The Catholic Poor Schools 1800–1845*, p. 2.
[11.] White, *London in the Nineteenth Century*.
[12.] Murphy, *The Associated Catholic Charities of the Metropolis*, pp. 38–9.
[13.] Ibid., pp. 104ff.

both the Agricultural and Industrial Revolutions were at their height, and brought in their wake the creation of new classes of rural and urban poor. Periodic bad harvests and slumps in trade both at home and abroad, together with the impact of the Corn Laws and the harshness of the Poor Law system, led to repeated outbreaks of rioting, machine breaking and rick burning. The wretched existences of millions are described in the fictional works of Dickens, Disraeli and Mrs Gaskell, as well as in factual accounts such as Engels' *The Condition of the Working Class in England* and Chadwick's *Report of the Commissioners for the Inquiry into the State of Large Towns and Populous Districts* of 1844–45.

The second cause of disturbance was political, and arose from the social distress and economic disorder that have just been outlined. There developed an increasing refusal to accept a situation in which political power was exclusively in the hands of a tiny minority of the wealthy. After 1804, Cobbett's paper, *The Weekly Political Register*, attacked anything savouring of oppression, and from 1821 began to feature the reflections of his *Rural Rides*. When, in 1816, he reduced the price from one shilling and a halfpenny to two pence, his influence became enormous. Behind him, and the philosopher Bentham, were a number of lesser-known agitators: Major John Cartwright, who founded the Hampden Clubs pressing for parliamentary reform; the Spencean Philanthropists, who preached a primitive brand of communism; and dangerous demagogues such as 'Orator' Henry Hunt, Arthur Thistlewood and the Watsons.

The demand for reform increased throughout the 1820s and was reinforced by the French Revolution of 1830, which followed bad harvests in 1828 and 1829.

The Reform Act of 1832 gave only a temporary respite from unrest, as it was soon realized that five out of every six working men were still excluded from the franchise. The late 1830s saw a further slump in home and foreign trade and a series of poor harvests. All this led to the establishment not only of the Chartist movement in 1838, whose programme was political and social reform, but also of the Anti-Corn-Law League, the following year, which pressed for free trade in order to provide cheaper food. Further riots and disturbances continued throughout the country for a number of years.

The urgent task of successive governments was therefore to attempt, by whatever means, to forge a society torn by these class antagonisms into a nation state. Education was seen by some as a way by which the regulation and transformation of the working class might be achieved.

In the very early nineteenth century, however, there was, in England, general indifference to the issue of education for the poorer classes and when, in 1833, the first state grants (£20,000) were approved for voluntary schools, the bill was easily passed in the House of Commons. Administrative structures to ensure that the money was properly spent were almost entirely lacking. It therefore had to be channelled through the two great religious societies that were responsible for schools at the time – the British & Foreign Schools Society (Nonconformist) and the National Society (Church of England). Until the Catholic Poor School Committee was established in 1847, there was no national body with oversight of the development of Catholic schools. The British & Foreign and National Societies, therefore, alone made recommendations as to which groups of citizens had established, and were continuing to maintain, schools which might be eligible for grant.

After the principle of state grant had been approved, interest in the education of the poor started to develop. Growing pressure developed in the House of Commons for 'universal and national education of the whole people'.[14]

The new funding system soon gave rise to difficulty: the British & Foreign Schools Society became dissatisfied with the grant arrangements, because in practice, the National Society gained almost eighty per cent of the available funds. These were difficult times for the Church of England. The repeal of the Test and Corporation Acts in 1828 had ended its monopoly over public appointments, and the Catholic Emancipation Act of the following year had allowed Catholics to enter Parliament. All this meant that the Church could no longer assume that those who ruled the country were its members.

From this time it was under increasing attack from liberals and radicals, and calls for disestablishment began to be heard with greater frequency. After the passing of the Reform Act, the Whigs embarked on a programme to remedy the more obvious abuses and failings manifest in the Established Church.

Perhaps as a reaction, in 1838, the National Society proposed a huge expansion of the Church of England's stake in education, from infant school to university level. This was too much for the Whigs and their Prime Minister, Lord Melbourne, who called on his Home Secretary, Lord John Russell, to attend to the problem.

Russell eventually arrived at two proposals. The first was that

[14.] Smith, *The Life and Work of Sir James Kay-Shuttleworth*, p. 74.

control of the administration of parliamentary grant for schools
should be removed from the Treasury. A special committee of the
Privy Council was established in 1839 (The Committee of Council)
to 'superintend the application of any sums voted by Parliament
for the purpose of promoting Public Education'. Membership of
this new committee was deliberately confined to laymen, in order
to keep church influence at bay: the Lord President of the Council,
the Lord Privy Seal, the Chancellor of the Exchequer, the
Secretary of State for the Home Department, and the Master of the
Mint. In appointing Dr James Kay (later Sir James Kay-
Shuttleworth) as its first Secretary, the Whigs assured him that
'their object was to frustrate the claims of the Church to the
national system of education and to assist the claims of the civil
power to control the education of the country'.[15]

Kay therefore set to work with four main objectives: the provision of much better and more extensive education for the poor;
more assistance by the state; increased state control of secular
education; and the general supervision of schools to be shared with
the laity. Wherever possible, there should be a lay majority on the
committee that had oversight of a school.

Russell's second proposal was the establishment of a single
school on the successful 'Irish system'. In 1831, Grey's government
had established a national state-funded education system for
Ireland which provided for the joint education of Protestant and
Catholic children together in the same school, with both undenom-
inational and separate denominational religious instruction. The
arrangement worked well. In the early days of the century, English
Catholics were not opposed to integration, but neither the National
Society nor the British and Foreign Schools Society would consent
to this in England. So great was the degree of anti-Catholicism and,
in particular, anti-Irish racism, that no such solution was possible in
this England. The government had to accept that a publicly
financed denominational, rather than a national, secular educational system was the only means of making progress. Russell's
modest proposal was, therefore, quickly dropped.

When the new Privy Council Committee made enquiries into the
condition of the schools requiring assistance, it appeared that, in
far too many cases, the various types of school trusteeship, governance and management that had run for so long had lost a sense of
purpose and direction, and were virtually non-existent, corrupt or
incapable. In practice, day-to-day management had passed into the

---

15. Chadwick, *The Victorian Church*, vol. 1, p. 340.

hands of the local vicar or clergyman. This situation could not continue now that state funds were involved, and suitable arrangements had to be made to protect public money. From 1847, the device was therefore adopted by the Committee of Council of requiring schools that wanted grant to be open to inspection, and to incorporate into their trust deeds a set of management clauses prescribed by the Committee that were intended to give due place to the three groups that had an interest in the school: the subscribers, the religious or educational society with which the school was connected, and the Committee of Council itself. Each school was to have a board responsible for its management, with moral and religious education being entrusted to the clergy.

Catholic Elementary Schools Begin to Receive Grant

These clauses were first applied to Church of England schools but were in December 1847 extended by the Committee to Catholic ones. As has already been described, the Catholic community had initially been unable to receive government grant for its schools, but it had entered into a period of intense activity after 1833, establishing day and Sunday schools. From their own resources, Catholics more than doubled day school accommodation (13,000 to 27,000 places) between then and 1845, and, in 1847, the bishops set up the Catholic Poor School Committee to be the national agency that would formally link the Church with the Privy Council Committee. Money was by now desperately needed.

The failure of the potato crop in Ireland in each of 1845, 1846 and 1847 caused the poorest, who could not afford the voyage to America or Canada, to flee to England, Scotland and Wales: crossings could be made for two shillings and sixpence to Liverpool or free (as ballast) to Cardiff. By the spring of 1847, tens of thousands of Irish destitute, many disease-ridden, spread from the ports throughout all three countries, and had to be provided for. Woodham-Smith describes the diaspora.[16] In the first five months of 1847, 300,000 had arrived in Liverpool, a town with a native population of only 250,000. By 1851, about 430,000 Irish Catholics were estimated to have settled in ten urban centres, principally Liverpool and London. Nearly half the worshipping Catholics in England lived in Liverpool and London. English-born Catholics at this time numbered no more than 250,000.

16. Woodham-Smith, *The Great Hunger.*

The Catholic percentage of the population in York rose from 2.7 per cent in 1841 to 7.2 per cent just ten years later. It totalled 3,500 by 1870. The Irish settled in Walmgate, one of the largest areas of slum housing in the city. Britannia Yard, off Walmgate, had sixteen two-roomed houses. In 1851, these were inhabited by 171 people, of whom 154 were Irish.[17]

By the same year, Irish immigrants made up ten per cent of the population of Bradford. These were, again, a largely poverty stricken group. They were received with animosity, and often deep hostility, by the local people, who saw them as a threat to their economic livelihood. Unwanted in the mills, they were forced to resort to the declining trades of hand-weaving and hand-combing. As in York, they were largely confined to an inner-city ghetto where disease was rife. In the 1840s, fifty per cent of infants born in Bradford did not survive their fifth birthday and the average age of death was fifteen.[18]

The funding of schools to provide for the needs of all these children could no longer be left to voluntary sources: public money had to be provided. In any event, there was a belief that the Irish immigrants of this period posed a social and political threat. The social unrest already referred to continued, and there was concern that the activities of Luddites, the Anti-Corn Law League, the Chartists, and the Trades Unions would create a breakdown in social order. The greater fear was that the Irish might combine with the English working classes and seriously threaten the state. The Catholic Church was seen as the only body able to control and educate the Catholic poor. Thus it was that grant aid became available to Catholic schools, for the first time, in 1847.

It was not without a struggle, but after prolonged correspondence with the Poor School Committee, that agreement was eventually reached. The model trust deed provided that the priest, acting under the bishop, had the management and superintendence of religious instruction and could use the school on Sunday for this purpose. The appointment and dismissal of the teacher and other aspects of management were vested in a committee composed of the priest and six other Catholics. Vacancies on the managing body were to be filled by the election of the remaining members, until the bishop directed that elections should be made by subscribers. Subscribers were allocated a number of votes in

[17] Roberts, *Catholic Childhoods: Catholic Elementary Education in York 1850–1914*, pp. 3ff.
[18] Jowitt and Perks, *Destination Bradford. A Century of Immigration.*

proportion to their subscriptions, up to a maximum of six. The priest was the chairman and had a casting vote. Only Catholics could vote, become a member of the committee, or be employed in any capacity. The priest could suspend any teacher or exclude any book on religious grounds, after having laid a written statement to that effect before the committee.

Kay-Shuttleworth's requirement to inspect grant-aided schools again caused controversy amongst Catholics (as it had previously in Church of England and Nonconformist circles). Because of failure to reach early agreement, the first inspector of Catholic schools, T. W. Marshall, was not appointed till the end of 1848. Many Catholic schools at first refused to accept grant because of concerns about state interference. The Privy Council Blue Book of 1856 recorded that of sixty Catholic schools built since 1847, only seven received grant.[19]

One school that was quick to apply for grant was St Anne's in Spicer Street, Spitalfields. Its committee, on receipt of the first grant, issued Rules on 28 September 1849 that prescribed what the curriculum would be; gave the committee power to hire and dismiss masters and mistresses 'who would carry out exactly all decisions of the committee'; forbade the teachers from accepting any children from outside the district without written authority from one of the priests or a member of the committee; prescribed the hours the school would be open; and required that all complaints be communicated to a committee member.[20]

The availability of grant was not an unmixed blessing. Some, for example the Christian Brothers (a Catholic Religious Order dedicated to teaching), would have nothing to do with it because of the fear of government interference. There were other reasons for caution, as shown by Fr Kelly, priest of St Mary & St Michael's, Commercial Road, on the feast of the Epiphany 1861:

> Our Schools cost the Rector much less for their maintenance before the connection with the Committee of Council than since that connection, and therefore it may be asked, of what use and profit is such a connection since it requires such local efforts to obtain and preserve it ... The 'Committee of Council' lays down certain definite conditions which entail very great expense, both as to the character of the School buildings, their tenure and state of repair, and the furnishing of the School Rooms with every requisite for a first-rate *elementary* education, indeed equal to any in first rate

[19.] Holland, *The British Press and the Educational Controversy 1847–1865*, p. 247.
[20.] Murphy, *Catholic Poor Schools in Tower Hamlets (London) 1765–1865*, pp. 14–15.

Colleges. But this is not all – the Committee requires Certificated Teachers to be appointed, and at a salary not less than a fixed sum which it names ... In reference to Books and Maps ... the Committee every three years will give Ten-pence a head for every child in the School ... but only on condition that the Manager gives Twenty-pence for every Ten-pence given by the Committee.[21]

Most schools could not hold out for long, however, and the acceptance of grant, with all the attendant constraints, quickly became the norm.

Catholic School Managers at Work

Glimpses of managers at work are to be found in records of one sort or another. In commenting on the poor quality of male teachers in Catholic schools, the London and Dublin Orthodox Journal of 16 April 1843 refers to 'irksome relations towards managers' as one of several reasons. On the other hand, T.W. Marshall HMI made favourable comment on a number of occasions. Whereas, in 1849, he reported that the St Marylebone girls school was 'decidedly the most unsatisfactory' he had ever visited and required the immediate attention of its managers, by 1851 he was able to say that great efforts had been made to improve the efficiency of the school and they had been successful. Again, in 1852, great improvements had been made due to the 'zeal and liberality' of the managers in the past year.[22]

The Log Book of St Ann's Boys School, Ashton-under-Lyne records the managers, at this time, observing lessons given by pupil teachers or testing children.[23] Those of St Patrick's (later St Wilfred's) and St George's York show the managers exercising their authority and, in particular, the 'Reverend Managers' visiting at least weekly, if not daily, to ensure the high standard of religious instruction that was essential if grant were to be received from the Catholic Poor School Committee.[24]

[21.] Ibid., p. 66.
[22.] Murphy, *The Associated Catholic Charities of the Metropolis*, pp. 162ff.
[23.] Lannon, *Catholic Education in the Salford Diocese*, p. 39.
[24.] Roberts, *Catholic Childhoods: Catholic Elementary Education in York, 1850–1914*, p. 17.

The Newcastle Commission 1858–61

Despite the provision of state funding and the consequential need for providers and managers to conform to the Committee of Council's requirements, the situation remained unsatisfactory. Over the years, the extent of parliamentary grant had soared: £30,000 in 1839, £40,000 in 1842, £75,000 in 1845, £100,000 in 1846 and £125,000 in 1848. The government became increasingly unwilling to pay for religious instruction, and anxious that its considerable financial input into public education should show some practical returns. In 1856, The Privy Council's Committee for Education was replaced by a new Education Department. In 1858, the new Department set up an enquiry under the Duke of Newcastle into the state of popular education in England. The ensuing report – The Newcastle Report into the State of Popular Education in England – (1861) described a situation of widespread apathy and neglect in the matter of school management, particularly in rural areas. The Commission had difficulty in investigating Catholic schools. Assistant Commissioner J. S. Winder's plaintive report is quoted at the beginning of this chapter. Comments of an almost identical nature were made by Assistant Commissioners Rev. James Fraser, George Coode, Patrick Cumin, John Middleton Hare and Josiah Wilkinson.[25] The information, however, was eventually obtained.

The main claim to notoriety of the Newcastle Commission's eventual report – the introduction of the practice of payment by results in the Revised Code of 1862, and many of the implications springing from it – lies outside the scope of this book. What is relevant is that the functions of managers were now codified as comprising the oversight of the spending of government grant, the employment of teachers (including negotiating their stipends), and supervising the registers and premises. All payments to a school were merged into a single capitation grant paid to managers, and no longer, in part, to teachers and pupil teachers.[26] The relationship between managers and teachers was, by this provision, changed irrevocably. However, at this point, Departmental Regulations were in force covering many aspects of school activity; managers had very little freedom, and elementary schools were

[25] Newcastle Commission Report 1861, vol. 4, pp. 178, 25, 288; vol. 5, pp. 24–5, 216, 325.
[26] Capitation is a method of funding schools based on the number of students on roll.

dependent on central government for initiative and development. Grant was now to be made available for good attendance and proficiency in basic subjects, but not for religious instruction.

The Revised Code had one further adverse effect on schools: the Department started to refuse building grants to denominational applicants when places were available for students in existing schools operated by other denominations.

The repercussions of the Revised Code for grant-earning schools lay in the future. What is clear is that, by 1860, Catholic elementary schools were an accepted part of the national pattern of grant-aided schools; that they, with those run by the two Protestant societies, were required to appoint managers who were to conduct their schools in accordance with a trust deed, whose terms were dictated by the state; and that there was already disquiet in the Catholic community about the nature and extent of state involvement in the running of the schools. The policy of seeking to provide a place in a Catholic school or every Catholic child was firmly established, as far as the Catholic hierarchy was concerned.

Cardinal Manning, Gladstone and the 1870 Education Act

Cardinal Edward Manning became Archbishop of Westminster (and therefore *de facto* leader of the English and Welsh Catholic communities) in 1865, a time when a new intellectual movement brought about by Lyell's *Principles of Geology* (1830–33) and Darwin's *On the Origin of Species* (1863) had thrown the Churches onto the defensive. Manning was deeply alarmed about the extent of lapsation amongst Catholics. An article in the Jesuit magazine *The Month* claimed that, since 1841, between 750,000 and one million Catholics had given up the practice of their faith. He believed that one way to maintain links with Catholic families was to encourage children to attend a Catholic school. In 1866 he alleged that there were between 7,000 and 12,000 Catholic children in London receiving no education because of the poverty of their parents. He notoriously refused to spend money collected from the rich and influential for the building of a new cathedral (the purpose for which it had been collected). Having secured the site, he spent the balance, instead, on providing elementary schools.[27]

[27.] McClelland, *Cardinal Manning, His Public Life and Influence.*

Bishop Turner of Salford agreed. Writing to the Catholic clergy in his diocese in 1868 he commented: 'There is but too much reason to apprehend that many of the household of faith become lost to us from ... the absence of religious teaching.'[28]

By now, various pressures were combining to create a climate of opinion that demanded universal education for the nation's children. The Churches between them were in no position to provide this. The Reform Act of 1867 extended the franchise and the political strength of the Nonconformists. In the 1868 General Election campaign, many Liberal candidates pledged themselves to work for a national system of elementary education free from 'sectarianism'. Manning realized that the state would have to make provision for educating the poor, but he was resolute in his belief that denominational schools must be retained. He envisaged a dual system, at least from 1868, in correspondence with Gladstone. Other Catholic bishops were opposed, as a matter of principle, to any state involvement in the provision of education. There is disagreement about the position of Ullathorne, Archbishop of Birmingham. The conventional view is that he was opposed to state intervention. Champ, in her recent biography, follows Selby in arguing that there was, rather, a wide level of agreement between him and Manning, and that the areas of dispute were limited: the surrender of denominational inspection, and whether Catholics should stand for election to the new school boards.[29]

Unfortunately for the Catholic Church, relations between Gladstone and Manning deteriorated at this critical time, because of Gladstone's hostility to the First Vatican Council of 1870, the promulgation of the doctrine of Papal Infallibility, and what Gladstone described as 'Vaticanism' on the part of the Catholic Church. The Catholic weekly the *Tablet* opposed the Church's official position. When the education bill was introduced, proposing secular schools financed from the rates, it reported, in its edition of 25 February, that 'the Catholic Community does not look with favour upon the Bill'. Many clergy and some laity were extremely critical. The Poor School Committee petitioned the House of Commons and the government, and interviewed individual MPs, but to little effect.

The bill became the Elementary Education Act of 1870. Its principal significance – the establishment of non-sectarian board

[28.] Lannon, *Catholic Education in the Salford Diocese*, p. 17.
[29.] Champ, *William Bernard Ullathorne, A Different Kind of Monk*; Selby, *Manning, Ullathorne and the School Board Question 1870–76*.

schools to be financed from the rates – again falls outside the scope
of this book. But it brought to an end building grant for voluntary
schools. To compensate for this, a proposal was made to increase
the annual grant per pupil to a maximum of fifteen shillings. The
calculations on which this decision was based were, unfortunately,
flawed. Gladstone had been advised that the average cost of
educating a pupil was then thirty shillings, of which roughly ten
shillings came from the state, ten shillings from voluntary contributions and ten shillings from fees. The problem was twofold: first,
the actual grant a school received would continue to depend on
income from other sources, and on payment by results. In most
cases it would, therefore, be unaffected by an increase in the
maximum that might be payable if all other circumstances were
favourable. Second, whilst it might have been true that the average
cost of educating a child at that time was thirty shillings, the
maximum grant was already fifteen shillings, and had been so since
1862. In practice, therefore, voluntary schools lost building grant,
and those serving the poorer communities received nothing in
compensation. The consequences for Catholic schools, in particular, were severe.

Growing Financial Problems

If financial pressures had been a problem for Catholic schools in
the past, they were as nothing compared with the situation that
developed as a result of the 1870 Act. The problem was that, in
practice, every penny a person paid in tax was a penny less that he
was either able or willing to contribute to a voluntary school. What
was worse, board schools usually charged lower fees than voluntary
ones. After 1870, board schools received on average seventeen
shillings per child from the rates, whereas voluntary schools
received only six shillings and ten pence from subscriptions.
Furthermore, where a board school claimed it had room for all
children in its own schools, the voluntary schools in the area
received no grant at all. Catholic schools serving urban poor
communities were therefore particularly hard hit. Poor Law
Guardians had the power to pay the fees of children whose parents
wished them to attend a voluntary school. They were not required
to do so, however, and seem to have chosen not to exercise their
discretion on many occasions.
   The developing practice of management after 1870 was interesting. With the notable exceptions of London and Liverpool, it

became customary for the larger (usually urban) boards to do without lay managers, relying, instead, on paid employees – officers and inspectors – to exercise oversight of their schools. A dual structure of elementary schooling therefore emerged, with voluntary schools and the board schools of mainly London and Liverpool having managing bodies, and the majority of the remainder of the country's board schools (including Birmingham, Bradford, Hull, Leeds and Manchester) being without them.

The Churches were given less than six months after the passing of the 1870 Act to establish what schools they could before the new boards began their work. The Catholic Church inaugurated a Catholic Education Crisis Fund which, by the end of 1873, had helped build or enlarge 257 schools, providing accommodation for 56,456 children. By this date, only four out of seventy six parishes in Salford had no day school. The rest had, between them, 146 schools. It was no doubt this activity that also enabled Bishop Bagshawe of Nottingham, in his first *Ad Limina* Report to be able to claim that, at St Patrick's Mission 'Adjoining [the chapel] three large and handsome schoolrooms have been built ... The building of these schools ... prevented the building of one of the godless government schools in the neighbourhood; that, in Lincoln, 'excellent new schools have lately been built'; that 'a large school has recently been erected' at Great Grimsby, and in Leicester 'a new School has recently been built by the zealous exertion of the Missioner'.[30]

In 1876, Disraeli's government increased the level of grant to seventeen shillings and sixpence, with an additional sum where this could be matched from other sources. Nevertheless, as time went by, the greater resources available to board schools continued to undermine church school provision of all kinds. In 1887, for example, Huddersfield board schools provided an average of 4.5 square yards per pupil whilst comparable voluntary schools offered an average of 1 square yard, and St Patrick's R. C. only 0.52 square yards. Average salaries for principal teachers were £148 3s. 9d. in board schools, £120 3s. 3d. in Church of England schools and £111 11s. 11d. in Roman Catholic ones.[31] Despite all these problems, however, the rolls of Catholic schools continued to rise. Writing to Pope Leo XIII on 16 April 1883, Thomas Allies, Secretary of the Catholic Poor School Committee, pointed out that the number of

[30] The Ad Limina Report is a report each Catholic bishop has to make to the Vatican every four years which gives an account of the state of his diocese.
[31] Chadwick, O., *The Victorian Church*, vol. 2.

Catholic elementary schools had grown from 666 in 1870 to 1562 in 1882, and the number of pupils in them from 75,127 to 190,540. Government grant had increased, during the same period, from £41,527 to £162,887.[32] In the Salford Diocese the number of school departments increased between 1873 and 1892 from 146 to 225, whilst the average attendance almost doubled, from 17,817 to 33,708.[33]

Manning soon wished to have the 1870 settlement reviewed, but found progress difficult, not only because of the hostility of the Liberal Party to church schools in general, but also because Archbishop Benson of Canterbury was opposed to the concept of rate aid for Church of England schools, and because the education question was now increasingly mixed up with that of Irish Home Rule.

The 1880s witnessed a deteriorating situation. The Mundella Education Act of 1880 made school attendance compulsory; fixed the leaving age at thirteen; but permitted half-time attendance for children over ten years of age who had reached the fifth standard, and whose earnings were considered necessary for the support of their families. Catholic schools suffered because the increased number of older children they had to accommodate made the provision of suitable books and equipment and extra teachers diffi-cult. They also had a high proportion of half-timers. In board schools, expenditure per child rose between 1880 and 1885 from forty-two shillings to forty-five shillings, whilst the comparable figures for voluntary schools were thirty-one shillings and thirty-three shillings. In 1880, voluntary schools earned more than board schools in grant, under the payment by results scheme, but the position was reversed by 1885. Catholic schools had by far the largest percentage of free admissions at this time: thirteen per cent compared with board schools (four per cent), Church of England (three per cent), and Wesleyan (under one per cent).

In 1883 the Catholic Poor School Committee met Gladstone to explain the increasing difficulties of Catholic schools in the light of rising expenditure on the part of the board schools, but they received an unsympathetic response. In 1884, therefore, the Voluntary Schools Association was set up by the Catholic bishops, encouraged by Archbishop Vaughan of Birmingham. Its aim was to co-ordinate the action of dioceses to secure educational reform, and also to marshal opposition to the Birmingham Radicals, who

---

[32.] Allies, *Thomas William Allies,* but see p. 23 below for a different assessment.
[33.] Lannon, *Catholic Education in the Salford Diocese,* p. 35.

were hostile to the concept of church schools as part of a national education system. It rapidly made the Poor School Committee redundant.

By 1884, over 1,000 voluntary schools had been taken over by school boards. By 1902 the figure had reached 1,500. How many were transferred because of financial pressures and how many for philosophical reasons cannot be ascertained. However, not a single Catholic school was involved. But finance continued to be a major problem. In 1885, the parish priest of St George's, York, urged his congregation to

> send children to schools and regularly. Schools a *heavy* burthen on the Mission, only one way to keep that burthen from being unbearable by obtaining a good grant by good examination. This impossible without good and regular attendance. Not only injury to children to be taken into account but injury to the Mission also by detaining the children without great and urgent necessity.[34]

'Great and urgent necessity' frequently arose, however. Insanitary housing and insufficient food and clothing made children susceptible to epidemics of measles, scarlet fever and whooping cough. In the winter, those with leaky boots, or no boots at all, could not get to school. At harvest time, children were often in the fields, or girls, if not, were at home looking after the family whilst their mothers were at work.

When the general election campaign started in the autumn of 1885, several Catholic bishops openly urged Catholics to support the Conservatives because of the intransigence of the Liberal government. The *Tablet* followed suit.[35] On 1 November, Manning wrote to Lord Salisbury pressing for a review of the 1870 Act. On 2 November the Catholic bishops wrote to *The Times*, 'The Catholic Bishops cannot confide in any candidate for a seat in parliament who will not equip himself to do his utmost to redress these present glaring inequalities.' At this juncture, Sir Richard Cross, who was to become Home Secretary, proposed at an election meeting just such an enquiry.

[34.] Roberts, *Catholic Childhoods: Catholic Elementary Education in York, 1850–1914*, p. 26.
[35.] *The Tablet*, 10 Otcober 1885, pp. 565, 588.

The Cross Commission

Even before the election results were known, work started on preparing for a Royal Commission – the Cross Commission. Its establishment turned out to be the Conservative government's only achievement, as it fell on 28 January 1886. The ensuing Liberal government, however, was also short-lived, so that by the time the Commission reported in 1888, the Conservatives were again in office.

Unlike the Newcastle Commission, which had no Catholics as members, the Cross Commission had two, including Manning himself, thus indicating that, by this time, Catholic schools were a significant enough part of the educational provision of the country to warrant recognition at national level. In giving evidence to it, E. H. Brodie HMI, one of the Commissioners, reported that town schools were carefully managed but country schools were less so; it was usually, again, left to the local clergyman, who dominated not only his voluntary school but the local school board as well. His account was confirmed by another Commissioner Rev. D. Stewart HMI. A third, J. G. Fitch HMI, found the managers of London voluntary schools much more in sympathy with their schools than their board school counterparts.

As with the Newcastle Commission, the Catholic community seems to have distanced itself from Cross. Little evidence appears to have been given by Catholics, in comparison with the substantial numbers who spoke on behalf of the Church of England and the Nonconformist Churches. Only five are recorded, in addition to the Catholic Poor School Committee: Mr L. Conway, Head Master of the Holy Cross school in Liverpool, Miss C. Fox, Head Mistress of St Patrick's Infants school in Manchester, Rev. Dr. Graham, Principal of St Mary's Roman Catholic Training College, Hammersmith, Mr J. Murray, Head Master of the St Francis Xavier schools, Liverpool, and Rev. Dr W. J. B. Richards, Diocesan Inspector of Roman Catholic Schools, St Charles College, Notting Hill. What emerges from their evidence reflects, again, one of the central themes of this book: acute tensions between the schools and the secular authorities.

Mr Conway complained about the inspection regime: inspections took place in January and February and therefore bore 'hard upon ill-fed and ill-dressed children ... of dock labourers and cotton porters'.[36] Out of 278 on the register, 90 paid no fees and

---

[36.] Cross Commission Report 1888, p. 242.

180 were paid for by the guardians through the school board. 'It is very difficult to get the guardians to pay fees. Parents must attend personally to apply for the payment of fees in the daytime, which is a great hardship owing to the difficulty of obtaining work.'[37]

Miss Fox had much the same to say. 'A great many of the children have only a piece of bread for dinner and a few come without having had any breakfast.' The fee at St Patrick's was two pence, or one penny for those who could not afford two pence. Before accepting the penny fee she always consulted the managers as to the circumstances of the parents. The school had to deal with many of the very poorest children, who were mostly Irish. Nevertheless, parents were unwilling to apply to the guardians for the payment of fees. The school thereby suffered. 'The tardiness of the guardians ... besides causing loss of school fees also means the loss of the children's attendance.'[38]

Mr Murray provided another dimension to Catholic poverty, which, he claimed, meant that many schools had insufficient staff and that teachers were underpaid, compared with their board school counterparts. He alleged discrimination: 'School board visitors do not exert themselves to get such good attendance in voluntary schools as in board schools.' Furthermore, 'Voluntary schools buildings suffer from want of means.'[39]

Dr Richards added his concerns about guardians: 'Most parents object to appear before the guardians, as it is humiliating, and they object to the harshness and oppressiveness of the guardians.'[40]

T. W. Allies, Secretary and Treasurer to the Catholic Poor School Committee, complained that, since 1877, difficulty between the school boards and the voluntary system had arisen over the supply of school places, the London School Board being the exception. 'The refusal of the School Boards to allow Catholics to supply school place deficiencies was a hardship and the decision should rest, not with the School Boards but with the Department.'[41] Curiously, in the light of evidence referred to below, he claimed that

> With the exception of the correspondents, there are no boards of managers for each of the Catholic schools owing to the action of the local school boards. The resident priest generally has the principal

[37] Ibid.
[38] Ibid., p. 278.
[39] Ibid., p. 271.
[40] Ibid., pp. 151ff.
[41] Ibid., p. 599.

management of the schools ... Some of the Catholic teachers are
solicited to go to board schools at higher salaries, which is a great
temptation to them ... Board schools, both in their building and in
their furnishing, have a great advantage over other schools. Board
schools, owing to their large income from the rates, can obtain
everything they require. Catholic schools obtain their support from
the poorest part of the population. The disadvantage is so great that
in the course of time the board school system will destroy the voluntary school system. Every effort is being made to bring the Catholic
schools up to standard, and the clergy sacrifice their health, and
even their lives in the attempt ... Another hardship is the obligation
to contribute to the rates which support the board schools, which
Catholics cannot use, and to support voluntary schools ... There is
more personal contact between the managers in voluntary than in
board schools. They take more interest in the schools and in the
children.

These views were supported by Rev. D. J. Stewart HMI who said that
'[t]he relations between managers and teachers are generally
more friendly than is the case with board schools' but that 'Board
schools appear to have too much management in London.'[42]

J. G. Fitch HMI added a similar view to that of Messrs Allies and
Stewart: 'Managers of voluntary schools take more interest and
show more sympathy than the managers of board schools do.'[43]

Allies was at odds with Manning over state aid. He said he had 'a
great dread' of financial assistance from the rates. Perhaps too
much should not be made of this. As stated above, the bishops had
established the Voluntary Schools Association in 1884 and this had
created growing tension with Allies' Poor School Committee.

The Cross Commissioners came to the conclusion that school
management could be divided into two branches: that which could
be conducted at a distance (the appointment and dismissal of
teachers, the equipment of the school), and that which required
personal involvement in the form of frequent visits. The
Commission praised the voluntary sector for the close contacts that
existed between managers and their schools. It wanted school
boards to become more like voluntary schools, and called unsuc-
cessfully for a combination of school board skill in dispensing
money, and the close personal involvement of the managers of
voluntary schools. This was not to be, however, for another
hundred years.

[42.] Ibid., p. 561.
[43.] Ibid., p. 852.

Because of the divisions in the Commission, there was very little practical change in the circumstances of Catholic schools.

Deteriorating Finances

The 1891 Education Act made elementary education free. This came about because the Conservative government was concerned that a future Liberal administration might provide free education only in the board schools, thus putting voluntary schools at a hopeless disadvantage. Manning opposed the move. It did have an adverse effect on Catholic schools: full-time pupils between the ages of five and fourteen would earn a grant of ten shillings. But many children in Catholic schools were half-timers and therefore attracted only five shillings The position of voluntary schools continued to deteriorate: in 1896 expenditure exceeded income in 166 schools. By 1900, this had increased to 245. The Log Books of the Catholic elementary schools in York record that they were reliant on the support of nuns, managers, and particularly parish priests, for donations in kind. The Bar Convent nuns took no salaries for their twenty-four years' service to St George's and they occasionally paid for cleaning and repairs, as well as books. The managers gave books and slates, pianos, hockey sticks and rocking horses. The nuns and the parishes also provided soup and bread, and hot milk or cocoa in the winter.[44]

Despite all these hardships, Cardinal Vaughan, who had succeeded Manning as Archbishop of Westminster in 1892, was able to write in *The Dublin Review* of January 1897 that the rolls of Catholic elementary schools had increased to 367,344 by 1895, and that the Catholic community had incurred debt of £1,700,000 in providing school sites and buildings in the same period.[45] By 1902, just over one half of the elementary school population still attended voluntary rather than board schools.[46] Of these, about 400,000 children were pupils at 1,066 Catholic schools.[47]

---

[44] Roberts, *Catholic Childhoods: Catholic Elementary Education in York 1850–1914*, pp. 27–8.
[45] *The Dublin Review,* January 1897, pp. 14–15.
[46] Cashman, *The 1902 Act and Roman Catholic Schools: a study of a community's efforts to gain and preserve denominational education in its schools*, p. 147.
[47] Evenett, *The Catholic Schools of England and Wales*, pp. 17, 20.

The 1902 Education Act: A New Beginning

The General Election of 1895 gave the Conservatives a very large majority in the House of Commons. This persuaded the denominationalists to press for a number of educational reforms: rate aid for their schools, the replacement of school boards by bodies more likely to be sympathetic to voluntary schools, and the provision of denominational education in board schools.

A further Royal Commission had been established in 1894 to consider what were 'the best methods of establishing a well-organized system of secondary education'. There is scarcely a mention of denominational schools in the ensuing Report (*The Bryce Report*) of 1899.

The Commission did not think that new local education authorities should supervise 'the details of administration which form a large part of the duties of the governing body of a school', but that governing bodies should be 'independent of the local authority'. They should be entrusted with the general supervision of the school, and with the exercise of such supervision over the management, teaching and curriculum as was usually conferred on governing bodies by schemes under the Endowed Schools Act of 1869. The head should be, as far as possible, unfettered in matters of discipline and teaching, for example the division of classes, school hours and school books; holidays in term time; the appointment and dismissal of assistant masters; and the general direction of courses and methods.

All this was very welcome to Sir Robert Morant, Permanent Secretary (1903–11) to John Gorst, vice president of the new Board of Education. He favoured voluntary schools, and wanted to abolish school boards. He also wanted to develop local authority secondary schools based on the endowed schools. The recently established county and county borough councils were the obvious authorities to take over unified control of both elementary and secondary education.[48] He came to the conclusion that the only way to achieve all this was to put a scheme to aid denominational schools at the heart of an education bill. His proposal was to fund voluntary schools from the rates. This, however, required subordinating managing bodies to the new local education authorities.

Cardinal Vaughan expressed concern to Morant about the posi-

[48.] County and county borough councils were new units of local government. County councils survive to this day. County boroughs – urban communities – were abolished in 1974.

tion that Catholic schools would be in if they should be put under the control of county councils without any voice on their education committees, and proposed that voluntary associations be allowed to nominate representatives to sit on them. The bishops proposed that, in return for public funding, one third of a school's managers should be nominated by the council providing the funds. This was accepted and became the legal requirement.

The first comprehensive education bill to reach the English statute book, in the form of the 1902 Education Act, therefore, removed control of the secular curriculum from voluntary school managing bodies. But they gained control of religious education (RE) and retained responsibilities for the buildings and buildings costs. Although they could appoint teachers, they could dismiss them only with the consent of the LEA except on grounds connected with RE.

The period between 1870 and 1902 can now, therefore, be seen as entirely typical of the history of Catholic education in England and Wales after 1847: despite huge financial problems caused by the inequitable funding arrangements introduced by Gladstone, voluntary schools in general, and Catholic schools in particular, retained their appeal; there was lack of agreement in the Catholic community about the relationship which the Church should have with the State in the matter of school provision, and the issue of state funding for church schools was attracting vociferous opposition. The 1902 Act removed entirely from managers' control of the secular curriculum. What now remained to be seen was how the Church would come to terms with this settlement, and, in particular, the loss of power by managers; and how English and Welsh society would react to the new funding regime. Since this had already been caricatured as 'Rome on the rates' the latter, at least, was fairly clear.

The Age of the Local Education Authority; Early Difficulties

The provision of rate funding for voluntary schools aroused fierce opposition throughout the land, but particularly in Wales. Clifford, writing in *The North American Review* of 15 March 1905, reported that 600 Passive Resistance Leagues had been established, with a central committee in London. 40,000 summonses had been issued, nearly 100 people had been sent to prison for refusing to pay their rates, and property had been confiscated and sold. Some LEAs refused to maintain their voluntary schools, whilst others tried to force them to reduce the amount of curriculum time devoted to religious instruction.

Four bills were introduced after the Liberal Party took office in 1905 (the Birrell bill of 1906, two McKenna bills of 1907 and 1908, and the Runciman bill of 1908), in each of which there was a proposal to transfer compulsorily to LEA control voluntary schools in single school areas, to extend public control of most of the others by transference, restriction of the amount of denominational instruction given at public expense, and limitation of the number of teachers whose appointment, promotion, retention or dismissal could be affected by their religious beliefs. All were unsuccessful, and gradually opinion started to tire of disputes between impassioned clergymen and their followers. In time, the 1902 Act came to be accepted, together with a preference for the spread and development of education rather than disputes about its management and funding.

It is worth pausing to note the detail of Birrell's proposals. Murphy records that the Catholics were prepared to accept his bill, albeit with modifications.[49] Pattison, however, argues that the Catholics were divided: the Irish Nationalists were anxious to support the Liberals in return for help with home rule, but the English Catholic press consistently opposed the bill. Cardinal Bourne, the Archbishop of Westminster, played an ambivalent role, lending support to the Nationalists without informing the Duke of Norfolk, who was leading the opposition.[50]

Birrell proposed that all schools were to be provided by the LEA, but a limited number of voluntary schools might be allowed to retain a quasi-denominational character. Rent would be paid for their use. Two types of voluntary school were envisaged: 'moderate', in which religious instruction would be indistinguishable from Cowper-Temple instruction, and 'extreme', in which distinctive religious instruction could be given every day of the week.[51] The entire conduct of these schools would be governed by the religious and historical point of view of the particular denomination. This second group of schools would be permitted only in urban areas where alternative schools were available, where four-fifths of the parents had asked for special religious instruction, and where the local authority had agreed. The purpose was clearly to ensure that Catholic schools

---

[49.] Murphy, *Church, State and Schools in Britain 1800–1970*, p. 98.

[50.] Pattison, *The Birrell Education Bill.*

[51.] Cowper Temple was an MP who proposed that religious instruction in board schools should exclude any 'catechism or religious formulary distinctive of any particular denomination' when the Education Bill of 1870 was being debated (Woodward, 1962, p. 283). This was savagely lampooned by Gladstone as 'the religion of no-one, taught by anybody at everybody's expense'.

in the larger urban areas would be left virtually undisturbed, whilst the Anglican rural schools would be taken over.[52]

Just how desperate had the plight of voluntary schools become by this time was revealed by G. L. Bruce in the *Independent Review* of June 1905: of 438 inspected by the London County Council, a quarter were considered wholly unsuitable for school purposes and incapable of adaptation, and of the remainder, the large majority, even with the suggested improvements, were thought unfit for permanent approval. 'Halls and teachers' rooms rarely exist. Playgrounds are scarce and scanty ... The classrooms are often ill-lighted, ill-ventilated and overcrowded. The drains are defective in three quarters ... the staff are inadequate, almost always ill-trained.'

The Board of Education exercised its powers through codes of regulations which, having been laid on the table of the House of Commons, became law. Codes and a system of inspection gave the board close control of what went on in schools. The board's overall powers were, however, limited, and the absence of any positive initiating power enabled LEAs to proceed as fast or as slowly as they chose. Thus began a period of atrophy which was to last for over eighty years.

Secondary Schools

As to secondary schools, Morant, whose concept of secondary education has already been explained, was in the tradition of the public and endowed grammar schools, shared the view of the Bryce Commission that they should have governing bodies that were distinct from, and independent of, the local authorities. The requirement that 'every secondary school must be under the super-intendence of a body of Managers responsible to the Board' was therefore written into the very first body of regulations for secondary schools (Regulation VII of 1902/3), though the self-same regulations provided, fatally in the event, that the LEA could be the managing body for a school or group of schools.[53] The term

[52.] Pattison, *The Birrell Education Bill.*

[53.] The effect of this provision was to deny the schools involved an independent governing body concerned, primarily, with the interests of a single school. As late as the early 1970s, the borough of Gillingham (Kent) education committee would first meet as the governing body for all its secondary schools, adjourn briefly, and reconvene as the borough education committee to receive the recommendations it had just passed to itself.

'governors' first appeared as an alternative to managers in the 1903/4 Regulations and superseded it altogether in 1904/5.)

In 1908 the board issued model Articles of Government. The Prefatory Memorandum to the 1909/10 Regulations stated that the model could be adopted 'with such adaptations as may be suitable for the particular School', but proposed alternatives had to make satisfactory provision for:

- the composition of the governing body;
- the appointment and dismissal of assistant teachers;
- the powers and responsibilities of the headmaster or head-mistress;
- the relations of the governing body to the LEA in respect of finance.

The head teacher should have a voice in the appointment and dismissal of assistant staff and a right to submit proposals to, and be consulted by, the governing body.

All this was opposed by some of the new education authorities, particularly in respect of schools they were providing. It is sufficient to note that, as a result of a series of oversights, the board eventually found it had slid into an untenable position and Morant had to concede defeat.

In summary, the position after 1902 was that non-provided (i.e. voluntary) primary schools had to have managing bodies, but their powers were tightly circumscribed by their LEAs. County boroughs and urban districts could appoint managing bodies if they chose, but most decided not to; county councils had to establish managing bodies for the schools they had provided, but, under Section 12 of the Act, grouped arrangements were permissible, and many county authorities availed themselves of this facility. Provided secondary schools might or might not have governing bodies depending on the view of the LEA. As with primary schools, many did not, and the practice of grouping was widespread. Whether a secondary school had a governing body, or was administered directly, depended on its history, academic or social standing, and the financial resources it had in its own right.

1902–44: Little Change

There is little to be said about the position between 1902 and 1944. There was virtually no development.

After the Birrell, McKenna and Runciman Education bills failed, the Liberal Government used Board of Education regulations to make it impossible for the Catholic community to open new secondary schools or gain recognition for existing ones. Later, when government pressure was not so great, many LEAs took the view that secondary education was their exclusive domain, and refused to support proposals for voluntary provision. In any event, demand for it from the Catholic community was not great. The absence of building grant, the improved standards required for elementary school buildings, which put perpetual strain on parish resources, and the fact that secondary schools did not belong to a single parish community, and no one parish felt responsible for them, all meant they were not an attractive proposition.

The Salford diocese was not untypical. Bishop Vaughan had founded a Commercial School in Manchester and Collegiate Institutes in Blackburn and Burnley, with limited success. By 1902, there was no secondary provision for boys outside Manchester and Blackburn, and for girls there were schools only in towns where there happened to be a convent. As secondary education had to be completely self-financing, there was no provision for the working classes.[54]

Writing in *The Month* for October 1917 in connection with the education bill then going through Parliament, Rev. S. F. Smith quoted a letter from Bishop Ward of Brentwood to the newspaper *The Universe*:

> At the present moment it is absolutely impossible to open a new Catholic Secondary School without being financially handicapped in competition with others, and being unable to receive public grants under the full scale ... It is necessary for any new school to be administered by a governing body, the majority of whom ... may be non-Catholics. This is a position which we cannot accept.

Accept it the Catholic community had to, however. The bill was piloted through Parliament by H. A. L. Fisher, whose view was that 'finance, indeed was at the heart of the problem. The cause which had been arresting educational progress in the country was lack of financial support'.[55] On appointment as President of the Board of Education by Lloyd George, he had found that 'education was a

---

[54.] Lannon, *Catholic Education in the Salford Diocese*, pp. 164, 166–7.
[55.] Fisher, *An Unfinished Autobiography*, p. 104.

popular subject and discussed in an atmosphere cleared of religious acrimony'.[56] Furthermore:

> I was well content with a scheme under which the public system of
> education ... was conducted by a partnership between the Board of
> Education and the local education authorities. It would have been a
> senseless extravagance to buy out the Church schools, and suicidal
> to derange the hard-won compromise on the religious question ...
> The general framework of the Balfour Act [the 1902 Education Act]
> seemed to me to be sound ... First, it was in actual, working.
> Second, it was clearly compatible with great improvements and
> developments.[57]

It comes as no surprise, therefore, to learn that, by 1924, out of
1,115 grant-aided secondary schools, only sixty-six were Catholic –
fourteen for boys and fifty-two for girls.[58]

The 1936 Education Act revived the policy of building grant for
voluntary schools that had been discontinued in 1870. LEAs were
given powers to make grants of between fifty per cent and seventy
five per cent towards the cost of new voluntary schools made necessary by a decision to raise the leaving age to fifteen on 1 September
1939. The arrangement was a temporary one: proposals had to be
made within three years, and only accommodation for senior children could be assisted in this way. Teachers at these 'Special
Agreement' schools were to be employees of the LEA except for an
agreed number of 'reserved' teachers employed to give religious
instruction. The onset of war meant that little progress was made
as a result of this legislation. By then just ten denominational
schools had been reorganized in this way.[59]

The 1944 Education Act – A Missed Opportunity

In the long gestation period of the 1944 Act, the Catholic bishops
yet again found themselves at odds with almost all the other parties
involved, in their opposition to the National Government's proposals: the National Union of Teachers, the Nonconformist Churches
and the Church of England. The President of the Board, R. A.
Butler, quotes the Archbishop of Liverpool: 'We shall continue to

---

[56.] Ibid., p. 94.
[57.] Ibid., p. 96.
[58.] Lannon, *Catholic Education in the Salford Diocese*, p. 201.
[59.] Evenett, *The Catholic Schools of England and Wales*, p. 28.

struggle for denominational schools even though we have to fight alone', and again 'Not long after I reached the Board, I had had to receive a massive deputation of Church leaders; but the absence of the Roman Catholics made it essential for me to say as little as possible at this stage.'[60]

Arrangements for the management and government of schools were reviewed prior to the 1944 Act, and the White Paper of 1943 *Educational Reconstruction* proposed that all secondary schools should have a governing body. There was no such proposal for managing bodies to support primary schools, but this emerged in the draft bill, which also advocated articles of government or rules of management be drawn up by the LEA for primary schools and county secondary schools, and by the Minister for voluntary secondary schools.[61] The Minister was to make instruments of government for both primary and secondary voluntary schools.[62] During the negotiations that took place during the passage of the bill, the LEAs got more or less what they wanted: pressure to give primary schools governing bodies was successfully resisted, as were proposals to include parent managers / governors. The ability to group was again conceded.

After the enactment of the bill, the Ministry issued a Command Paper (1944 Cmd 6523) setting out in some detail its philosophy of school government. Every school was to have 'an individual life of its own ... reasonable autonomy ... and freedom to exercise legitimate and appropriate functions' (paragraph five). The functions of the governors were described in some detail, but since the model instrument for county secondary schools gave the LEA absolute discretion as to the numbers of governors, the manner of appointment, and grouping, the significance of these guidelines should not be overstated – fifty-seven out of seventy-eight county boroughs indulged in grouping, as did twenty-two out of forty-five counties. The dichotomy between county and voluntary schools that had developed from the middle of the nineteenth century was, therefore, reaffirmed, with voluntary school bodies exercising responsibilities for the buildings, equipment, staffing and pupil admissions.

For the next fifteen to twenty years all involved in education were fully engaged in coping with the huge problems that faced

[60.] Butler, *The Art of the Possible*, pp. 99–100.
[61.] Legal documents prescribing the duties of managing and governing bodies.
[62.] Legal documents establishing governing bodies, and prescribing the nominating bodies and the number of members.

them: making a start on remedying the decades of neglect of voluntary school buildings, repairing war damage, raising the school leaving age, coping with the post-war baby boom, and reorganizing elementary schools into the new pattern of primary and tri-partite secondary schools.[63] There was little time, energy, or money for much else.

The Second Vatican Council 1962–65; Consequences for Catholic Schooling

Despite its reputation for conservatism, the Catholic Church began to modernize itself in advance of the movement that swept through Western European secular society later in the decade. Pope John XXIII had decided that the Church had become too introspective and hidebound, and needed to re-align itself with the urgent needs of mankind. He summoned the Second Vatican Council to work out how this might be done. The concept of a hierarchical institution rigidly controlled by clergy was, at least in theory, modified. The new vision of the Church was of a pilgrim body in which each individual had a unique vocation, and where the laity were called upon to exercise their skills and talents in spreading the Gospel.

The consequences of the Council for Catholic education were both profound and long-lasting. They not only shaped the English system as it is to be found today, but also sowed the seeds of the various issues that are the subject of this book, in particular a reconfiguration of the role of the laity and its relationship with the clergy. A small number of seminal texts relating to education emerged from the Vatican in subsequent years. These will be examined in detail later. For the present, it is sufficient to note a number of key statements made in the document on education *Gravissimum Educationis*:

> As a mother, the Church is bound to give these children of hers the kind of education through which their entire lives can be penetrated with the spirit of Christ.[64]

> The Catholic school aims to create for the school community an atmosphere enlivened by the gospel spirit of freedom and charity. It

---

[63.] Grammar, technical and secondary modern schools, which catered for varying degrees of what were then perceived to be intellectual ability.

[64.] Abbott, *The Documents of Vatican II*, p. 642.

aims to help the adolescent in such a way that the development of his own personality will be matched by the growth of that new creation which he became by baptism. It strives to relate all human culture eventually to the news of salvation, so that the light of faith will illumine the knowledge which students gradually gain of the world, of life, and of mankind.[65]

This sacred Synod earnestly entreats pastors of the Church and all the faithful to spare no sacrifice in helping Catholic schools to achieve their purpose in an increasingly adequate way, and to show special concern for the needs of those who are poor in the goods of this world or who are deprived of the assistance and affection of family or who are strangers to the gift of faith.[66]

What this meant in simple terms was that Catholic schools were intended to be communities that are to derive their ethos from the two great Christian commandments that mankind should love God and neighbour; where all members, whether staff or pupils, are uniquely valued in the eyes of God and have an eternal destiny; that the curriculum should be based on a belief that all knowledge comes from God and that the universe is God's creation; and that the schools have a special mission to the poor and underprivileged.

The 1960s – The Spirit of Educational Reform

In the 1960s the mood of the country began to change. The governance of teacher training colleges, polytechnics and further education colleges was reformed following pressure from the Association of Teachers in Colleges and Departments of Education The result of this was to free these institutions from LEA dominance.

There was increasing unwillingness to accept the moribund condition of many school managing and governing bodies. Sharp argues that two national pressure groups – the Campaign for the Advancement of State Education and the Advisory Centre for Education – began to draw attention to the fact that there were matters regarding school governance that required attention.[67]

Curiously, though, in 1965 the DES,[68] in issuing Circular 10/65,

[65.] Ibid., p. 646.
[66.] Ibid., p. 648.
[67.] Sharp, *School Governing Bodies in the English Educational System: An Historical Perspective*.
[68.] DES is the acronym for the Department of Education and Science.

which 'requested' LEAs to prepare schemes of secondary school reorganization on comprehensive lines, did not advise LEAs to consult governing bodies. Though stress was placed on the need to consult parents, all that was said about governing bodies was that those of voluntary aided schools had to consult LEAs, as indeed they had to, as they would need to find substantial sums of public money to fund any building adaptations. In this regard, Baron and Howell were wrong in claiming that the Circular expressly advised LEAs to consult governing bodies.[69] It did not.

Then, in 1966, the Plowden Committee of enquiry into primary education submitted its report. It included a complete chapter on 'The Status and Government of Primary Education' and found that 'The whole subject of school management requires reconsideration.'[70] A salvo of recommendations was fired: parents should be represented on managing bodies; each school should have its own managing body; where this was not practicable, groups should be as small as possible; managers needed to be more actively concerned in their schools; and their responsibilities must be increased.

In the same year, a Royal Commission was set up to consider the reform of local government. In their evidence to the Commission, though it was not made till towards the end of the decade, Baron and Howell provided ample evidence about the unsatisfactory nature of school governance:

> There are many authorities ... in which managing and governing bodies are mere formalities and are accorded a minimal role within strong and highly bureaucratised structures ... Managing and governing bodies operate on the periphery of the network of relationships that constitute the educational system ... The provisions of the Education Act 1944 and the prescribed machinery of instruments, rules and articles are clearly ineffective in securing to them a place of significance, [though] the position of voluntary aided governors and managers is stronger .[71]

In commenting on this, Sharp argues that Baron and Howell's research provided all the facts, the detail and the empirical data necessary to support the case for major change. As none of this had

---

[69.] Baron and Howell, *The Government and Management of Schools.*

[70.] Central Advisory Council for England, *Children and their Primary Schools,* para.1131.

[71.] Baron and Howell, *The Government and Management of Schools,* pp. 189, 193.

been readily available before, he concludes that the importance of the research in this regard could hardly be overstated.[72]

Unfortunately for my purposes, Baron and Howell confined their research, so far as the voluntary aided sector is concerned, to Church of England schools.[73] There is, accordingly, no direct evidence in their work on which judgements about the situation in Catholic schools might be formed. There is no reason to suppose, however, that the position was significantly different.

Even the Department of Education and Science (DES) gave evidence in favour of enhanced powers for governing bodies, and for the automatic appointment of parent governors, as did the Association of Education Committees, the County Councils' Association and the National Union of Teachers. Against this background, it is not surprising that the Commission, reporting in 1968, recommended that the 'sphere of action open to managers and governors of schools should be widened' (vol.1 Report para. 318). In the same year, the *Skeffington Report* on people and planning recorded a growing demand by many groups for more opportunity to be involved in working out policies that affect people.[74]

In their evidence to the Commission, the DES had pointed out that both parents and teachers could be introduced to governing bodies without the need for legislation by simply amending the Instruments of Government. The Inner London Education Authority and Sheffield were quick to do this and where, in the latter, just over 100 people had been serving as governors in the 1960s, by the mid 1970s over 3,000 were participating, thus giving the lie to the (mainly county borough) chief education officers who opposed strengthening managing and governing bodies on the ground that not enough people would be interested.[75]

Circular 10/65, The Plowden Report, and the rapid expansion of higher education at this time, gave rise to the '*Black Paper*' movement – the publication of three documents (two in 1969 and one in 1970) that sought to argue that the country was witnessing the collapse of an educational system that had served it well for many

---

[72.] Sharp, *School Governing Bodies in the English Educational System: An Historical Perspective.*

[73.] This omission is typical of the marginalization of Catholic schooling in many researches at this time.

[74.] *Report of the Committee on Public Participation and Planning*, 1969.

[75.] Sharp, *School Governing Bodies in The English Educational System: An Historical Perspective*, pp. 50–1.

years, brought about by the ill-considered views of left-wing politicians and educationists. The documents will be examined later.
The important point to note at this stage is that it strengthened the
growing view that education was too important to be left in the
hands of educationists.

William Tyndale Junior School and the Taylor Report

In 1975, what came to be known as *The William Tyndale Affair* developed as a national scandal, and appeared to many as evidence that
what the *Black Paper* essayists had complained about was amply
justified. The events concerned a primary school in the London
Borough of Islington, where a newly appointed headteacher
decided to change fundamentally the ways in which the school was
organized and the children worked. The report of the Public
Inquiry into events at the school set up by the Inner London
Education Authority will be examined later. It is sufficient, at this
stage, to note that it concluded that 'by the time Mr Ellis [the newly
appointed headteacher] had completed his first two terms there,
the School was in complete turmoil'.[76]

It was scarcely surprising, therefore, that by this time, all the major
political parties had become interested in parents' rights. In 1975 the
Labour government of James Callaghan set up the Taylor Committee
of enquiry into school management and government. In the same
year, the Prime Minister gave what came to be regarded as a keynote
speech at Ruskin College, Oxford, which called for a national
debate about education 'to examine its priorities and to secure as
high efficiency as possible by the skilful use of existing resources'.[77]

The Taylor Committee's report, *A New Partnership for our Schools*
(1977), recommended for county schools equal representation for
four groups – LEA, parents, staff and the local community; and
that governors should assume responsibility for the curriculum.
According to Arthur, covert pressure from the Catholic Education
Council had led the Secretary of State to withdraw from the
Committee's terms of reference those aspects of the government
and management of voluntary schools which arose from their
voluntary character.[78] He, however, provides no evidence to

---

[76.] Auld, *William Tyndale Junior and Infants Schools Public Enquiry, A report to the Inner
London Education Authority*, p. 274.

[77.] Callaghan, *Ruskin College speech*.

[78.] The Catholic Education Council was the successor to the Catholic Poor School
Committee.

substantiate this claim, and, indeed, it is far from clear what it means.

Nevertheless, the ensuing Education Act of 1980 made sweeping changes to the composition of voluntary school managing and governing bodies: indeed, primary school managing bodies were abolished altogether and replaced by governing bodies; provision was made for the headteachers of voluntary schools to become governors if they wished, and for both elected teachers and parents to have a place; the appointment of elected non-teacher governors was provided for, but not made mandatory.

At a stroke, therefore, a voluntary primary school managing body of six became a governing body of eleven to fourteen, and whilst secondary school governing bodies could remain at twelve, the Catholic Education Council advised that this was likely to be too small. There was therefore an immediate need for the recruitment of thousands of new, and necessarily inexperienced, foundation governors, particularly since a limit of five was imposed at the same time on the number of governing bodies of which any one person could be a member.[79] At this stage, little was done to address the powers of governing bodies other than in the field of pupil admissions. Nevertheless, the majority that foundation governors enjoyed over the other interests represented in the governing body was sharply reduced in proportionate terms. From this point, it was going to be much more uncertain that trustees' wishes could be made to prevail through the influence of the local clergy.

[79.] A foundation governor is defined in Regulation 8 of the School Governance (Constitution) (England) Regulations 2007 as 'a person appointed to be a member of the school's governing body other than by a local education authority and who

    (a) is appointed for the purpose of securing the character of the school, including where the school has a particular religious character, such religious character, is preserved and developed, and

    (b) Where the school has a foundation, is appointed for the purpose of securing that the school is conducted in accordance with the foundation's governing documents, including, where appropriate, any trust deed relating to the school.'

Although these regulations clearly post-date the 1980 Act by many years, the definition of a foundation governor has in essence not changed over many decades. The reference to a local education authority is erroneous. As indicated in note 1 above, LEAs ceased to exist as a result of the 2004 Children Act. It should read 'local authority'.

1986 – The Conservative Strong State

By the mid 1980s the Thatcher government was looking for more
radical reform of governing bodies. Kogan had shown wide varia-
tions in the extent of delegation, and that it was impossible for
governing bodies to be free-standing from the political and administrative systems surrounding them.[80] It was not at all clear whether
governing bodies were expected primarily to support and advise
the head or to govern the school.

His research provided the Government with the evidence it
needed, and in 1986 the Education Act (No. 2) Act was passed,
which not only defined both the composition of governing bodies
and their functions in more detail than ever before, but also
attempted to prescribe the respective roles of governing bodies,
LEAs and heads over a wide field. The one conspicuous omission
was the trustees of voluntary schools, no doubt on the ground that
the legislative changes did not impact on their role. Nevertheless,
the balance of partnership changed decisively in 1986, and the
position of the LEA was considerably weakened in comparison with
that of governing bodies.

The Education Reform Act of 1988 was even more radical in
terms of the powers of governing bodies. The National Curriculum
was introduced, LEAs were compelled to delegate budgets to the
majority of schools, and aided school governing bodies were given
the power to appoint, suspend and dismiss staff as they thought fit.
A new type of school was introduced – the grant-maintained school
– and it was here that the first major dispute since the 1940s arose
between the Catholic bishops and the government. The bill
proposed that governing bodies and parents be given the power to
decide whether to seek grant maintained status. The bishops
protested that, as the schools involved actually belonged in law to
the trustees, the consent of the trustees should be sought before
any application could be made. Their position is set out by
Cardinal Hume in Haviland.[81] The Secretary of State, Kenneth
Baker, described his three meetings on the issue with Cardinal
Hume in his autobiography:

> The Cardinal argued that there was a fundamental doctrinal objec-
> tion to grant-maintained schools which made them unacceptable to
> the Catholic Church. It centred upon the position of the Bishop,

---

[80.] Kogan et al., *School Governing Bodies.*
[81.] Haviland, *Take care, Mr Baker*, pp. 128–9.

who derived his authority over his flock directly from the Pope, who had received his from St Peter and thence from God. The Bishop was the father of his followers and nothing should come between them and him. So our opting-out proposals by which Catholic parents could choose to make their school independent of the LEA, even though it would remain Catholic, destroyed that relationship ... The Cardinal in effect was saying that all Catholic schools should be excluded from the provisions of the Government's legislation. The Church should prevail over the State.[82]

The Secretary of State was unmoved.

I was reminded of the same arguments which Henry VIII used to challenge the powers of the Papacy ... *cuius regio, eius religio* ... and ... *imperium in imperio*.[83] [These were] now being re-argued in the last decade of the twentieth century. In the Anglican tradition I argued for the supremacy of Parliament, for at the end of the day the issue was who should determine the law relating to the education of English children in England.[84]

The furthest Baker was prepared to go was to concede that schools contemplating this course should consult their trustees as part of the general process of consultation that was required. In this way were the foundations laid for a major conflict of principle between Catholic school governing bodies and their trustees.

Though the spate of legislation has continued unabated since 1988, it can be argued that most of the Education Acts between then and the Children, Schools and Families Act of 2010 – the last piece of education legislation of the thirteen-year-old Labour government – has simply reinforced the position that was then established. Of the many education acts passed during this time, the two of greatest significance were probably the School Standards and Framework Act of 1998 and the Children Act of 2004. The first of these imposed an upper limit on the size of infant classes, thereby removing from both schools and LEAs any discretion in the matter; required LEAs to prepare and submit to the secretary of state education development plans for their area; gave the secretary of state powers to intervene in an LEA if

---

[82.] Baker, *The Turbulent Years*, pp. 217–18.
[83.] *Cuius regio eius religio* may be roughly translated as 'the sovereign chooses the religion of the state', and *imperium in imperio* as 'a state within a state', that is, in this instance, that the Catholic Church in England and Wales is entitled to certain rights and privileges because of its nature as a universal church.
[84.] Baker, *The Turbulent Years*, pp. 217–18.

he thought it necessary to secure the proper performance of the LEA's functions; and established School Organization Committees, Education Action Zones and Forums, and the office of the Schools Adjudicator, all of which impacted on the powers of LEAs.

The Children Act of 2004 carried central government involvement and regulation to unprecedented lengths. In response to the report into the death of a young child, Victoria Climbié, new local children's services authorities had to be set up to take the place of the century-old local education authorities. They were required to appoint an officer and designate a member to be the lead on children's services matters. Even the title of the chief officer was prescribed. Needless to say they had to prepare a children and young people's plan for the discharge of their functions which had to be approved by the secretary of state. They had to establish a local safeguarding children board whose membership was made up of representatives of partners all of whom were designated.

Reference has already been made to the early challenge made by LEAs to the attempt by Sir Robert Morant and the Board of Education to control the way in which secondary schools were administered. This was the work of James Graham of Leeds and his colleague John Robson of Durham. Later in the chapter, I argued that few developments took place in the organization of schools between the two world wars. The situation is described by Godsden in gloomy detail.[85]

> The Years between the wars were not a happy period for the Board or, indeed, for the education service more generally. The standing of the Board of Education in Whitehall sank low, partly because of the thrust of government policies and partly because the attitude of presidents ... undermined the Board's position with the local authorities.[86]

He quotes The Deputy Secretary, R. S. Wood, writing to the Permanent Secretary Maurice Holmes in 1940 about Eustace Percy, President from 1924–29:

> [His] general policy was to belittle the powers and position of the department, and to circumscribe their control. I do not think that we have ever recovered from the damage of that period.[87]

---

[85] Gosden, *Public Education in England 1839–1939*.
[86] Ibid., p. 12.
[87] Ibid., p. 13.

There were few exceptions. An important one was undoubtedly the development of village colleges by Henry Morris of Cambridgeshire. Then, in the run-up to the Second World War, it was Edmund Rich, Education Officer of the London County Council, who planned and organized the evacuation of the capital's children in the teeth of indifference and open hostility from various government departments.[88]

After the war, a number of LEA chief education officers of remarkable vision and tenacity pioneered advances across the board: men like Sir Alec Clegg of the West Riding of Yorkshire; John Haynes of Kent; Sir Graham Savage and Sir William Houghton of London; and Stuart Mason of Leicestershire. They had the freedom, power and resources, for example, to liberate primary education, develop the concept of comprehensive secondary education, establish youth orchestras, introduce circulating art collections, and encourage and co-ordinate the establishment of new universities in the late 1950s and early 1960s (not waiting, as popular myth has it, for the *Robbins Report*). As I will show later, local authorities now have neither the powers nor the resources to act in this way. They are nothing more than area offices of the Secretary of State, and their officers civil servants in all but name. It may be only a matter of time before much of the edifice is swept away in the name of efficiency and economy. But that is another story.

It seems incontrovertible in the face of all this activity that for a very long time, power over schools has been moving in one direction. So, what is notable about the first piece of legislation to be introduced by the new Coalition administration in 2010 – the Academies Act – immediately began to drive one aspect of the administration of education into reverse.

Reference has been made to the dispute between the Catholic Church and the previous Conservative government over the matter of the trustees of voluntary schools' locus in the matter of applications for grant-maintained status. Grant-maintained schools were abolished by the succeeding Labour government. Those Catholic schools that had become grant maintained reverted to voluntary-aided status. The successors of grant maintained schools were to be academies, and an ambitious programme was introduced aimed at creating a significant number of these establishments by September 2010. Like grant-maintained schools, they were to be completely independent of local authorities, and accountable only

[88.] Gärtner, N., 'Administering "Operation Pied Piper"'.

to the secretary of state. The initial concept had to be modified at least twice before the Labour government fell in 2010, for reasons that do not concern us here. But it has been taken over by the incoming Conservative government, and reformulated so that any school might apply for academy status.

On this occasion, however, clause 3(4) of the Act requires that any voluntary school wishing to apply must first obtain the consent of its trustees before application may be made. This is a remarkable and unheralded change in the approach of the government to trustees. Whether this proves to be an isolated incident, or the operation of the legislation in practice effectively counteracts what appears to be at face value a significant exercise in subsidiarity, or really does mark a sea change in government / voluntary relationships seems doubtful. It is claimed that the 2011 Education Bill will confer on the Secretary of State about fifty additional powers.[89]

The Impact of Globalization

This book investigates how governors of Catholic schools exercise their powers in such a way that the distinctive character of the school is both preserved and developed against the background that has been described. This includes the emergence of an empowered Catholic laity exercising greatly increased legal authority in Catholic schools that exist in a globalized society.

The social theorist Anthony Giddens argues that globalization is political, technological and cultural, as well as economic, and affects intimate and personal aspects of people's lives. Writing before the invasion of Iraq, he tended to see it, certainly in its economic aspects, as synonymous with Americanization. He cited the apparently universal triumph of commodities such as Coca Cola and McDonalds, as well as the influence of multinational business corporations, many of which are based in the USA, to justify his thesis. If this were true at the end of the twentieth century, it may no longer be so at the beginning of the twenty-first. Even if it is, the rapid growth of the Chinese and Indian economies, not to mention the increasing militancy of some Islamic states, may very well mean an early end to American cultural, economic and political hegemony.

In the political sphere, he proposes that it is globalization which underpins the inexorable spread of liberal democracy: the instantaneous electronic dissemination of knowledge has been an

[89.] *Times Educational Supplement*, 4 February 2011, p. 20.

invincible weapon in the struggle for power in authoritarian regimes, and whilst much of this lies well outside the parameters of this book, the inherent characteristic of democracy: the ability of the individual to sift and assess knowledge, and the power of the individual to make decisions in the light of this process that will effect change, is central to it. It is at this point that the political aspects of globalization merge inexorably into cultural ones.

Giddens develops his politico-cultural thesis by proposing that the processes of globalization work in a contradictory fashion, not only pulling upwards but pushing downwards, and creating new pressures for local autonomy. Institutions that appear the same as they used to be from the outside have become quite different on the inside. These he calls 'shell institutions' and include the family, work, tradition and nature. Assumptions and perceptions have changed irrevocably. He goes on to assert that, in western countries, not only are public institutions becoming opened up from the hold of tradition but also everyday life. There is much here of direct relevance to the issue of the relationship of the Catholic Church with its adherents, and I reflect on this matter at the end of the concluding section of this chapter.

Conclusion

The chapter has sought to establish the historical and political context in which school trustees and governors are now operating. From it, a number of significant features emerge. First, the Catholic Church was not, in the early years of the nineteenth century, opposed to the notion of inter-denominational schools, but when it became clear that in England this would be unattainable, the drive to have sufficient schools for the needs of the Catholic population was embarked upon, and has been pursued consistently ever since. Second, tensions have existed between the Church and successive governments throughout the whole of the period over a variety of issues: the extent of government control over the schools; the nature and purpose of education; the supply of places to meet the needs of the Catholic community; and levels of funding. Third, the powers and responsibilities of managers and governors have waxed and waned over the period in the light of changing governmental perceptions. Fourth, following the legislative changes that have been made since 1980, the government of the day offered scant recognition to the interests of school trustees on the single occasion the issue was raised. The strain this has subsequently put on relationships between trustees and governors of Catholic schools will be examined later.

The implications of globalization for an organization like the Catholic Church both in general, and in its work of education within a secular context in particular, appear interesting. The first observation that needs to be made, because it is so easy to overlook, is that the Catholic Church is itself a global organization, and has been for many centuries. It has somehow repeatedly survived cultural and political assaults, in the absence of rapid intercontinental travel facilities and instantaneous communication systems, and appears still to be flourishing in many parts of the world.

The second is that, at least in theory, the Church defused at least some of what could have been the ruinous consequences of globalization, by abandoning its hierarchical structures and adopting a more democratic philosophy during the Second Vatican Council. Indeed, it is possible to argue with some conviction that it is precisely in those areas where such a change is not manifest: the role of women, the nature of marriage, artificial birth control, for example, where it has suffered its most obvious failure to relate to the needs of the world at the end of the twentieth and the beginning of the twenty-first century.

The third is that, despite all this, tensions remain, and many still see the Church as a male-dominated, authoritarian organization more or less out of touch with society in general, and the young in particular.

Chapter 2

The Catholic Church's View of School Education and Contemporary School Governance

Rappresentanti in Terra

The Catholic Church has had a good deal to say about school education in the last eighty years. A convenient starting point is the encyclical of Pope Pius XI *Rappresentanti in Terra* issued in 1929, and written at a time of rising concern about the growth of aggressive nationalism.[1] The backdrop to this encyclical was the then emergent communist and fascist views about the citizen's relationship with, and responsibilities to, the State, and the perceived duty of schools to serve the political systems of the nations in which they were situated.

About the only topic not referred to in this encyclical is the duty of Catholic schools to serve the needs of the poor. Perhaps the reason for this omission was that, given the prevailing social structures of most nation states at that time, the proposition was so self-evident as not to need rehearsal.

Matters such as the recognition that parents are the prime educators of their children; the need for schools to prepare students both to meet their obligations as members of civil society and for their eternal destiny, and to reach out to those who are without faith; the proposition that there is a concept of the common good, to which all education must be directed; the need for co-operation between Church and State in the provision of education; are all to be found within it. In particular:

> It is necessary that all the teaching and the whole organization of the school, and its teachers, syllabus and textbooks in every branch

---

[1.] Pius XI, Pope, *Rappresentanti in Terra* (1929).

be regulated by the Christian spirit ... so that Religion may be in very truth the foundation and crown of the youth's entire training.[2]

The Second Vatican Council 1962–65

On 25 January 1959, the newly elected Pope, John XXIII, announced his plan to convoke the Church's Twenty-First Ecumenical Council, the first since the Council of 1869–70. It opened on 11 October 1962, and was a meeting of all the bishops, world wide. Its aim was to enable the Catholic Church to renew itself by adjusting its thinking, and its mission, to the needs of modern world. In particular, it emphasized the imperatives of concentrating on the needs of the 'lowly, poor and weak', of striving for peace, and of pleading for social justice.[3]

Grace endorses Hastings' view that 'There can be no question that the Vatican Council ... was the most important ecclesiastical event of [the last] century.'[4] Arthur, on the other hand, points out that, as far as education is concerned, the changes were much less significant, arguing that it 'substantially reaffirmed' the contents of the 1929 encyclical of Pope Pius XI.[5]

The document *Lumen Gentium* 'hailed as the most momentous achievement of the Council', and 'the most imposing achievement of Vatican II' laid the foundations for many of the changes and challenges that were to arise in Catholic education in the ensuing decades.[6] Here is not the place to undertake a detailed examination of its contents. It is sufficient to note that it defined, for the very first time in its history, the Church's understanding of its nature. In many respects it was revolutionary: the Church saw itself not, as it had in the past, as a hierarchical, self-serving organization, but as a pilgrim body with a missionary duty to take the Gospel message to the whole world, and one where the laity had a crucial role to play. The consequences of all this, for its work in the field of education, in the light of societal changes that were only then beginning to affect the western world, and which I describe below, cannot be overstated. On the other hand, it is equally important to recognize that *Lumen Gentium* 'does not actually define any new dogmas'.[7]

[2] Ibid., para. 80.
[3] Abbott, *The Documents of Vatican II*, p. 5.
[4] Grace, *Catholic Schools, Mission, Markets and Morality*, p. 55.
[5] Arthur, *The Ebbing Tide, Policy and Principles of Catholic Education*, p. 49.
[6] Abbott, *The Documents of Vatican II*, pp. 10, 13.
[7] Ibid., p. 11.

Gravissimum Educationis

The same contrast is apparent in the Council's work on education. Of the sixteen documents produced in its three-year life, only one concerned this subject – *Gravissimum Educationis,* one of the shortest documents to emerge from its deliberations. Rynne describes its origins in somewhat comical terms. It had been intended to produce a detailed document on the subject of Catholic schools, but the decision was taken, instead, to publish a series of broad principles which were to be developed in the post-conciliar period by a special commission.

The debate on these principles initially showed a general consensus amongst the bishops in favour of the draft document. Most comments on it were accepted for incorporation. But then a major dispute arose over the Declaration on Religious Liberty, and the Council broke down in confusion and disarray whilst it was being debated. Towards the end, no one was paying the slightest attention to the speakers, though order was eventually restored.[8]

Thus, *Gravissimum Educationis,* continuing one of the themes of *Rappresentanti in Terra,* claims that education is the concern of the Church, because the Church has the duty of proclaiming the 'way of salvation to all men, of communicating the life of Christ to those who believe, and of assisting them so that they may be able to attain the fullness of that same life'.[9] More particularly, the Church is under an obligation to provide for its children 'the kind of education through which their entire lives can be penetrated with the spirit of Christ'.[10]

The crucial role of teachers in the success or otherwise of the school is unequivocally stated, and Catholic schools are urged to pay particular attention to the needs of the poor, those who are without the help and affection of family, and those who do not have faith.

Overall, therefore, Vatican II signals a position of continuity in the educative activity of the Church. A more developed view was left to a special postconciliar commission and to the various conferences of bishops.

---

[8] Rynne, *The Third Session,* pp. 225–8, 257–8.
[9] Abbott, *The Documents of Vatican II,* p. 642.
[10] Ibid.

The Catholic School

In accordance with the decision of the Council, the Sacred Congregation for Catholic Education was set up, in 1968, by enlarging the remit of the already existing Sacred Congregation for Seminaries and Universities, to build on the foundations laid by the Council about the Church's thinking about its educative role in schools. Its first major publication was *The Catholic School*, which concerned itself with what it perceived to be the nature and purpose of Catholic schools.

If it is correct that little that was new found its way into *Gravissimum Educationis,* the same cannot be said of this treatise, which set out the nature and purpose of Catholic education in a school setting. Though it has one or two weaknesses, to which I draw attention below, it is, on the whole, difficult to criticize as a basic, but comprehensive, manifesto.

It begins by claiming that the Catholic school is part of the overall mission of the Church to bring the Christian faith to the whole of mankind – particularly important in the contemporary climate of cultural pluralism, materialism and secularism. It proposes that 'the Catholic school has its place in any national school system', and proceeds to address objections that are ranged against them.[11]

A definition of a school is offered as a 'place in which, through a living encounter with a cultural inheritance, integral formation occurs'.[12] On the basis of this there follows what has, perhaps, since become the most frequently quoted defining feature of a Catholic school: 'Christ is the foundation of the whole educational enterprise in a Catholic school.'[13] It is this single basic fact that makes the Catholic school different. The task of the school is to provide 'a synthesis of culture and faith, and a synthesis of faith and life'.[14]

The synthesis of culture and faith is to be achieved by 'integrating all the different aspects of human life in the subjects taught', but the latter are to be treated 'not as mere adjuncts of faith'.[15] At the same time, a cautionary note is sounded that this process is not simply 'the attainment of knowledge, but the acquisition of values and the discovery of truth'.[16]

[11.] *The Catholic School,* p. 9.
[12.] Ibid., p. 12.
[13.] Ibid., p. 14.
[14.] Ibid., p. 15.
[15.] Ibid.
[16.] Ibid., p. 16.

It is at this point that the argument may be seen to falter slightly. It proceeds in this fashion: 'In the measure in which subjects are taught by someone who knowingly and without restraint seeks the truth, they are to that extent Christians.'[17] This seems to suggest that a teacher who is an atheist might be defined as a Christian, a somewhat difficult concept, particularly when 'the achievement of this specific aim ... depends not so much on subject matter as on the people who work there'.[18]

The 'integration of faith and life is part of a life-long process' and '[y]oung people have to be taught to share their personal lives with God'.[19] The concept of the common good begins to emerge at this point: 'they are to overcome their individualism and discover ... their specific vocation to live responsibly in a community with others', and 'to serve God in their brethren and to make the world a better place'.[20]

Whilst religious education must not be confined to specific classes, it must nevertheless be 'imparted explicitly'.[21] Returning to the theme of Christ at its centre, emphasis is placed again on the need for the Catholic school to have 'constant reference to the Gospel and a frequent encounter with Christ' through scripture, liturgy and the sacraments.[22]

The proposition that Catholic schools are divisive, which did not feature in the document's early and brief rehearsal of objections to Catholic schools, now appears. In the context of England in the twenty-first century, this is not an argument that can be disposed of as simply as it is here, but it has to be remembered that the document has worldwide application, and it was expected that individual Bishops' Conferences would apply it to their own local circumstances. It is, perhaps, enough for it to argue that 'since it is motivated by the Christian ideal, the Catholic school is particularly sensitive to the call ... for a more just society' and that 'First and foremost, the Church offers itself to "the poor or those who are deprived of family help and affection or those who are far from the faith".'[23]

The document then moves to review what it loosely describes as 'the practical possibilities open to those who work in, or are

[17.] Ibid.
[18.] Ibid.
[19.] Ibid., p. 17.
[20.] Ibid.
[21.] Ibid., p. 19.
[22.] Ibid., p. 20.
[23.] Ibid., p. 21.

responsible for' Catholic schools.[24] Importantly for the argument
developed in this book, after endorsing the principle of subsidiarity and the legitimate role of the laity, it then appears to revert to
a hierarchical concept by arguing that 'lay involvement in Catholic
schools is an 'invitation to cooperate more closely with the aposto-
late of the Bishops'.[25] By the same token, whilst it is the duty of the
whole Catholic community 'to ensure that a distinctive Christian
educational environment is maintained in practice', '[w]here difficulties and conflicts arise about the authentic character of the
Catholic school, hierarchical authority can and must intervene'.[26]

The key role of teachers is acknowledged, and the need 'to
ensure their continuing formation through some form of suitable
pastoral provision' is stressed.[27] Although there is no explicit
acknowledgement of the existence of school governors throughout
the whole of the work, the need to make appropriate provision for
them has, I suggest, to be extrapolated from this.

It ends by appearing to contradict the difficult claim made
earlier: only a Christian can contribute to building up a Catholic
school, whose success 'cannot be measured by immediate efficiency'.[28] 'Freedom and grace come to fruition in the spiritual
order which defies any merely temporal assessment'.[29] Whether
and how this should be assessed is not explained.

In summary, therefore, what defines a Catholic school is that the
living Christ is at its centre, and its task is to provide a synthesis of
culture and faith, and of faith and life, in order to provide the
pupils with values to work for a more just society. Prayer, study of
the Scriptures, liturgy and the sacraments are all essential features.
The synthesis of faith and life is a life-long process, and the success
of a Catholic school cannot be measured in terms of 'immediate
efficiency'. Whilst the contribution of the laity is recognized, this is
unambiguously subordinated to the bishop.

Lay Catholics in Schools: Witnesses to Faith

Having defined the nature and purpose of Catholic schools, the
Sacred Congregation moved, in *Lay Catholics in Schools: Witnesses to*

24. Ibid., p. 25.
25. Ibid., p. 26.
26. Ibid., p. 27.
27. Ibid., p. 29.
28. Ibid., p. 31.
29. Ibid.

Faith, to examine the role of lay Catholics in them and other types of school. This is accurately described by Grace as 'daunting in its expectations'.[30] Much of the content is not, however, strictly relevant to this book.

There are a number of presentational difficulties. It claims to have application to all 'who are responsible for the direction of the school' but admits that it will concentrate on the role of the teacher.[31] There are, thereafter, few references to, or acknowledgements of, any other members of the school community, or to how they may contribute to the school's mission. Nor is there any discussion about how lay non-Catholics may be successfully inducted into a Catholic school's life.

That said, it is arguably essential that governors have a thorough knowledge of what are the Church's expectations of teachers in their schools. Much of what is written about teachers here must equally apply, then, to governors themselves in the light of the responsibilities that have been placed upon them by successive English governments.

The Catholic educator is called upon to live his vocational identity, '[a]nd if there is no trace of Catholic identity in the education, the educator can hardly be called a Catholic educator'.[32] Does this mean that non-Catholics have no place in Catholic schools as teachers? This is the point at which some comment should have been offered on the problems and opportunities presented by the issue, but the document is silent about it.

Picking up one of the central themes of *The Catholic School*, the Catholic teacher's task is to create for his students a synthesis of faith, culture and life. This involves the presentation of

> the responses Christian revelation brings to questions about the ultimate meaning of the human person, of human life, of history, and of the world, and, derived from this, a set of values which generate human attitudes such as freedom (including respect for others); conscientious responsibility; a search for truth; a calm and peaceful critical spirit; a spirit of solidarity with and a service toward all other persons; a sensitivity for justice; and a special awareness of being called to be positive agents for change in a society that is undergoing continuous transformation.[33]

[30.] Grace, *Catholic Schools, Mission, Markets and Morality*, p. 20.
[31.] *Lay Catholics in Schools: Witnesses to Faith*, p. 9.
[32.] Ibid., p. 15.
[33.] Ibid., pp. 17–18.

We therefore have here a document that presents a number of difficulties. Whilst it claims to have general application to all who work in and for Catholic schools, it is in reality addressed solely to teachers, whose responsibilities are described in terms that verge on the hyperbolic. No satisfactory account is taken of other contributors to the life of the school, and nothing is said about the role of non-Catholic employees in Catholic schools.

The Religious Dimension of Education in a Catholic School

An idealized approach to Catholic education is repeated in the third document to emanate from the Sacred Congregation. The blueprint drawn here again requires schools to provide a comprehensive and ongoing programme of induction and in-service training that embraces the entire staff as well as governors. The implications for schools, particularly primaries, in terms of time and money, are once more, in Grace's word 'daunting' as they are in terms of the time commitment required of governors.

A bleak picture is painted of the materialist and secular societies in which young people are today growing up, and the issues they have to confront. The significance of some of the latter may have altered in the last twenty years: 'the threat of nuclear annihilation, vast unemployment, the high number of marriages that end up in separation or divorce, widespread poverty'.[34] Whilst the threat of nuclear annihilation may, at least for the time being, have diminished, and no one in contemporary Britain can know how serious is the threat of immediate structural unemployment, following the global financial crisis of 2008 and the steps taken by the new Conservative / Liberal Democrat coalition government in 2010, those of climate change and AIDS may well have more than taken their place. Many young people, accordingly, find their lives have no meaning. 'Others live in an environment devoid of truly human relationships; as a result they suffer from loneliness and a lack of affection',[35] and abandon their faith.[36]

The document claims that, despite, or perhaps even because of, this background, 'Positive signs give us reason to hope that a sense of religion can develop in more of today's young people.'[37] Its

[34.] *The Religious Dimension of Education in a Catholic School*, p. 8.
[35.] Ibid., p. 7.
[36.] Ibid., p. 8.
[37.] Ibid., p. 10.

purpose is to show how the Catholic school might respond to this challenge.

The first essential is what is described as 'the school climate'. This comprises seven elements: 'persons, space, time, relationships, teaching, study and various other activities', all of which must have a religious dimension.[38] The religious dimension is defined as an awareness of 'the living presence of Jesus' which influences the entire life of the school community 'through the celebration of Christian values in Word and Sacrament, in individual behaviour, in friendly and harmonious . . . relationships, and in a ready availability' [of the teachers].[39]

The relationship between faith and culture, found in earlier documents, is reiterated. The centrality of religious instruction is also emphasized, and a distinction is drawn, not altogether persuasively, between this, defined as the transmission of knowledge, and catechesis: 'passing on the Gospel message to those who accept it "as a salvific reality"'.[40] The document ends with an outline scheme of religious instruction. Nothing is said, explicitly, about the place of comparative religion in the Catholic school.

The Catholic School on the Threshold of the Third Millennium

By 1998, the Sacred Congregation had been renamed simply the Congregation for Catholic Education. In that year, concern about negative developments, both in society and in the field of education, led to its fourth publication *The Catholic School on the Threshold of the Third Millennium*.

The authors note 'a crisis of values which . . . assumes the form . . . of subjectivism, moral relativism, and nihilism'; a widening gap between rich and poor, 'a growing marginalization of the Christian faith', together with military conflict, hunger, and poverty in many parts of the world, and the spread of urban crime.[41] There is also 'a tendency to reduce education to its purely technical and practical aspects' rather than to foster 'values and vision', and 'to forget that education always presupposes and involves a definite concept of man and life'.[42] Catholic schools are therefore

---

[38] Ibid., p. 12.
[39] Ibid., pp. 12–13.
[40] Ibid., p. 34.
[41] *The Catholic School on the Threshold of the Third Millennium*, pp. 35, 38.
[42] Ibid., p. 40.

confronted with children and young people who experience the difficulties of the present time. Pupils who shun effort, are incapable of self sacrifice and perseverance and who lack authentic models to guide them, often even in their own families. In an increasing number of instances they are not only indifferent and non-practising but also totally lacking in religious or moral formation. To this we must add ... a profound apathy where ethical and religious formation is concerned.[43]

Catholic schools are urged to 'Take up this challenge and respond to it in the conviction that "It is only in the mystery of the Word made flesh that the mystery of man truly becomes clear."'[44] It is notable that there is little reflection on the possibility that the model of Catholic schooling as promulgated at least since the Council might have been less than successful in addressing some of these problems, still less that it might have been, possibly in part, a cause. Thus 'The Catholic school must be firmly resolved to take the new cultural situation in her stride.'[45]

As before, they must remember they always form part of the pastoral work of the Church, and the need to provide pupils with a synthesis of culture and faith, which has run through the previous documents, is reiterated, so that what is taught produces 'a Christian vision of the world, of life, of culture and of history ... a set of values to be acquired and truths to be discovered'.[46]

Other previously enunciated concepts are reaffirmed: that Catholic schools are open to all, and need to pay special attention to the weakest; that the school is a community; that teachers have a central role in creating a Christian climate; and that parents have an important part to play in the educating community. In passing it should be noted that the document comes close to specifying a new category of poor: the materially affluent but emotionally deprived, but does not quite get there. Reinforcing the theme of self-confidence that runs through its pages, Catholic schools should be 'an example and stimulus to other educational institutions'.[47]

These, then are the defining documents that established the framework within which the bishops of England and Wales conduct their network of schools.

[43] Ibid., pp. 37–8.
[44] Ibid.
[45] Ibid., p. 44.
[46] Ibid., p. 43.
[47] Ibid., p. 44.

Spiritual and Moral Development Across the Curriculum

This statement formed a response to a discussion paper of the National Curriculum Council (NCC) on the subject of spiritual and moral development.[48] Stress is laid, in this document, on the concepts of community and the common good, and how Catholic schools, because of their very nature, make a positive contribution to both.

Catholic schools are reminded that they are an expression of the life of the Church in a particular place at a particular time. Their purpose and tasks arise from the sense of purpose of the whole Church. So, any question about the purpose of the latter is also a question to be posed of the distinctive nature of Catholic education. 'The Church does not exist for its own sake ... faith and all its demands are given ... for the well-being of our wider society and of all creation.'[49]

The document proposes that 'This understanding of the nature of Catholic education rests on ... the insistence, in the Catholic synthesis, that the human and the divine are inseparable ... Nothing which is truly human is foreign to God.'[50]

Echoing The Sacred Congregation's texts, it asserts that 'Religious education ... is the foundation of the entire educational process. The beliefs and values it communicates should inspire and draw together every aspect of the life of a school.'[51] Then in a direct challenge to the NCC paper, it goes on to assert that 'Spiritual development across the curriculum is concerned with the individual's growth in faith through his or her deepening knowledge of creation and revelation. Moral development across the curriculum is about how individuals – pupils and teachers – increasingly live that faith within the community.'[52]

The teacher's task in spiritual development 'is to ensure that pupils come to understand that what they are learning in all subjects of the National Curriculum is not an end in itself ... all this

---

[48.] The National Curriculum Council was established under S.14 of the Education Reform Act of 1988. It had duties, amongst other things, to keep all aspects of the National Curriculum in England as defined in that Act under review; to advise the Secretary of State on the curriculum; to carry out programmes of research and development into curriculum matters; and to publish and disseminate information relating to the curriculum for schools. Its remit was confined to the maintained sector. A similar body was set up to cover Wales.

[49.] *Spiritual and Moral Development across the Curriculum*, p. 7.

[50.] Ibid., p. 8.

[51.] Ibid., p. 9.

[52.] Ibid., p. 10.

contributes to our understanding of the way God works in the
world and in our lives and thus of our understanding of and
response to Him'.[53] 'The way in which we and our pupils work is
then seen as contributing to God's creation and continuing
purpose.'[54]

Moral development is defined in the document as 'a growing
awareness of, and a positive response to, the demands of living as
an individual with others in community'.[55] It is then postulated
that 'one of the current features of society in this country is its lack
of any common system of values' and that for Christians, the
natural search for happiness finds its end in the beatitudes.[56] How
they understand and interpret Christ's new commandment 'love
one another as I have loved you' depends on a deepening understanding of God's love for mankind. They work for the good of all
God's creation increasingly as they comprehend the extent of his
love. So, spiritual and moral development are inseparable and
interdependent.[57]

Those concerned with the spiritual and moral development of
young people are reminded that they need to agree on their
shared values and how these are to be put into practice. 'The
extent to which we ... uphold, for example, honesty, respect for
each other, integrity of effort, contributes, or fails to contribute, to
the moral development of children ... Since, for young people,
witness is more effective than words, we need to be particularly
aware of the tendency to say one thing and do another'.[58]

Schools are told explicitly that they need to ensure that their
admissions policies do not exclude pupils with alternative educational needs. If the mission statement includes an aim to help all
pupils achieve their full potential, there is a need to ensure that
the monitoring and evaluation policies are capable of fulfilling this
and that they are effectively implemented. The way the timetable is
constructed and staff are allocated must not sacrifice the weak and
vulnerable.[59]

Teachers are reminded that opportunities must be identified
and used to help pupils to become increasingly aware of moral
issues, and the complexity of moral choices. In the Catholic tradi-

[53.] Ibid., p. 13.
[54.] Ibid., p. 14.
[55.] Ibid., p. 19.
[56.] Ibid.
[57.] Ibid., p. 20.
[58.] Ibid., p. 21.
[59.] Ibid.

tion, making moral decisions is about the judgement of conscience. Young people need to be helped to understand that conscience is not the same as instinct or personal preference, but a responsible and informed judgement based on the moral teaching of Christ and his Church. A crucial element in the moral development of young people is the question of motivation, which needs to be based on the conviction that we are made to live with, in and through community, and find fulfilment in giving rather than receiving. There are many opportunities in school life to promote this.[60]

Finally, Catholic schools are reminded that they need to show the interdependence of spiritual and moral development and that moral development hinges on the practice of self-denial, on the willingness of the person to see his own good in relation to that of others and in terms of a living God who calls us, through generous self-giving, to a true fullness of life.[61]

In the Catholic discourse, therefore, spiritual and moral matters are distinct but interdependent. The ways in which individuals exercise moral choices have inevitable and powerful consequences for the common good, and for the welfare of the societies in which they live.

The Common Good in Education

These arguments were reaffirmed in this document, which was a frank and explicit challenge to the ideology that had underpinned the Education Reform Act of 1988, and which had been developed thereafter.

It opens by expounding a set of propositions on the dignity of the human person, and the social dimension of faith:

> Every human being is made in the image of God ... Christ challenges us to see his presence in our neighbour, especially the neighbour who suffers or who lacks what is essential to human flourishing ... The test, therefore, of every institution or policy is whether it enhances or threatens human dignity.[62]

---

[60] Ibid., pp. 22–3.
[61] Ibid., p. 27.
[62] *The Common Good in Education*, p. 6.

But

> There appears to be increasing confusion in society about the
> nature and purpose of education, stemming from the tendency to
> judge the success of both individuals and of society as a whole by
> economic criteria ... However, economic self-interest should not be
> the basis of ... a commitment [to education]. Education is, primar-
> ily, about 'human flourishing ... the development of the whole
> person.[63]

For a Christian, the aim of education is defined as the drawing out
of young people 'their God-given potential, to enable them to fulfil
their unique role in creation within the human community'.[64]

All involved in Catholic education are reminded they are challenged by Christ 'to see his purpose in our neighbour, especially
the neighbour who suffers or who lacks what is essential to human
flourishing. That is why the poor and the disadvantaged – in financial, social, academic or spiritual terms – must be our primary
concern'.[65] Ways in which this might be effected are listed, and it
is notable that in doing so, the needs of staff, governors and
parents are not overlooked.

The concepts of subsidiarity and solidarity are examined, and
schools are again reminded that they need to have regard not only
to their own interests but also to those of the diocese, other
schools, and also to the common good.

The argument then moves to a consideration of morality in what
it describes as 'the market place'. It is unequivocally and
presciently proclaimed that the Catholic Church explicitly rejects
belief in the automatic beneficence of market forces:

> Catholic social teaching has constantly been aware of the tendency
> of free market economic theory to claim more for itself than is
> warranted. In particular, an economic creed that insists the greater
> good of society is best served by each individual pursuing his or her
> own self-interest is likely to find itself encouraging individual self-
> ishness ... Christian teaching that the service of others is of greater
> value than the service of self is sure to seem at odds with the ethos
> of a capitalist economy.[66]

[63.] Ibid.
[64.] Ibid., p. 7.
[65.] Ibid.
[66.] Ibid., p. 12.

Education is not a commodity to be offered for sale ... Teachers and their pupils are not economic units whose value is seen merely as a cost element on the school's balance sheet. To consider them in this way threatens human dignity. Education is a service provided by society for the benefit of all its young people, in particular for the benefit of the most vulnerable and the most disadvantaged – those whom we have a sacred duty to serve.[67]

Furthermore:

There is already concern that the philosophy of the market place is limiting educational opportunities for the disadvantaged in our society ... The desire to 'succeed' at all costs has encouraged some schools and colleges to discriminate in their selection procedures against pupils with special educational needs or from disadvantaged families ... Others are permanently excluding pupils with emotional or psychological problems ... In some schools, the most able and experienced staff are deployed to teach the most able pupils ... The less able may not be permitted to enter public examinations ... Where specialist resources ... are limited, these are sometimes made available only to the more able students. In all these ways, institutions are neglecting their Christian duty to have a particular care for the weak and disadvantaged.[68]

Ways in which schools might promote the common good are described as

- supporting teachers in their vocation to serve young people;
- promoting excellence as part of a spiritual quest rather than in a spirit of competition against others;
- accepting their responsibility for the education of all, particularly the most disadvantaged in society;
- making joint provision with other schools for those with severe behavioural problems;
- ensuring that those most in need have the best resources available;
- working in partnership with other schools...in order to improve the quality of education for all;
- resisting the temptation to ignore the reasonable aspirations of neighbouring schools.[69]

[67] Ibid., p. 13.
[68] Ibid., p. 14.
[69] Ibid.

The document proceeds to show how the ideology being pursued at that time acted against the interests of those who are most at risk in society. Quoting again from *The Common Good*, it states categorically that '[T]hose most likely to suffer from over-reliance on competition are the poor, vulnerable, powerless and defenceless.'[70] Unlimited free markets tend to produce what is, in effect, an option against the poor. Unrestricted market forces frequently reduce the ability of schools in poor urban and inner city areas to achieve high rankings in test league tables and the lack of a 'value added' factor is unjust and demoralizing. 'It is crucial to ensure that those who do not succeed academically are valued by the community ... All have God-given gifts. What is important is that these should be used to the full.'[71]

Finally, governors are reminded that, as employers, they have a number of specific obligations towards their teaching and support staff:

- ensuring that contracts of service and employment practices are based on Gospel values;
- ensuring that all staff are valued for their contribution to the work of the community;
- linking staff appraisal with staff development;
- promoting a sense of dignity and self-worth among all staff;
- supporting the professional and spiritual development of all staff;
- involving chaplaincy in support of staff as well as students;
- ensuring that the school is run according to Gospel, not market, values.[72]

Governing a Catholic School

Catholic schools and colleges are reminded that they are at the heart of the Church's mission. The legal duty of foundation governors is quoted, and put into a Catholic context: they 'take on the ... responsibility of safeguarding the Catholic nature of their school and the education it provides'.[73] They are advised that they represent those who appoint them and have a legal duty to protect their interests. They play a leading role in the Catholic community:

[70.] Ibid., p. 15.
[71.] Ibid., p. 16.
[72.] Ibid., p. 20.
[73.] *Governing a Catholic School*, p. 5.

they collaborate with the bishop in his ministry in education. It is therefore, important for them to

- know and implement the Bishop's policies on education, including religious education;
- understand and promote the distinctive nature of Catholic education;
- act for the good of Catholic education as a whole within the diocese;
- secure the long term future of Catholic education.[74]

All governors of Catholic maintained schools, not just those of the foundation, are told they 'have legal rights and responsibilities which ensure that they safeguard and promote their school's denominational character'.[75] This is defined as 'appointing Catholic teachers wherever possible; admitting pupils first and foremost on religious grounds; and ensuring that the whole curriculum of the school ... is taught in the light of Gospel values and actively promotes the spiritual and moral development of pupils'.[76]

Finally, again, 'All governors of Catholic schools are partners in the Church's mission in education.'[77]

Evaluating the Distinctive Nature of a Catholic School

This is a revised version of an earlier document that set out to assist governors and school leaders in the task of assessing the extent to which their school is distinctively Catholic. As such, it has important messages with regard to school ethos, a concept which forms a significant element in my enquiry. It carries forward the work of the Sacred Congregation texts in proclaiming that Catholic schools see all life as God's gift, and that every part of the school curriculum is religious and relates to God.[78] Of particular relevance to this book, a school's mission statement should 'provide the foundation for all school ... policies and practices, [and its] review and development ... provide the opportunity to focus on the distinctive identity and character of the school as a Christian community'.[79]

[74.] Ibid., pp. 13–14.
[75.] Ibid., p. 14.
[76.] Ibid., pp. 14–15.
[77.] Ibid., p. 16.
[78.] *Evaluating the Distinctive Nature of a Catholic School*, p. 8.
[79.] Ibid., p. 11.

Schools' activities are grouped under four headings: first, mission, which embraces the mission statement itself; leadership; the admissions policy; the school as a worshipping community; chaplaincy; home, school, parish relationships; the school environment; and equal opportunities; second, the curriculum, both with regard to policy considerations and its implementation; third, the pastoral care of pupils; and, finally, staffing matters. There is much in these pages that ought to inform the policy and practice of any good school. The unique thread that runs through them all, and identifies the distilled essence of the Catholic school is, however, in the words of *The Catholic School* that have already been scrutinized: 'Christ is the foundation of the whole educational enterprise in a Catholic school and its task is to provide 'a synthesis of culture and faith and a synthesis of faith and life'.[80]

Conclusion

The Second Vatican Council proclaimed the principles of modern Catholic education policy, as a result of which schools were reminded they had a key role in the missionary work of the Church, and charged with the task of synthesizing human culture and faith. They were given particular responsibility to serve the poor, the disadvantaged and those without faith, and were to be fully involved in all aspects of the society of which they formed a part.

These themes run through all four publications from the Sacred Congregation (subsequently renamed the Congregation for Catholic Education), and those later developed by the English and Welsh bishops. The latter reflect, as they were required to, the societal background of England and Wales at the end of the twentieth century, and increasingly stress the requirement for schools to enable their students to flourish as unique individuals created in the image of God, rather than simply as economic units in a wealth-creating machine, who have a duty to contribute to the common good. This has led to an increasing tension with the policies of successive Conservative and Labour governments.

What we therefore see is continuity of principle, but also powerful elements of incongruity and challenge in the light of developments in secular society. Some of these developments are the decay of traditional political structures in the western world,

80. Ibid., pp. 14–15.

the decline of respect for formal authority, and the emergence of the cult of the individual. All have implications for the Catholic Church and could, indeed, produce internal incongruities and challenges relating to the conduct of Catholic schools. It is to this I now turn.

Chapter 3

Contemporary School Governance in a Time of Changing Concepts of Power, Politics, and Democracy

Introduction: The Age of 'And'

It is now desirable to place the work undertaken by school governors in its social context.

Governors bring to their work – and, indeed, are expected to do so – a distillation of the totality of their life experience, including, amongst other things, their own education, their employment, their marital status, their position and role in the community, and their personal responses to the social and cultural mores of the society in which they live; in other words, all the ingredients that make up their own personal identities.

Is it possible to isolate the major cultural influences that may be shaping and influencing the thinking and actions of people in contemporary Britain? If it is, how might these be interacting with the thinking of the post-Vatican II Church?

The social theorist Ulrich Beck endorses Kandinsky's thesis that, whilst the nineteenth and twentieth centuries – an era established by the storming of the Bastille – were characterized by 'separation, specialization, efforts at clarity and the calculability of the world', the new order, initiated by Chernobyl and the collapse of the Berlin Wall, which he calls 'the age of "And"', was one of simultaneity, multiplicity and uncertainty. The old political structures were in decay and a new political order was evolving. At the end of the twentieth century, people were being cut loose from the ways of life of industrial society, and a new concept of individualization was emerging. This he sees as a new mode of arranging life, no longer obligatory and embedded in traditional models, but where the individual must produce, stage and assemble his biography himself. He is 'actor, designer, juggler and stage director of his own biography, identity, social networks, commitments and convictions'.[1]

Beck proposes that one important phenomenon to emerge at the end of the last century was political subjectivity. Citizen initiative groups have taken power politically and have created a new social agenda for the future in a movement from below, which Beck defines as subpolitics.[2] Subpolitics, he argues, is distinguished from politics in that it allows agents from outside the political or corporatist system to appear on the stage of social design, and not only social and collective agents but individuals as well compete for the emerging power to shape politics.[3]

He continues that, everywhere, there is a demand for forms and forums of consensus-building and co-operation, but for this to happen, the model of unambiguous instrumental rationality must be abolished. Though this is plainly a hyperbolic claim, since a moment's reflection makes it clear that many people in the contemporary world have much more basic problems of survival to be concerned with matters such as consensus building and co-operation, he makes his point in this way:-

People must say farewell to the notion that administrations and experts always know exactly, or at least better, what is right and good for everyone: de-monopolization of expertise.

The circle of groups allowed to participate can no longer be closed according to considerations internal to specialists but must instead be opened up according to *social* standards of relevance: informalization of jurisdiction.

All participants must be aware that the decisions have not already been made and cannot now simply be 'sold' or implemented externally: opening the structure of decision making.

Negotiating between experts and decision makers behind closed doors must be transferred to and transformed into a *public dialogue* between the broadest variety of agents, with the result of additional uncontrollability: creation of at least partial disclosure.

Norms for this process – modes of discussion, protocols, debates, evaluations of interviews, forms of voting and approving – must be agreed on and sanctioned: self-legislation and self-obligation.

[1] Beck, *The Reinvention of Politics*, p. 95.
[2] Ibid., p. 100.
[3] Ibid., p. 103.

Negotiation and mediation institutions of this type must experiment
with novel procedures, decision-making structures, overlaps of
competence and incompetence and multiple jurisdictions.[4]

Beck's thesis articulates well with Zygmunt Bauman's, who proposes
that we are currently in the throes of what can best be called the
second – this time the secular – reformation, whose catchword is
human rights, that is the right of every individual to use her or his
freedom of choice to decide what the bliss she or he wants ought to
be like, and to select or design her or his own track which may or
may not lead to it. Thus is emerging 'the modular man' of Ernest
Gellner, a creature with mobile, disposable and exchangeable qual-
ities, a man without essence, a self-modelling man who can do well
without a fixed code of rules and yet steer clear of the Hobbesian
nightmare of a life which is bound to be nasty, brutish and short.

Bauman argues that, in face of the globalization of capital,
finance and information, national governments are inclined to
divert the deepest cause of anxiety – that is the experience of individual insecurity and uncertainty – to the popular concern with
threats to safety, by demonstrating their energy and determination
in the war against foreign jobseekers and other alien gate-crashers.
To this must surely be added, in the context of the United
Kingdom, an endless war, however unjustified, against waste, inef-
ficiency and low standards in the public sector in general, and in
health and education in particular.

Market pressures are replacing political legislation as agenda
setters, and the world is increasingly perceived as a container of
potential objects of consumption. Individuals are induced to view
the arousal of desires clamouring to be satisfied as the guiding rule
of the chooser's life. Among the values toward which the choosers
are trained to orientate their choices, the entertainment potential
of objects and events is assigned a superior place. The effects by
which the successful application code of choosing is assessed are
the experiences lived by the agents themselves – self-centred, self-
preoccupied individuals, little interested in the repercussions their
choices might have on anything other than their own sensations.[5]
The resulting decomposition of community finds its correlate in
the fragmentation of life of each one of its constituting units. The
life process of every agent tends to split up into a series of episodes,
each being self-confined and self-sustained.

[4.] Ibid., pp. 122–3.
[5.] Bauman, *In search of Politics.*

Anthony Giddens sees things similarly. According to him, the self is a reflexive project for which the individual is responsible, and must now adopt new mechanisms that are shaped by – yet also shape – the institutions of modernity.[6] Individual societies, rituals and cultural habits kept things more or less the same from generation to generation. Modernity offers no equivalent structure, but it does provide individuals with the ontological security they need to form their self-identities. This security is grounded upon the certitude of rational knowledge. The problem is that knowledge in modernity is always open to revision. Each moment in life is a new moment at which the individual can ask 'What do I want for myself?' 'What to do? How to act? Who to be?' 'These are the focal questions for everyone living in the circumstances of late modernity.'[7]

As a result, in modern social life, the notion of 'lifestyle' takes on a particular significance. The more tradition loses out, and the more daily life is reconstituted in the dialectical interplay of the local and the global, the more individuals are forced to negotiate lifestyle choices among a diversity of options. Personal meaninglessness becomes a fundamental psychic problem in the circumstances of late modernity. This is a repression of moral questions which day-to-day life poses but which are denied answers. 'Existential isolation' is not so much a separation of individuals from others as a separation from the moral resources necessary to live a full and satisfying existence. But lifestyle choices raise moral issues which simply cannot be pushed to one side. Such issues call for forms of political engagement which the new social movements both presage and serve to help initiate.

One possible lifestyle choice is to look to traditional authorities for guidance, of which religion is one. It is for this reason that religion not only refuses to disappear but undergoes a resurgence. As to new forms of political engagement, Giddens argues elsewhere that citizens are developing growing confidence to challenge authority, particularly that vested in political and state institutions, and this is creating a movement to democratize democracy both above and below.[8] The precise term was fashioned by Giddens.[9] He proposes it as a process that democracies need to embark upon in order to counter the growing apathy of their citizens about the

[6.] Giddens, *Modernity and Self Identity*, p. 75.
[7.] Ibid., p. 70.
[8.] Giddens, *Beyond Left and Right: The Future of Radical Politics*.
[9.] Giddens, *Runaway World*, p. 75.

nature of the political process. In order to reconnect with them, he argues that there has to be a devolution of power in relation to the issues that really concern them, together with the creation of new democratic processes to encourage people to participate. The old mechanisms do not work when citizens have access to the same information as those in power over them.

As with Beck, Giddens' argument is somewhat exaggerated. There are many parts of the world where citizens are not growing in confidence to challenge authority, either because of grinding poverty or political or military oppression or, as he argues, and is evidenced elsewhere, because the prevailing mood is one of increasing political apathy. These considerations apart, the proposition certainly seems to hold some validity in its application to western Europe in general, and Britain in particular, though whether his caveat with regard to political apathy is correct may now be open to challenge. One of the 2010 coalition government's first proposals to deal with the deficit it inherited by raising higher education tuition fees brought immediate and serious public disorder and even more public comment and debate. The extent to which this will be replicated when the effects of expenditure cuts on the delivery of public services, and the substantial job losses that form a concomitant part of them, remains to be seen.

Subpolitics, Subsidiarity, Associationalism, and Communitarianism

The political theorist, Paul Hirst sees things rather differently.[10] For him, the collapse of socialism and the stagnation of liberal democracy are creating a climate favourable to the revival of associationalism after a long period of eclipse. He proposes that 'Human welfare and liberty are both best served when as many of the affairs of a society as possible are managed by voluntary and democratically self-governing associations.' He traces the movement as far back as Robert Owen and Pierre Joseph Proudhon through F. W. Maitland, John Neville Figgis, G. D. H. Cole, and Harold Laski to its zenith in 1925, after which it went into a rapid and almost total decline.

It is worth spending some little time examining Hirst's proposals because they seem to have been a major influence on the

---

[10.] Hirst, *Associational Democracy*, p. 112.

thinking of David Cameron, the post-2010 Conservative prime minister, in the development of his proposals for a 'big society' by reducing the role of the state in the lives of (at least) English people.

Hirst claims that the concept of associationalism aims to limit the scope of state administration without diminishing social provision, and enables market-based societies to deliver the substantive goals desired by citizens by embedding the market system in a social network of co-ordinative and regulatory institutions.

Modern associative democracy can only be a supplement to liberal representative democracy. It does not seek to abolish the individual right to vote, nor abolish the state as a public power that attempts to protect the rights of individuals and associations. It extends and enhances liberalism, and does not seek to supersede it. Its central claim is that individual liberty and human welfare are both best served when as many of the affairs of society as possible are managed by voluntary and democratically self-governing associations.

Associationalism seeks to square the aims of freedom for the individual with the effective governance of social affairs. Individualism is rejected because in a purely competitive market society, many lack the resources to achieve their objectives, and the capacity to control their affairs. Freedom can only be pursued effectively by the majority of persons if they are enabled, and supported by society in joining with their fellows in voluntary associations in order to do so. Associations must therefore be protected by a public power that can enforce the rule of law and also, where necessary, be funded by the public through taxation.

The institutional changes proposed in an associative democratic reform are that voluntary self-governing associations should become the primary means of the democratic governance of economic and social affairs; that power should, as far as possible, be distributed to distinct domains of authority; and administration within such domains should be devolved to the lowest level consistent with the effective governance of the affairs in question – in effect the Catholic social doctrine of subsidiarity, which, he notes with approval, has been adopted by the EEC as one means of distributing functions between different levels; and that democratic governance consists in the flow of information between governors and the governed, whereby the former seek the consent and co-operation of the latter.

The state should, accordingly, cede functions to such associations, and provide finance to enable them to undertake them. This means that an associative order in civil society needs to be built up through the establishment of 'private' voluntary bodies that are accountable both to their members and the public power. Associationalism would, therefore, gradually change the primary role of government from that of service provider to a means of ensuring that services are adequately provided and the rights of citizens and associations protected. Self-governing bodies become the primary means of both democratic governance and organizing social life. The state becomes a secondary public power that ensures peace between associations, and protects the rights of individuals.

It is essential, however, that decentralization and de-bureaucratization go hand in hand. There is little point in decentralizing if the result is large and bureaucratically administered local authorities or quangos.[11]

These ideas are developed by Hirst in a set of essays published together under the title *From Statism To Pluralism*. Here he affirms that the state would fund and supervise, but not be directly responsible for, the voluntary self-governing associations that would deliver services in areas like health, education, and welfare. Citizens would choose to join these associations and would have certain entitlements to services, and the associations would receive public funds proportionate to their membership. They would be guaranteed a right of exit. Associational voluntarism would allow the affluent to choose the services they please, and to use their public entitlements to pay for them – at least in part. The poor will still get only the minimum entitlements ... but they could begin to deal with their own problems in their own way, to gain control of their affairs.[12]

It is at this point that questions begin to arise, just the same questions that arise from Cameron's exposition of a reduction in governmental activity in the lives of the people. One looks in vain for an 'education' or 'schools' entry in either volume. Hirst concedes that the success of his system presupposes a mixture of social crusading by those 'haves' who care, and the empowerment of the 'have nots'.[13] But knowledge of the English educational system, where selective schools continue to exist, seems to show that it is precisely this manifestation of philanthropy that does not exist. In Kent, the archetypal selective authority, which I have

[11.] The acronym for quasi-autonomous non-governmental organizations.
[12.] Hirst, *From Statism to Pluralism*, p. 33.
[13.] Ibid., p. 41.

observed and experienced as an officer of the education authority, a member of the education committee and a parent for over forty years, co-operation between schools is severely limited at best. The system is ruthlessly competitive and hierarchical: each community has prestigious grammar schools, where the free school meal entitlement is around two per cent and, at the other end of the scale, a struggling secondary modern school where AEN and working-class children are concentrated, and which most parents will go to great lengths to avoid for their children, if there is any available alternative.[14] This hierarchical system affects all the authority's primary schools as well: they are judged by parents according to their success in obtaining grammar school places for their pupils. Even in comprehensive areas, education reforms of the last fifteen years have made secondary schools, in particular, just as competitive as those in selective LAs. The middle classes have their favoured schools.[15]

If the affluent can use their entitlement to buy into private education, is not this just another manifestation of the neo-liberal voucher system that has been proposed on a number of occasions in the past and then dropped when its practicalities were found to be unworkable?

More fundamentally, just what is a voluntary association in the education sector? Is it a single school or a group of schools? If a group, how will it differ from the school boards that were discontinued over a century ago? If a single school, how will funds be allocated? Schools cannot expand and contract in accordance with the demands of the members of the voluntary association, as successive governments have discovered to their cost in trying to make available 'parental choice', or to introduce voucher systems. Will free transport be available to enable children to reach their first-choice school and if so, who will provide and pay for it? If not, how will the children of the poor be able to exercise their associational rights? What mechanisms will be available to ensure some sort of social justice for those who have alternative educational needs?

Attractive though the concept may be in outline, it is clear that a good deal more detailed work needs to be done to establish its practicability in the education sector. This was recognized by Whitty who called for 'new forms of association in the public

---

[14.] The acronym for alternative educational needs; in this context, children with learning difficulties of one sort or another.

[15.] Ball, *Class Strategies and the Education Market;* Power et al., *Education and the Middle Class.*

sphere within which citizen rights in education policy – and indeed
other areas of public policy – can be reasserted against current
trends towards both a restricted and authoritarian version of the
state and a marketized society'.[16]

More recently, Wolf has issued a note of caution from a different
perspective.[17] She points out that the transformation that has
taken place in the lives of women in the West since the end of the
Second World War has had a number of consequences that get far
less attention than they deserve. One of these is what she describes
as 'the erosion of female altruism'.[18] During the period from the
mid nineteenth to the mid twentieth century, '[a] path once
followed by able women across the developed world led to university, teaching and then motherhood, homemaking and voluntary
work. Such women are now too busy' and, as a result, today, the
middle-class working-age female volunteer has all but vanished:
'The old unpaid female labour force is now otherwise engaged.'[19]
She cites the average amount of time that today's British citizen,
male or female, devotes to volunteer activities as four minutes a
day, though the authority for this claim is not given. In other
words, if associations were set up to do the work Hirst envisages,
who, in hard fact, would join them to do it?

A similar approach is being pursued by the proponents of
communitarianism, a loose movement that emerged in the late
twentieth century in opposition to the concept of radical individualism encapsulated in Mrs Thatcher's famous maxim 'There is no
such thing as society.' The term is used in two senses: philosophical communitarianism and ideological. It is the ideological model
that concerns us here: a belief that many social goals call for co-
operation between government and private groups. The
resonances in contemporary Conservative thinking could scarcely
be more obvious. Arthur and Bailey have examined what this might
mean in educational terms:

- The family should be the primary moral educator of children;
- Character education includes the systematic teaching of virtues
  in schools;
- The ethos of the community has an educative function in school
  life;

[16.] Whitty et al., *Devolution and Choice in Education, The School, the State and the Market*, p. 134.
[17.] Wolf, *Working Girls*, pp. 28, 31–2.
[18.] Ibid., p. 28.
[19.] Ibid., pp. 31–2.

- Schools should promote the rights and responsibilities inherent within citizenship;
- Community service is an important part of a child's education in school;
- A major purpose of the school curriculum is to teach social and political life skills;
- Schools should provide an active understanding of the common good;
- Religious schools are able to operate a strong version of the communitarian perspective;
- Many existing community based education practices reflect features of the communitarian perspective;
- Schools should adopt a more democratic structure of operating.[20]

As with associationalism, there are a number of problems here, for example the apparent assumption that there is an agreed moral code into which all children should be inducted, and that all families are capable of performing this function; and that there is agreement on what virtues should be taught, and how a community and its ethos are to be defined and by whom.

Perhaps this is all irrelevant. There is, as yet, no consensus about what the 'big society' really is. The most recent attempt to define it is by Norman.[21] According to him, the big society already exists, and is evidenced by numerous charitable activities of all shapes and sizes. The problem for him is that this big society is constantly at risk from interference at the hands of government, trespassing in activities that do not concern them.

So far so good, but as with the issues canvassed above, it leaves awkward questions unanswered about what happens when a sectional pursuit of an aspect of the big society clashes with the common good. In the terms of this book, how do you justify the establishment of a free school, which in reality is likely to be the creature of articulate, wealthy middle-class parents, and which then runs the risk of undermining the existing neighbourhood school? No answer has yet been forthcoming.

[20] Arthur and Bailey, *Schools and the Community: The communitarian agenda in education.*
[21] Norman, *The Big Society.*

Education Legislation and School Governance

I have described in Chapter 1 how public opinion in England began to shift in the 1960s and 70s, when there was growing disquiet, both about what was perceived to be the failure of schools to deliver a satisfactory level of education, and about the inability of parents to exert any influence over the course of events. It is now necessary to survey a number of key documents that have already been referred to, in passing, in the first chapter, that illustrate this.

The first of these is the Department of Education and Science Circular 10/65. This requested LEAs to prepare schemes showing how secondary education could be reorganized so as to bring to an end the process of selection by ability at the age of eleven plus. Requiring, as it did, the abolition of grammar schools, this proved to be as contentious a policy as could be imagined, and immediately gave rise to accusations that the quality of secondary education either would be, or, after the event, had been, fatally undermined.

Then, in 1966, the report of the Central Advisory Council for Education (England), *Children and their Primary Schools,* more commonly known as the Plowden Report, after its Chairman Lady Plowden, was published. Reference has already been made in Chapter 1 to its views on the inadequacy of primary school management arrangements. It is necessary here to look at the Report in more detail because of its repercussions, either real or perceived, on the quality of educational provision in primary schools throughout the land.

The enquiry was asked 'to consider primary education in all its aspects and the transition to secondary education'.[22] Overall, [its] 'Report was neither radical nor particularly innovative'.[23] For example, on the curriculum, it had this to say: 'The appraisal we have made ... confirm (sic) many or most of the suggestions that our predecessors made. Their insights have been justified and refined by experience. "Finding out" has proved to be better for children than "being told", and 'The gloomy forebodings of the decline of knowledge which would follow progressive methods have been discredited.'[24] These were, no doubt, references, to, amongst other things, the Hadow Report *The Primary School* published almost fifty years before, which had concluded

[22.] Plowden Report, p. 1.
[23.] O'Connor, *Plowden plus ten.*
[24.] Plowden Report, pp. 460–1.

During the last forty years, and with increasing rapidity in the twelve years since 1918, the outlook of the primary school has been broadened and humanised. Today ... it appeals less to passive obedience and more to the sympathy, social spirit and imagination of the children, relies less on mass instruction and more on the encouragement of individual and group work' ... We see that the curriculum is to be thought of in terms of activity and experience rather than of knowledge to be acquired and facts to be stored.[25]

Nevertheless, reaction to Plowden rapidly polarized, and many were quick to attribute to it perceived failures which had other causes. Lady Plowden was reported to be 'disturbed by the "sloppy thinking and "lack of comprehension"' which attended the implementation of many changes allegedly in line with the report. Much of this she attributed to the 'incompetent expansion' of teacher training, the substantial turnover of teachers, and comparable mobility among senior staff. She was also reported to be 'increasingly concerned that some of her camp followers [were] threatening to throw the baby out with the bathwater, neglecting basic skills and "the sheer knowledge which is an essential of being educated"'. She stressed the report 'never denied the need for computational exercises, nor for leading children towards the stage of reading-readiness'.[26] O'Connor continues:

There are many instances of teachers apologising to inspectors or other visitors when they are discovered actually teaching a whole class, or checking up on tables, as though these are practices that have somehow been proscribed. Either advisers have actually conveyed this impression, or teachers have drawn a false inference: either case implies a distortion of Plowden. Publicity has not helped teachers, but teachers cannot simply blame the media's misrepresentation, for they themselves have compounded this by their mishandling of the publicity that really matters, with their own parents.[27]

It was against this background that the notorious *Black Papers* were published. Brief reference was made to these polemics in chapter 1, when I was describing the growing demand for educational reform that began in the 1960s. Each of the three *Papers* consists of a series of essays, and was concerned with what the editors, Cox and Dyson, saw as the progressive collapse of education, not only

[25] Hadow Report, pp. xvi, 75.
[26.] O'Connor, *Plowden plus ten*.
[27.] Ibid.

in schools, but in higher education, too. They suggested that the first *Black Paper's* major achievement was 'to have broken the fashionable left-wing consensus on education', though what that was is not made explicit.[28] They claimed, in preparing *Black Paper Two*, to have been 'astonished by the naiveté of major documents such as the Plowden Report'.[29]

Perhaps the nature and tone of the *Black Papers* is best summed up by quoting one or two extracts from *A Short Educational Dictionary* compiled for them by the novelist Kingsley Amis and Robert Conquest:

> *Academic.* 1) (Pejorative) Used of knowledge difficult to master, irrelevant (qv) to contemporary reality and deriving from dead or elderly authorities'.
>
> 2) Used of qualifications for university posts: e.g. 'Having beaten up the Vice Chancellor's office in the course of a relevant protest, he is academically qualified for a post as Lecturer in Sociology'.[30]
>
> *Spelling.* A bourgeois pseudo-accomplishment designed to exclude, or penalize, students distinguished for *either* concern *or* creativity *or* both.[31]

The *Black Papers* had an enormous impact. About 80,000 copies were sold, and there was widespread reporting of, and comment on, them in the national press, on radio and on television, and exchanges in the House of Commons (6 May 1969, *Hansard*, pp. 259–62).

The William Tyndale Affair

It is now necessary to return to what became known as 'The William Tyndale Affair' of 1975, described in the Report of Robin Auld QC. This was a series of events that led to the complete breakdown of one of the Inner London Education Authority's Islington primary schools in 1974. As with the *Black Papers*, this was briefly referred to in Chapter 1.

A new headteacher, Mr Ellis, took up duty at the beginning of the spring term of that year. The school was, by all accounts,

---

[28] Cox and Dyson (eds), *Black Papers*, p. 12.
[29] Ibid.
[30] Ibid., p. 215.
[31] Ibid., p. 222.

reasonably successful, and well regarded by parents, but Mr Ellis did not approve of the way it had been conducted. He was of the view that it did not serve the interests of children, 'particularly those from deprived backgrounds and / or who were of low academic attainments or had disturbed personalities', and that the best way to put matters right was to give them 'scope to express their own personalities in their own way and at their own pace'.[32]

The Public Enquiry set up by the Inner London Education Authority to investigate what eventually transpired as a result of this ill-judged initiative, which had been pursued without any planning or consultation with any other party, made a very large number of disturbing findings, at least some of which had nationwide significance. Most importantly for this book,

> It is difficult to determine the precise nature of the oversight that managers are expected to exercise. Although some oversight of the conduct and curriculum of the school by someone other than the headteacher is no doubt necessary, one of the many questions that this Inquiry has brought to the fore is whether managing bodies as presently constituted, or at all, are the bodies best qualified to exercise that function.[33]

It is difficult to over-estimate the effect this matter had on public opinion. The affairs of the school had become a national scandal, with extensive coverage in the media. The message was stark: parents, the education of whose children was at stake, had found it virtually impossible to have their concerns addressed; the ability of managers to cope with a situation such as this had been called into question by a public enquiry; and the largest, and to many the most prestigious, local education authority in the land had shown itself unwilling to intervene until too late.

The Beginnings of Change – The Education Act 1980

Against this backdrop, it is hardly surprising that the government of the day (by now a Conservative one) decided that action had to be taken. The transformation of the nature and functions of governing bodies since the Education Act 1980 has been outlined in chapter 1. It is necessary, here, to look into the matter in more

[32] Auld, *William Tyndale Junior and Infants Schools Public Enquiry. A report to the Inner London Education Authority.*
[33] Ibid., p. 25.

detail. In doing so, I shall examine whether governing bodies have been given power to govern or, on the contrary, have simply reverted to the role of managers, with real power transferred from the local education authority to the Secretary of State.

As has been stated (p. 37), the 1980 Education Act, which was the first time for almost forty years that questions of school governance had been addressed in legislation, made what were, without question, fundamental changes to the constitution of all governing bodies. Symbolically, perhaps, primary school managers were re-designated governors. Provision was made for elected parent and teacher governors; the head could be a governor if (s)he wished; and discretionary powers were set up to provide for the election of non-teaching governors. The virtual monopoly of power exercised by the LEA in the case of county schools and the trustees in the case of voluntary ones appeared, as a result, to be irrevocably shattered.

As to powers and duties, Parliament moved more cautiously. Governing bodies were required to publish their arrangements for the admission of pupils and the number of pupils to be admitted to any year group. They were required to comply with a preference for the school expressed by a parent other than in three defined situations, and had to make arrangements to enable parents to appeal against a decision of theirs not to admit a child. Finally, a restriction was placed on anyone being a governor of more than five schools; and any governor who failed to attend meetings for a period of twelve months automatically ceased to hold office, unless the absence was with the consent of the governing body.

The question that immediately arises is this: although the size and membership base of governing bodies has considerably expanded, to what extent have their powers of governance, as opposed to management, increased? In this connection, Kogan et al. were quite clear that the 1980 Act, despite the best of governmental intentions, left LEAs still very much in control of their operations.[34] There can be little doubt that they were right: although the composition of school governing bodies had changed radically, almost nothing had been done to give them greater powers, something that was, perhaps, even more urgently required than before, since one of the objects of the reform of local government in 1974, after the 1966 Royal Commission reported in 1969, was the creation of larger, more efficient and more powerful LEAs.

[34.] Kogan et al., *School Governing Bodies*.

Parliament Tries Again – The Education (No. 2) Act 1986

The background to this piece of legislation has, again, been described in chapter 1. On this occasion, the conduct of every school was put under the direction of the governing body, but subject to a large number of exceptions.

Every LEA was required to draw up a curriculum policy. The 1944 Act gave control of the secular curriculum to the LEA in all schools except aided secondaries. This Act transferred control to aided primary governors as well, but they were required to 'have regard' to LEA policy.

Governing bodies were to publish information about the school as required by the Secretary of State. Control of the terms, session times and holidays was transferred to governing bodies, but, since many schools were constrained by home-to-school transport and meal arrangements organized and co-ordinated by the LEA, this concession did not amount to much, in many cases.

Discipline policy was put in the hands of the head, subject to any general principles laid down by the governing body, which was given power to re-instate a pupil permanently excluded by the head. The governing body and LEA were also given power to re-instate a pupil excluded for a fixed period or indefinitely. LEAs were to give schools budgets to spend, at their discretion, on books, equipment, stationery 'and such other heads of expenditure (if any) as may be specified by the authority and prescribed by the Secretary of State'. Governors were required 'to comply with such reasonable conditions as the authority think fit to impose'. Governing bodies that were admissions authorities were also to consult the LEA at least once a year as to whether their admissions arrangements were considered satisfactory, and also before determining or varying them.

The Education Reform Act 1988

Whilst the balance of power might have begun to move in the direction of governing bodies, in the light of the 1986 Act, there can be little doubt that LEAs were still a major factor in the provision of school education in England and Wales and that governing bodies were still largely subservient to them.

The 1988 Act changed all that. For the first time in England and Wales, a National Curriculum was introduced, consisting of

religious education; core subjects that were defined as mathematics, English and science, together with Welsh in
Welsh-speaking schools; and foundation subjects that comprised
history, geography, technology, music, art, physical education and
Welsh in non-Welsh speaking Welsh schools. All pupils were to be
assessed at prescribed times – the end of what were named key
stages one to four.

The Secretary of State was to establish, and keep under review,
the content of the National Curriculum, the targets pupils were
expected to attain, all programmes of study for the National
Curriculum, except RE, and the assessment arrangements that
were to be put in place at the end of the four key stages. Clearly this
measure amounted to a massive and unprecedented transfer of
power from the local community, whether that be defined as the
LEA or the individual school governing body, to the state.

Other provisions of this Act transferred power from the LEA to
governing bodies: provisions for financial delegation were greatly
extended, and schools were to have greater freedom and responsibility in staff matters. Aided schools were given powers to appoint,
suspend, and dismiss staff as they thought fit.

Finally, secondary schools and voluntary primary schools with
three hundred or more registered pupils on roll were given the
ability to become 'grant maintained'. These were to be completely
independent of the LEA, and funded directly by the Department
for Education and Science. They remained, however, subject to
much the same statutory requirements as all other maintained
schools and to the authority of the Secretary of State on a significant number of matters. The initiative to seek grant-maintained
status lay either with the governing body of the school or with
parents.

The minutiae of the arrangements are not central to the argument. What is important here is that, whilst it was open to a school
to make a proposal for grant-maintained status, the ultimate decision rested with the Secretary of State.

There can be no doubt that the overall effect of the 1988 Act was
to strengthen enormously the power of central government
through the Secretary of State at the expense of LEAs. The
Secretary of State now controlled what was taught in schools, and
the arrangements for a programme of national testing at both
primary and secondary levels. He could decide which schools
acquired complete freedom from the LEA. Increased restraints
were placed on governing bodies' ability to control the admission
of pupils as they saw fit. True, governing bodies now had greater

financial freedom from LEA control, but what this amounted to was no more than an extension of their ability to manage a budget, the size of which was, to all intents and purposes, determined by the LEA, even if the money came, as in the case of grant maintained schools, from the Department. Furthermore, once account is taken of the very substantial proportion of the budget allocated to staffing costs, the bulk of which is required to service the demands of the National Curriculum, there must be doubt as to the extent of any genuine delegation of power, even in financial matters.

Further Centralization

The next major piece of legislation, the Education Act 1993, continued the trend towards central control. LEAs were removed from responsibility for providing an education service. Under S.1 of the 1993 Act the Secretary of State was now to 'promote the education of the people of England and Wales', and under S.2 (2) to 'exercise his powers with a view, amongst other things, to improving standards, encouraging diversity and increasing opportunities for choice'.

A new body was created, the Funding Agency for Schools, to take responsibility for financing grant-maintained schools. In certain circumstances this body or the LEA could direct an admissions authority (in the case of a Catholic school the governing body) to admit a pupil to a school who had either been refused admission or permanently excluded from a school, and the Secretary of State was given powers to modify school trust deeds if this became necessary, should the school seek grant-maintained status. Sex education was made obligatory in secondary schools and had to include education about AIDS, HIV and other sexually transmitted infections.

It is hard to see anything in this Act that extends the concept of delegation of power. On the contrary, the movement is again all one way: from governing bodies and LEAs to the Secretary of State.

A change of government in 1997 produced a need for further extensive legislation. A full account is not required here. It is sufficient to note, first, that, although LEAs were given responsibility for promoting high standards in primary and secondary education, their subordinate role was re-emphasized by the reiteration of S.1 of the 1993 Act. A prescribed limit on the maximum size of infants' classes further reduced governors' discretion, and overall, the power of the Secretary of State to make regulations was greatly augmented, as were his powers to give 'guidance' and issue codes of practice. In particular, the restricted power to modify an aided school's trust deed was replaced by a general one applicable in any circumstances. As with the 1993 Act, it is difficult to identify anything of significance that enhances the powers of governing bodies, parents or the local community.

School Governance Examined

I now return to my proposition that the literature on school governance manifests both an emphasis upon good management at the expense, often, of democracy, representation and participation, and a failure, adequately, to address concerns specific to Catholic school governance.

One of the earliest commentaries on the issue of school governance was *Improving Schools* (1994), where the role of governors in school improvement was first highlighted. School improvement was then defined as the ways in which schools:

- raise standards;
- enhance quality;
- increase efficiency;
- achieve greater success in promoting pupils' spiritual, moral, social and cultural development.

In 1999, Scanlon concluded that there was a clear association between effective schools and effective governing bodies, and identified no fewer than ten factors, of which a positive attitude on the part of the head was held to be crucial.[35]

Ofsted has continued to reflect on the role of governors over the years: in 2001, a study of schools that had been taken out of special measures[36] defined eleven functions of governing bodies that made a difference to the performance of their schools.[37]

[35] Scanlon et al., *Improving the Effectiveness of School Governing Bodies.*

[36] A term used to describe a school which has been found, by Ofsted, following an inspection, to have serious failures in one or more areas of its activities.

[37] Ofsted (2001), *Making It Better: Improving School Governance* identified the following characteristics of effective governing bodies and governors:
- Governors are clear about the aims of the school and the values they wish to promote;
- The governing body, and all its committees, have clear terms of reference and an inter-related programme of meetings;

In 2003, the work of governing bodies was given a high profile in the arrangements for the ensuing cycle of inspections. This seemed to be substantially undermined in the 2005 *Framework* (the document that defines the basis on which school inspections will be carried out). Governing bodies, however, were then charged with responsibility for the self-evaluation form that lies at the heart of the inspection process. They also remain responsible for the annual performance review of the headteacher.[38]

- Governors bring a wide range of expertise and experience and attend meetings regularly;
- The chair of governors gives a clear lead;
- Meetings are chaired well and efficiently clerked;
- There is a school plan, understood by all, which focuses on improving the school;
- Relationships between the governors and the staff are open and honest;
- Governors' training is linked to the school's priorities, and the needs of individual governors;
- Individual governors are clear about their role;
- The school's documentation is systematically reviewed;
- Governors have rigorous systems for monitoring and evaluating the school's work.

[38.] The 2003 Handbook for Inspections contained specific references to the need for inspectors to evaluate governance, which was to be judged on fixed criteria and graded from 2 (very good) to 6 (poor). The questions the inspectors were required to answer were:
- To what extent do governors help shape the vision and direction of the school?
- Do governors ensure that the school fulfils all its statutory duties, including
- promoting inclusive policies in relation to race, disability and sex?
- Do governors understand the strengths and weaknesses of the school?
- Do governors both challenge and support the senior management team?

None of this found its way into the next (2005) Framework, which was explicit that the new regime was to be one of 'short, focused inspections that ... concentrate on close interaction with senior managers in the school' (*Framework for Inspections in England 2005*, p. 1.). Though the basis of the inspection is now the school's self-evaluation form for which the governing body takes responsibility, the inspectors' focus during the on-site visit is on staff and pupils. Given the short notice of an inspection (zero to two days) that schools now receive, and that inspections do not normally last more than two days, it is entirely possible that no appropriate governor will be available to meet the inspection team. The current arrangements (Ofsted's *Framework for Inspection* from 2009), require that the self-evaluation form is to be used by the lead inspector to plan the inspection. It is also to be the basis for discussion with the school's senior leadership team and *where possible* [my italics] members of its governing body. The schedule of judgements in assessing the school has but one brief reference to the governing body: its effectiveness in challenging and supporting the school so that its weaknesses are tackled decisively. Given all the

Meanwhile, the DfES and its predecessors the DfEE and the DFE[39] produced a series of publications. *Governing Bodies and Effective Schools* sought to define the main roles of governing bodies in raising standards and improving schools. *The Governors' Role in Raising Standards,* following the Education Act 1998, reinforced this, claiming that governing bodies should have a strategic view of their main function, which is to help raise standards, and clear arrangements for monitoring against targets. *Roles of Governing Bodies and Headteachers* largely restates this position, but refers to 'progress' rather than improvement. The *Steering not Rowing* Conference urged governing bodies to undertake their own process of self-review and to be prepared to act as leaders with a vision, and to be prepared to act as agents for change. The *Guide to the Law for School Governors* has gone through a number of revisions over the years, the latest version – 2010 – lists a number of detailed matters on which voluntary-aided school governors are required to consult their trustees: the content of the instrument of government, and proposals with regard to federation, or to change the status of the school. But the basic requirement to conduct the school in accordance with the trust deed seems nowhere to be referred to. This is surprising, as it is explicitly referred to in the School Governance Regulations 2007. The matter is not a hair-splitting one: governors are aware of the *Guide to the Law,* and have ready access to it. The same cannot be said of the *School Governance (Constitution)(England) Regulations 2007.*

At the same time, others have sought to explore the broader role of governing bodies. One of the seminal studies is that of Deem et al. This was a research project involving at first fifteen, later reduced to ten, primary and secondary governing bodies in two contrasting LEAs. One limitation of this work is that voluntary-aided schools were deliberately excluded from the investigation, on the ground that the changes brought about by the 1986 Act were less far-reaching in voluntary aided schools than in others. This does not, however, limit the significance of their findings for my study.

In order to place English experience in context, the researchers examined school governance and educational reform in a

---

constraints that bear down on the inspection process, there has to be considerable doubt about the extent to which Ofsted now considers governing bodies to be of any real significance.

[39.] DfEE is the acronym for the Department for Education and Employment; DfE is the acronym for the Department for Education.

number of different countries, including Australia, New Zealand and the USA, as well as Scotland and Northern Ireland. They discovered that in all but the USA and Scotland, site-based management had been 'developed within a strong framework of centrally controlled curriculum, which seems to contradict some of the wilder claims for the autonomy afforded to schools'.[40] They also pointed to the creation of quangos, with substantial powers, particularly over the distribution of resources, and argue that, 'at the same time the powers of the central state have been increased rather than diminished'.[41]

They recall that the White Paper, *Better Schools* (DES 1985), which preceded the Education (No. 2) Act 1986, claimed that the extension of opportunities for citizens to participate in school governance 'would make governing bodies more effective instruments for giving schools identities of their own as opposed to them simply being agencies of the LEAs'.[42] However, they concluded that:

> Governing schools has become an important arena for the exercise of citizenship. It is however an imperfect one, because while there has been a numerical redistribution in tipping the balance between 'bureau professionals' (i.e. teachers and local authority administrators) to the lay governors, the latter have not gained power over schooling in any real sense ... This is in part because, alongside the rhetoric of subsidiarity and the devolution of decision making, the state has taken close control of the curriculum and had pressurized teachers to adopt certain pedagogical styles. Governors supposedly have power over the way that the school's finances are allocated, but the amount of money a school receives is subject to central regulation and so much is taken up by salaries that most governing bodies have very little financial discretion. Thus what tend to be devolved are the problems but not the means to their solution.[43]

They go on to argue that 'Site-based management itself does not necessarily give governing bodies and their schools autonomous decision-making powers if they are still constrained by the requirements and demands of central and local government.'[44]

In summary, they conclude that governors are 'agents of the state at a distance', working within the parameters of national criteria which they have had little or no part in formulating, but that

[40] Deem et al., *Active Citizenship and the Governing of Schools*, p. 15.
[41] Ibid., p. 17.
[42] Ibid., p. 44.
[43] Ibid., pp. 62–3.
[44] Ibid., pp. 131–2.

it is not acceptable for lay people to do the state's work for it under the guise of semi-autonomous devolved management, which is falsely seen to empower schools, parents and the community.[45]

Creese and Earley (1999), unlike Deem, did include a Catholic mixed comprehensive in their study. This concluded that, when governing bodies are working well, they are capable of making a difference to a school. They reported a growing body of evidence that there is a significant link between an effective school and an effective governing body. What was not so clear was the direction of that link. They found that the inspection process made many governing bodies give serious thought to the way in which they operated and were much involved in the post-Ofsted action plan. The inspection process had therefore empowered many governing bodies. Church schools are, of course, doubly involved in this because they are open to a separate inspection of their denominational RE and worship in addition to the standard Ofsted inspection. It is possible, therefore, that this double process is having a proportionately greater effect on the work of the governing bodies concerned than those of other schools.

According to Deem and her colleagues, school governing bodies do not provide examples of the democratization of democracy, as envisaged by Bauman, Beck and Giddens. They take the view that the reforms of the 1980s and 1990s seem to have removed from the governance of education both the experiences of participation in democratic politics, and the accompanying mechanisms of accountability, inadequate though they may have been. They call for the retention of some intermediary democratic layer which, by that stage, English educational reforms had striven so hard to obliterate. This is a process which has continued apace in the intervening decade, notwithstanding a change of national government from a neo-liberal one to a New Labour one, between 1997 and 2010.

The new political backdrop to governance was examined towards the end of the Labour Government's first term of office by Newman (2001). She paints a picture of a government, increasingly frustrated by its evident lack of power to make things happen in the public sector, struggling to exert ever tighter control from the centre rather than being able to re-configure the relationship between the citizen and the state, with a new emphasis on the values of community and the role of civil society.

Newman argues that, as a result, we are confronted by a situation

---

[45.] Ibid., p. 161.

where appearances are deceptive. In her analysis, although the literature suggests a series of shifts which push responsibility for, and decision making in, public services downwards, the reality of the contemporary situation is very different.

Rather than a coherent and unidirectional change from markets and hierarchies towards governance through networks, Newman argues that the process has been uneven and ambiguous, and cross-cut by strong counter-pressures. There are, she says, severe limitations to the process of decentralization, and alongside partial decentralization there is a clear recentralization of political control, manifested in the promulgation of a plethora of performance standards such as the literacy and numeracy hours, performance review procedures, audit and inspection measures, and the threat of the removal of powers from 'failing schools', with which school governors will be all too familiar.

Newman concludes that the overall dominant pull was therefore towards vertical integration, centralising power to government. Whilst its impact was uneven, it was strongest in the fields of health, education, social services and probation, and this could be viewed as continuing an uncompleted part of the Thatcherite programme of public sector reform. In other words, school governors are just as much the 'state volunteers' of Deem et al. as ever they were, if not more so.

Others continue to hope for better times. Halpin (1999) saw signs for a more inclusive politics of education in the (then) new Labour Government's Education Action Zones, though he cautiously admitted he had worries, most of which, unfortunately, appear to have been realized. He noted that the first wave of zones was inaugurated with very little preliminary debate among the various interests who were intended to run them. Thus, LEAs authored the first bids and teachers, parents and other community concerns, particularly business ones, were barely consulted. What is interesting for the purposes of this study, and taking up one of the two themes highlighted at the beginning of my historical survey, is that the Archdiocese of Southwark advised schools not to agree to cede any powers to the Education Action Forum. It took the view that it would be unacceptable for its governing bodies to yield control of their schools to another statutory body which had no concern for, or interest in, maintaining their distinctive religious character, for which the trustees were accountable to the Charity Commission.

Even so, Halpin, writing earlier, with others, was ready to concede that '[In] the compulsory phases of education ... the introduction of quasi-markets usually involves a combination of parental choice and school autonomy, together with a considerable degree of public accountability and government regulation.'[46] He supports Johnson, who argues that the new opportunities afforded by recent policies are narrow in scope.[47] He goes further and postulates that 'The imposition of the National Curriculum has taken out of [governors'] hands many of the issues connected to teaching and learning which they may have previously debated.'[48] In summary, he concludes that 'The reduction in bureaucratic and democratic control within education has actually enabled the contemporary state to consolidate its strategic position and steer institutions more effectively.'[49]

Dean et al., reporting in 2007 a study of three contrasting areas characterized by social and economic disadvantage, found that governing bodies often lacked the capacity to be effective and were confused about the real purpose of their work.[50] They suggested that successive waves of school reform had taken place without real consideration of the implications for governance, and argued that a national debate on this was needed, linked to questions about the nature of democracy in disadvantaged areas. In particular, they reported that governors in the schools surveyed did not feel able to challenge decisions made by their local authority, and, perhaps more worryingly, that governor support services in the local authorities by and large experienced low status. There are significant questions here for the proponents of the big society.

Amidst all this activity, little attention had been paid specifically to Catholic schools. Arthur's work, *The Ebbing Tide, Policy and Principles of Catholic Education*, has already been cited. This is a difficult book to interpret. In its central argument it reads like a polemic rather than an impartial work of scholarship. From the outset, the author makes his position clear: 'Many Catholics, both clerical and lay, are deeply concerned about the direction that Catholic schools have taken ... This book aims to fuel the fire of these concerns.'[51] The principal argument is that the Catholic Church's current leaders have failed to develop not only a credi-

---

[46] Whitty et al., *Devolution and Choice in Education, The School, the State and the Market*, p. 4.

[47] Johnson, *Thatcherism and English education: breaking the mold or continuing the pattern?*

[48] Ibid., p. 99.

[49] Ibid., p. 138.

[50] Dean et al., *Schools, Governors and Disadvantage in England*.

[51] Arthur, *The Ebbing Tide, Policy and Principles of Catholic Education*, p. 1.

ble educational policy, but any policy at all, other than a restate-ment of the need to secure a place in a Catholic school for every child whose parents wanted one. However, in response to the bishops' attempts either to follow long-established principles in the matter of the appointment of Catholic teachers or to evolve a policy which argued against the concept of grant-maintained schools based on the Church's teachings on social justice, Arthur is scathing in his condemnation of their alleged attempts to usurp the rights of governors. It is difficult to see how these positions can be reconciled.

Grace's work, on the other hand, provides a framework and it is, indeed, on its foundations that this book is substantially constructed. He points out that the manifest success of Catholic schools in terms of the yardsticks designed by the secular authori-ties is generating

> its own contemporary threats to the integrity of the holistic mission caused by undue emphasis upon ... the visible and measurable in education to the detriment of the invisible and more intangible outcomes of schooling; the potential for Catholic schools to be incorporated into a secular marketplace for education which may weaken their relation with the sacred and spiritual.[52]

He confined his study to maintained Catholic secondary schools in London, Liverpool and Birmingham. I both widened the focus, by extending it to both primary and secondary schools in different social environments, but simultaneously narrowed it to concen-trate exclusively on work of governors.

Grace answers Arthur's thesis by proposing that, in the absence of a fully articulated Catholic philosophy of education for modern culture, Catholic educators have in practice used as a resource the formal publications and declarations on Catholic education of the institutional Church that have been cited earlier in this text.

He proceeds to apply social theory, in particular aspects of the work of Bourdieu and Bernstein, to a deeper understanding of Catholic education. He argues that Bourdieu's concept of 'field' reveals at least two areas of struggle: legitimation and control.[53] The legitimation struggles fall outside the scope of this study, but struggles over control lie at its heart, and, as might be expected, centre round clergy-laity relations. Bourdieu stresses that one of

---

[52.] Grace, *Catholic Schools, Mission, Markets and Morality*, p. 4.
[53.] Ibid., p. 27.

the important ideological consequences of symbolic power is that 'the dominated accept as legitimate their condition of domination'.[54] Grace claims that this describes very well the general pattern of response by the Catholic laity to clerical leadership in schooling till the late 1980s.[55] The 1980s and 1990s were to demonstrate the limitations of Catholic symbolic powers in education in changed cultural, ideological and political conditions. At this time, the rise of the ideology of parentocracy in schooling presented the Catholic hierarchy with two major challenges. In the first place, parents were given precedence in educational decision making over the Catholic community of which they were only a part, and control of the governance of specific Catholic schools could pass from clerical leadership to parental leadership, with radical implications for the Catholic ethos of the school.[56]

Grace postulates that there is no simple unitary habitus of Catholic socialization but rather a number of varieties of which the comprehensive school is one. Although he pays little attention to primary schools, it is clear that they do have such a habitus and that it is closely linked to the secondary one.

Grace cites Bernstein's proposal that a major cultural transformation can be discerned in Europe from a faith-based conception of knowledge and pedagogy to a secular, market-based conception of education. He argues that the pedagogy of a faith-based curriculum has to acknowledge, at least at the formal level, the Christian value and dignity of every pupil and student, regardless of achievement. The pedagogy of the market curriculum has no similar principled constraint, and its potential danger is that pupils and students may become differentially valued as 'output assets'. The problem facing Catholic schools is that they are caught up in the working of the secular, market curriculum, a performance-based pedagogic regime, and a system of accountability and evaluation where measurable and visible outcomes are dominant.

Grace suggests that Catholic education institutions are now more weakly insulated from external agencies than in earlier historical periods. The issue which this generates, he argues, is whether this represents a progressive development of the mission of Catholic schools, and a fruitful realization of the openness principles of Vatican II reforms, or a loss of distinctive voice, character and integrity for the Catholic faith in the modern world.

[54.] Swartz, *Culture and Power: The Sociology of Pierre Bourdieu*, p. 89.
[55.] Grace, *Catholic Schools, Mission, Markets and Morality*, p. 31.
[56.] Ibid., pp. 34–5.

Comparable problems arise over Bernstein's concept of framing. Historically, the framing of Catholic curricula, pedagogy and evaluation was determined by the institutional Church. The educational reforms of the 1980s and 1990s made the state the principal framer. Has this dealt a fatal blow to concepts of a Catholic curriculum and pedagogy?

The answer is, predictably, not clear cut, as will become manifest in subsequent chapters. For while the diocesan directors are very largely sanguine about the context in which they are working, several of the governors appear to be unaware that there might be a problem, and others, indeed, seem to indicate that the secular ideology holds sway in their particular school.

Grace proposes that Bourdieu's concept of 'cultural capital' can be extended to include 'spiritual capital'. This he defines as 'resources of faith and values derived from commitment to a religious tradition'.[57] It is not, therefore, a characteristic exclusive to Catholic schools, but has application to all that are faith-based. Nevertheless, he argues that the Catholic school system has benefited from the presence of spiritual capital, found in school leaders drawn from 'priests, teaching Brothers and Sisters of various religious orders and from lay men and women who have acquired a sense of vocation through their own Catholic schooling and college experiences'.[58] His thesis is that future generations of school leaders and teachers in Catholic education are unlikely to benefit from this matrix of sources for spiritual capital and that this is already producing 'a major contradiction in a system of schooling which exists to give the nurture of spirituality a top priority and [is demonstrating] that the traditional spiritual capital of Catholic school leadership is a declining asset'.[59]

As stated above, this study aims, amongst other things, to take Grace's work a stage further by examining the position in primary as well as secondary schools, probing the awareness of governors of the issues, and seeing what strategies, if any, are being developed to deal with them. The approach was twofold. First, all the governors who returned questionnaires were asked to comment on three issues where tensions may exist: the appointment of senior staff, the admission of pupils, and the application of the Church's teaching about sexual morality to Catholic teachers. Second, those governors who were interviewed were questioned about a range of

[57.] Ibid., p. 236.
[58.] Ibid.
[59.] Ibid., p. 237.

issues that explored their relationships with their bishop, the diocese, and the LA. Although this part of the study was not a formal ethnography, there is, nevertheless, a strong ethnographic element about it. The conversations were lively, and in many instances revealed ambivalences as the individuals strove to articulate views on issues which they had not explicitly faced or discussed before. The aim at all times was to try to establish where, as it were, the school's compass is calibrated: Rome or Sanctuary Building via the LA.

Conclusion

What does all this tell us?

First, it tells us that there are clear elements of continuity in the Catholic Church's position on school education in England and Wales. The policy of a place in a Catholic school for every child who wants one, which emerged in the early nineteenth century, continues to this day, and was last vociferously reiterated as recently as November 2006, when the Catholic community vigorously objected to a proposal made by the former Conservative Secretary of State for Education, Lord Baker, that all Catholic schools be compelled to admit a proportion of non-Catholic pupils, even if this meant refusing places to Catholic children. Second, the Catholic Church continues to see the provision of schools as an essential part of its mission. Third, its belief in a supreme being who created the universe, and in whose image all mankind is created, continues, as it must, to inform and shape its thinking and actions in all matters pertaining to education.

These convictions have found their way into the work of the Sacred Congregation for Education, at the behest of the Second Vatican Council, and latterly into that of the Conference of English and Welsh bishops, whose publications I have examined.

Second, it tells us that the last forty years have seen massive changes, not only in the perception of the Church about the nature and purpose of Catholic education, but also in the way in which the state perceives its own role, and its relationship with the Catholic Church and other major providers of schools in England and Wales. These have taken place during a time when the developed world has experienced equally massive adjustments in beliefs about the nature of society and the role of the individual.

Related changes encompass the newly perceived role of the laity in the work of the pilgrim church, as envisaged by the Council, and the decline in religious observance, which has led to a widespread fall, not only in the numbers of parish clergy, but also in those of male and female religious Orders whose vocation is in teaching. This is the field that has been closely examined by Grace (2002), whose recent work I have extensively quoted.

Third, it tells us there are increasing incongruities between the Church and government, because of what the Church sees as an undesirable emphasis on competition, testing, and market forces.

Successive Education Acts have altered the balance of power in schools. Whilst the explicit objective of governments of both political persuasions has been to strengthen the powers of governors at the expense of LAs, there is argument as to whether the real beneficiary has, in reality, been the government itself, which has reduced governing bodies to the role of volunteer agents of government policy, in the same way that they were agents of the LEAs before 1944.

What is beyond argument is that the interests of Catholic school trustees have been almost entirely ignored whilst these adjustments have been made. Where, as in the case of Kenneth Baker, the issue of trustees' rights was explicitly raised, they were ruthlessly subordinated to the requirements of the state. The state challenged the Church in central issues relating to the latter's role in maintained school provision in England and Wales, and prevailed. The position remained unchanged during the subsequent thirteen years of Labour government. It is too early to tell how a new coalition administration will deal with the issue.

These changes, in combination, have produced a situation in which two challenges have already been made to the Church's leaders over educational matters, one of which centred upon the validity of a bishop's view of the Church's moral teaching. One purpose of my study was to gauge the extent to which these internal challenges were isolated events, brought about by unique sets of circumstances, or whether they presage a new era in which, as predicted by Grace, the spiritual capital inherited by the Catholic schools is finally exhausted, and they become indistinguishable from secular institutions.

Chapter 4

Catholic School Governing Bodies
Under the Microscope

'Further research is urgently required into Catholic education.'
Thus concluded James Arthur in his book *The Ebbing Tide, Policy
and Principles of Catholic Education*, to which reference was made in
the previous chapter. In both opening and closing the book, he
drew attention to the lack of attention given to Catholic education
policy by educational researchers.[1] That his comment went unre-
marked is attested by Grace:

> While Catholic schools, in some societies, may have come 'out of the
> ghetto' in terms of their relationships with external agencies this
> process does not seem to have happened to the same extent in
> educational scholarship and research. There still seems to be a
> 'secret garden' of Catholic education research known, in general,
> only to the cognoscenti.[2]

Invaluable though *Catholic Schools Mission, Markets and Morality* is
in providing insights into the working of a large number of urban
Catholic secondary schools, it has little to say either about the
much more numerous Catholic primary schools or about the
pivotal role governors currently exercise in English and Welsh
maintained schools. Indeed, apart from a very small survey of
Arthur's, in 1993, which involved seven governors from eighteen
Catholic schools in the north and south Oxford Deaneries of the
Archdiocese of Birmingham, there is virtually nothing on this
topic.

In the light of the acknowledged dearth of interest in and, conse-
quently, knowledge of, Catholic education, it might be helpful to
set down briefly some very basic facts about the Catholic Church in

[1] Arthur, *The Ebbing Tide, Policy and Principles of Catholic Education*, pp. 5, 253.
[2] Grace, *Catholic Schools, Mission, Markets and Morality*, p. xi.

England and Wales and its schools.There are five provinces, each under the leadership of an archbishop: Birmingham, Liverpool, Southwark, Wales and Westminster. In addition, there are seventeen dioceses led by a bishop. Each diocese has a number of trustees, of whom the archbishop or bishop is always one. One of the trustees' functions is to supervise the diocesan schools, which they, in secular law, actually own.

In each case the archbishop or bishop has delegated day-to-day responsibility for his educational responsibilities to a person who is usually described as the diocesan schools commissioner. Other titles are also used, very often director of schools or director of education. Up till about thirty years ago, the schools commissioner was almost always a priest.[3] By then, however, the growing complexity of the work persuaded most of the archbishops and bishops that this was no longer satisfactory and educational professionals began to be recruited from the ranks of HMI, LEA officers and advisers, and headteachers. By 2009 only four commissioners in England and Wales were priests, and one was a religious sister. All the rest were lay women and men.[4]

The latest available statistics (2009) show that there are, in the maintained sector in England and Wales, 1,835 Catholic primary schools, with 401,745 children on roll, and 389 secondary schools with 313,299 students. (Sixth form colleges are not included in this research.) It can be seen, therefore, that Catholic schools make up a significant proportion – around ten per cent – of maintained schools and pupil numbers in England and Wales. This proportion has remained virtually unchanged for thirty years.[5]

In the 1980s and 1990s, two incidents of litigation arose, one involving the Archdiocese of Westminster, the other the Archdiocese of Southwark. It is impossible to overstate their significance to the Catholic Church in England and Wales, and in understanding the changing nature of Catholic school governance.

The dispute at the heart of the Westminster case was about who had the power to determine whether a Catholic secondary school should retain its sixth form, or surrender it for what was argued to be the greater good of the establishment of a diocesan sixth form college. Was it the trustees or the governors? The salient point was that a group of lay people had been prepared, not only to challenge the head of the Roman Catholic community in

[3] Hornsby-Smith, *Catholic Education: The Unobtrusive Partner*, p. 128.
[4] *Catholic Directory 2010*.
[5] Hornsby-Smith, *Catholic Education: The Unobtrusive Partner*, p. 3.

England, but also to take that challenge into the domain of the secular courts.

The second case was, in essence, potentially much more worrying for the Church, because what lay at its heart was a matter of the Church's teaching and practice about an issue of morality. The governors of one of Southwark's primary schools wanted to appoint as their headteacher a Catholic man who had divorced and remarried in a register office. What was being argued by some of the governors (including most of the foundation governors) was not only that the bishops' view was wrong and that that of a governing body was to be preferred, but also that a secular court should decide the matter. The diocese held that to have proceeded in this way would not only have been a clear breach of the policy of the bishops of England and Wales but also of the teacher's contract of employment.

The High Court declined to become involved in the latter case, so the issue was never determined. It seemed to me, however, that, given the lack of understanding, at the time, of the position of trustees of church schools and the continued governmental drive to strengthen the powers of governors, here were important issues that should be investigated. Were these two incidents no more than isolated aberrations arising from the special circumstances of each case, or were they, rather, forerunners of a new phase in the development of the Church in which its doctrines and practices could become subject to scrutiny by the state? It seemed important to try to find out, and that was the originally conceived purpose of my enquiry.

As it developed, however, the focus moved to incorporate an enquiry into the extent to which Catholic schools may be said to be different qualitatively from other types of school in terms of how they are governed. If they are, in what ways are they different? This area of investigation seemed to be, in a very real sense, a corollary of the first, and one which had potentially far more significance for the tens of thousands of pupils who attend Catholic schools over the years. To what extent are governing bodies conducting schools where a distinctive Catholic ethic is being propagated, both inside and outside the classroom, which could be said to articulate clearly with the expectations of the Sacred Congregation and the Bishops' Conference of England and Wales? Conversely, to what extent had pressure from secular authorities (particularly in the light of the findings of Arthur and Grace) eroded this?

The passage of time justified the shift in emphasis: there has been no explosion of litigation between governors and trustees.

Indeed, only two subsequent disputes have come to national prominence, and since they involved both the Archdiocese of Westminster and the Archdiocese of Southwark (indeed, The Westminster case involved the self-same school as before), it seems safe to conclude that the problem, if there is one, is entirely London focused. My first thought was to investigate governors' attitudes and opinions on such matters as their relationship with their trustees, and on issues that appear to be of central concern to trustees and governors alike: the appointment of staff, admission of pupils, and maintaining a distinctive ethos, for example.

The method proposed was, initially, the circulation of a questionnaire in two dioceses I considered likely to produce a number of schools working in different social contexts, and therefore with the potential to provide a rich experience relating to the issues with which governors were having to grapple. It was planned to survey all the governors in ten schools in each diocese – seven primary and three secondary. It was expected that this number of schools and governors would produce a large enough return to produce statistically significant results. It was proposed, subsequently, to interview a number of respondents.

At this stage, it was intended to complement the interview element of the research with a case study involving a school which was experiencing a significant event, such as the appointment of a new headteacher, or the consequences of an adverse Ofsted report. The aim was to compare and contrast the support offered by the diocese and the LA, and to evaluate the extent to which secular, as opposed to Catholic, considerations influenced the thinking and consequent decisions of the Governing Body. The degree to which the various publications of the Sacred Congregation and the Bishops' Conference of England and Wales appeared to be of influence, and the input of the diocese, were to be taken as evidence of the latter.

It quickly became clear that there was an almost complete absence of any information about Catholic school governors similar to that provided by Scanlon for the generality of governors.[6] The decision was made, therefore, to take the opportunity to attempt to remedy this deficiency.

A research project was therefore planned on the basis of a questionnaire that was sent to a representative group of governors, followed by in-depth interviews with a smaller sample, and also with a number of diocesan directors. The schools were chosen

---

[6.] Scanlon et al., *Improving the Effectiveness of School Governing Bodies.*

from dioceses which served inner city, urban, suburban and rural communities in order to ensure, as far as possible, that a broad sociological field was surveyed. In each case the consent of the diocesan director was sought and readily obtained.

The Questionnaire Design

The content of the questionnaire emerged entirely from my own working knowledge of Catholic school governing bodies, the problems that they face and the tensions that can arise as they grapple with what can so easily appear the irreconcilable demands of Church and State. It is reproduced as Appendix 2.

Governors were asked to provide information about what category of governor they were, their age group, gender and ethnic background. They were also asked at what level they had completed formal education, what was, or had been, their occupation, if they were a governor of any other school, and if they played any other role in Catholic life. It is of interest to know how foundation governors were appointed. They were therefore asked to indicate who had, initially, asked them to serve.

Much is made of the difficulty appointing bodies experience in finding people who are willing to undertake the role of a school governor. Respondents were therefore asked whether they thought their work was of value to the school, and if so why; what aspects of it particularly appealed to them, and whether, if invited, they would seek reappointment. They were also asked about their length of service and whether they had experience of governing other schools.

A group of questions was asked concerning their induction and training experiences. The reasoning behind this was to enable some judgement to be formed as to the relative influence of the diocese and LA, particularly in matters that might seem to lie at the heart of a Catholic school's distinctive character: admissions, staffing appointments, buildings matters and the curriculum, including, but not exclusively, religious education and worship. They were asked if the diocese had arranged a commissioning ceremony at the start of their term of office, and, if it had, whether they had attended it. Questions were put as to whether the school had a mission statement, and the extent to which it had adopted its LA's curriculum policy in subjects other than RE. Three specific issues were then raised about matters that were considered to be possible areas of conflict between trustees and governors in the light of the Southwark dispute already referred to: the Bishops' Conference policy that headships, deputy headships and heads of RE posts should be reserved for practising Catholics, the admission of pupils, and the policy that Catholic teachers should be seen to uphold Catholic teaching on sexual morality in their private lives.

Finally, respondents were asked to raise any issues not covered by the questionnaire that they thought were relevant to my study, and to indicate whether they would be willing to undertake a face-to-face or telephone interview during which issues might be explored in greater depth.

The purpose of the interviews with diocesan directors was to raise with them the preliminary results of the governor question-naire and, more particularly, so that any themes that had begun to emerge in the subsequent governor interviews I had conducted could be discussed in depth. The opportunity was taken to enhance the representative nature of the research by involving diocesan directors in as many parts of the country as possible. This was successful: the only part of the country not involved in some way was the south west. When all the information was put together, it was expected that the findings would provide a reasonable overview of the English position at the beginning of the twenty-first century.

Ninety-nine completed questionnaires were returned. Although this was tantalisingly close to 100, the temptation to press for a further response was resisted.

The interviews with diocesan directors revealed a significant lack of convergence with those involving governors. This led to a further adjustment of the focus of the project to incorporate that finding.

The Interviews

The questionnaire asked if respondents would be prepared to be interviewed, either by phone or face to face, about some of the issues that had been raised. About half said they would. Decisions had to be made as to who to select. Not all the obvious categories could be included if this part of the project were to be kept within manageable proportions. It was therefore decided to include both men and women; foundation, LA, parent and teacher governors; an ethnic minority representative; representatives of various age groups; and those from both primary and secondary schools. In the event, the initial selection had to be modified when two of those who had indicated willingness to be interviewed (an ethnic minority male foundation governor and an elected non-Catholic female teacher governor in the twenty to thirty age group), declined to participate when invited to do so. I thought it would be interesting to interview (separately) two governors from the same school in order to evaluate the extent to which their views converged.

The following are brief descriptions of the schools from which the interviewed governors came, together with a note about the governor(s) to whom I spoke.

The Research Schools

- *Our Lady's* is a ten-class primary school serving an urban community with 'quite a lot of problems'. Over ninety per cent of the pupils are Catholic, as are the majority of the teachers. The pupils include an increasing number of travellers' children from Eastern Europe, and some Muslims. Two governors were interviewed from this school: the chair, a white male foundation governor, aged sixty-one to seventy, who is a retired retailer. He had been asked to serve by his parish priest and, at the time of the survey, had done so for two years; and a white female foundation governor, aged thirty-one to forty, a teacher by profession who had, again, been invited to serve by her parish priest and was in her first year.

- *St Joseph's* is a two-form-entry primary school serving an urban area. The chair, a black British female foundation governor, aged forty-one to fifty, said that the parents were mainly middle class, and most of the pupils' mothers were at home rather than out at work. The proportion of ethnic minority children had increased over the years, and now numbered fifteen to twenty per cent. She was a senior administrative officer working for a neighbouring LA, had been invited to serve by her parish priest and was in her fifth year.

- *English Martyrs* is a two-form-entry urban primary school with a nursery. It admits children from all over the borough in which it is situated, though the children come predominantly from its own parish. It is a very popular school and the roll is 100 per cent Catholic. There are a large number of pupils from one particular eastern European country. The governor interviewed was a white male LA governor, aged fifty-one to sixty, who had been a local authority councillor for many years, and on this governing body for fifteen. He had also served as a governor of upwards of a dozen schools over a thirty-year period. He was unsure about how many of the teachers in the school were Catholic, but thought the majority were. He is a Catholic, a member of the parish, and an accountant by profession.

- *St Edmund's* is a ten-class urban primary school in a deprived area. Seventy-five per cent of the pupils are Catholic, and the roll now includes a few black South African boys and several Chinese children. It used to have a number of Vietnamese boat children. The majority of the non-Catholic pupils are practising Anglicans. It was formerly oversubscribed, but now is not. About eighty-five per cent of the teachers are Catholic. The governor interviewed is a white female LA governor, aged fifty-one to sixty, who had twelve years' experience as a governor of the school at the time of the survey. She works for Ofsted, and is not a Catholic.

- *Corpus Christi* is a school of fewer than ninety pupils with no nursery. It is located in what is described by the governor as 'a mining town without a pit', where there is little employment other than in shops and service industries. Workers have to find jobs in the adjacent city, and the town is now essentially a dormitory. There is a high level of deprivation, and it suffers from a significant amount of illegal drug abuse. Almost half the pupils in the school are not Catholic. It suffers from competition from what are perceived to be more desirable Catholic schools in two adjacent LAs. The governor interviewed is a female foundation governor, aged sixty-one to seventy, who was the chair at the time of the survey. She did not give her racial background. She was in her second year of service, and had been invited to become a governor by the parish priest. She is a retired university administrator.

- *Holy Cross* is another two-form-entry school in a prosperous suburban location. It is said by the respondent governor to be well supported by the parents. Catholic children predominate, though the governor was unable to offer a percentage, nor did she know the proportion of Catholic teachers. She said it was small. The governor is a white female elected parent, aged forty-one to fifty, who has been on the governing body for three years, and is a part-time lecturer by profession.

- *Sacred Heart* is a very large (1,000+ pupils) inner-city secondary school which is for boys only from eleven to sixteen and has a joint sixth-form arrangement with an adjacent Catholic girls' school. It is the best performing secondary school in the LA, and also has a strong reputation for excellence in sport. The roll is virtually 100 per cent Catholic, but the elected teacher governor alleged that a number of very intelligent non-Catholics, including Muslim and Hindu boys, were also admitted by the former head in contravention of the published admissions policy, and without the knowledge of the governing body. More than half the Catholic boys are of African descent, and there are also those of Sri Lankan, Indian, and Filipino descent. The white boys are predominantly of Irish descent. The governor is white, and had been on the governing body for four years at the time of the interview. He is in the thirty-one to forty age group, and a Catholic. He did not offer a percentage for Catholic teachers, but said that there was a policy to recruit from Ireland.

My ninety-nine respondents include sixty-two who are foundation governors,[7] twelve LA,[8] ten elected parents,[9] seven elected teachers,[10] three heads, two sponsors,[11] one elected staff,[12] one minor authority,[13] and one who did not reveal her / his status.

Just over forty per cent (40.4 per cent) of the respondents are

[7.] See footnote 79 to Chapter 1 for the definition of a foundation governor.

[8.] The School Governance (Constitution) (England) Regulations 2007 define an LEA governor (Regulation 6) as a person who is appointed as a governor by the local education authority. As already explained in footnote 79 to Chapter 1, this is technically incorrect. Local education authorities no longer exist, and have been replaced by local authorities, or LAs.

[9.] A parent governor is a person elected as a governor by parents of registered pupils at the school and is himself a parent at the time when he is elected (Regulation 4 and schedule 1).

[10.] The 2003 Regulations changed the separate categories of staff governor: that is, headteacher, teacher and staff, that had hitherto been used, and provided for them within the umbrella term 'staff governor', whilst continuing make provision for all three (Regulation 5 and schedule 2). Transitional arrangements allowed for the retention of existing instruments of government, with the old nomenclature and categories, until 31 August 2006. For the purposes of clarity, the three pre-2003 categories are retained in this book, so the reference to 'staff' here indicates a member of the non-teaching staff.

[11.] Regulation 10 and Schedule 5 of the Regulations define a sponsor governor as a person who has given substantial financial assistance or services to the school.

[12.] See note 10. 'Staff governor', in the context of this research project, means a governor elected from and by the non-teaching staff.

[13.] A minor authority governor was appointed to a primary school governing body by a borough or district council in a place where the county council was the LEA. Minor authority governors were discontinued by the 2003 Regulations, but again, transitional arrangements provided for their retention until 31 August 2006.

men, and nearly sixty per cent (56.6 per cent) women. The remaining three per cent did not record their gender. The corresponding figures for foundation governors were 38.7 per cent, 58.1 per cent and 3.2 per cent. This does not accord well with the findings of Deem, whose own survey of 170 governors found that only thirty-one per cent were women.[14] Deem, at that time, drew attention to the 1989 NFER study of Streatfield and Jefferies, which had found forty-one per cent of governors in the schools they used were women, and the 1990 study of Keys and Fernandes, which had identified fifty-three per cent as women.[15] Whilst they admit that these figures might suggest some deficiencies in their research design, they postulate that the reason for the high representation of women in the NFER surveys is that many are teacher governors drawn, in the primary sector, from a feminized workforce.[16] This is not so in my study: whilst it is true that two-thirds of the elected teachers are women, the total number of teachers (men and women) taking part was only six, whereas between half and two-thirds (58 per cent) of the much greater number of foundation governors (sixty-two in total) are women, and only rather more than a third (38 per cent) men.

A more recent survey by Dean of seventy-three governors from fourteen community schools in three contrasting areas of social and economic disadvantage also reports findings that contrast with Deem's.[17] Here, it was common for women to make up sixty to ninety per cent of their school's governing bodies.

Nor is it true in my study, as Deem suggests in hers, that the women appear less powerful than the men. Whilst only two of the ten governing bodies surveyed by Deem were chaired by women, two of those I interviewed were women chairs, and a third referred to her chair as a woman. In three schools out of the seven I surveyed, therefore, a woman was in the chair. What is certainly true is that in the only secondary school where I interviewed a governor, the chair was a priest.

Deem also compares membership of governors' subcommittees and the average number of contributions made in meetings by male, female, black and white governors. She concludes from this that power, in the majority of cases, tends to be exercised by white males. Whilst I did not carry out enquiries of this kind, it was

[14.] Deem et al., *Active Citizenship and the Governing of Schools.*
[15.] NFER is the acronym for the National Foundation for Educational Research.
[16.] Ibid., p. 146.
[17.] Dean et al., *School Governors and Disadvantage,* p. 146.

manifest from the content of the interviews I conducted that the
women had a very well-informed view of the issues facing their
governing bodies, and did not appear inhibited from making
their views known to colleagues or the diocese when they considered it appropriate.

Thus, the female foundation governor of Our Lady's said she
originally became interested in becoming a governor

> because decisions were being made, and I thought 'I don't agree,
> and I have strong views on that, and I don't think that's in the best
> interests of the school, or best for the children.'

As a teacher herself, she had a very definite view about what she
considered good contemporary primary education practice, and
was assessing the newly appointed head's performance against
this. She was the link governor in her specialist field (maths), ran
workshops for both children and parents, and took an informed
part in budgetary discussions within the governing body, one of
the areas in which Deem et al. report women tend not to be
involved.

The LA governor of St Edmund's had, again, very clear views
about what constituted good primary practice. She had stood out
against the diocesan director's views on the appointment of a
previous headteacher, and had succeeded in persuading her
colleagues to her point of view. More recently, having become
concerned that the majority of the foundation and parent governors were employed at the school, in one way or another, she had
made representations directly to the diocesan director, albeit to no
avail at the time of the interview.

The foundation governor of Holy Cross, who was, perhaps, the
most hesitant of those to whom I spoke, believed the governing
body was run by a clique of which she was not a member. She had,
nevertheless, been involved in raising a large amount of money to
facilitate a building project, and was, at the time of the interview, a
member of the curriculum committee.

The overwhelming majority (90.9 per cent) described themselves
as white; a little over 5 per cent (5.1 per cent) black British; 1 per
cent black; and 1 per cent Chinese or other related group. The
corresponding figures for foundation governors were 87.1 per cent
white, 6.5 per cent black British, 1.6 per cent black, and 1.6 per cent
Chinese or other related group. Deem reports the 1989 NFER
study, which found that less than 3 per cent of governors were black
or Asian,[18] and the 1990 NFER study, where the figure was just over

1 per cent.[19] Whilst they give a figure for their pilot study (8 per cent), there is no corresponding figure for the main one.

Although the picture on ethnicity could, therefore, seem satisfactory, at least in comparative terms, this may not be necessarily so. Grace, in a recent analysis of the challenges facing urban education, especially in London, has identified contradictions of race as one of the factors contributing to the underachievement of pupils in inner-city schools.[20] He supports Gillborn's view[21] that institutional racism will not be easily changed, and proposes, *inter alia*, that 'Schools [should] draw upon the ethnic and racial resources of the city by bringing into classrooms various groups who could speak, from personal experience, of their encounters with racism in school and society' and that '[T]he presentation of role models ... may be the most powerful counter to the "ingrained stereotypes" and, in itself, the most influential form of anti-racist education that any school can provide.'[22]

While Grace does not suggest that governing bodies might have a powerful part to play in addressing a problem of this kind, it could be argued that the one statutory body responsible for formulating the policies of a school and monitoring its performance – the governing body – is uniquely well placed to make a major impact on it, and that the best way to accelerate the process of change would be to increase the representation of the ethnic minorities, better to reflect the ethnic composition of the community the school serves.

In my interviews with diocesan directors, it emerged that not one was monitoring the ethnic make-up of the governing bodies for which they are responsible. All acknowledged that this was a weakness in their arrangements.

The age profile of my respondents is given in Figure 1. It can be seen from this that the great majority (57.6 per cent) are aged between forty-one and sixty. Of foundation governors, slightly more (62.6 per cent) are in this age group. In other words, members of the governing bodies that took part in the survey are predominantly middle aged.

My respondents were asked to indicate at what stage they had

[18.] Streatfield and Jefferies, *The Reconstitution of School Governing Bodies.*

[19.] Keys and Fernandes, *A Survey of School Governing Bodies.*

[20.] Grace, *Urban Education; confronting the contradictions: an analysis with special reference to London.*

[21.] Gillborn, *Education and institutional racism.*

[22.] Grace, *Urban Education; confronting the contradictions: an analysis with special reference to London,* p. 125.

Fig. 1 Age Profiles of Governors

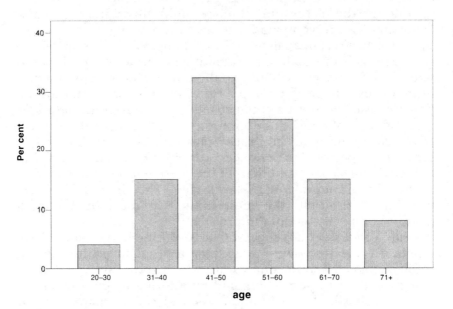

completed their formal education. The results are shown in Figure 2. The corresponding figures for foundation governors are almost identical, so they are not separately shown. The G(C)SE column includes those who took the School Certificate before the introduction of GCE, and the 'A' level column, likewise, includes those who passed the Higher School Certificate. Those who are included in the column labelled 'Other' have a variety of professional qualifications. The respondent who failed to answer this question was a foundation governor. It can be seen from this that the great majority of governors are well qualified academically, and are therefore likely to be able to take an informed and articulate interest in the matters they have to handle.

Respondents were asked to record what their occupations are or had been. Excluding ex officio heads and elected teacher governors, seventeen of the remaining categories of governor are or had been teachers, and then, in descending order, five are accountants, five are involved in higher education, five in nursing, four are stay-at-home mothers, three barristers, three scientists, two administrators, two bankers, two civil servants, two education advisers, two parish priests, two surveyors and two teaching assistants. The rest are single respondents covering a very diverse range of

Fig. 2 Qualifications of Governors

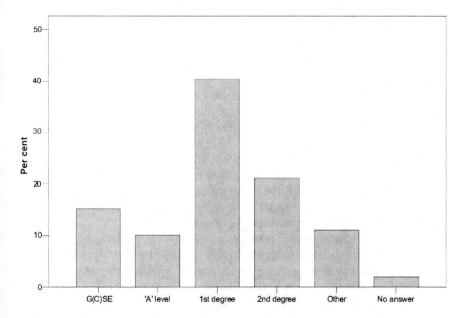

activities. Only one person reported an occupation that might be classified as 'blue collar.' The full list is given in Appendix 1.

Experience on the governing body varies from four respondents who have served for less than three months to one who has served for thirty-five years. The mean is nearly six years. Eleven of the group have experience of governing another school; seven of the schools concerned are Catholic, one is a community school, two are foundation schools and one is unspecified.

Leaving aside the foundation governors and head teachers, two of the elected teachers said they played a special role in the activities of their church, one did not, and three did not answer. The elected staff governor did not answer. Of the LA governors, four played some part in Catholic church life, three others did so in other Christian churches, and four made no answer. Only one gave a negative response.

The overall picture, therefore, differs somewhat from that described by Deem et al. who excluded voluntary schools from their 1995 enquiry. Catholic school governing bodies may be dominated by the white middle-aged middle and upper classes, but one is as likely to meet women as men serving on them. The caveat made by Deem about the influence of elected teacher governors on the gender balance appears not to apply in my survey.

My survey also indicates that the individuals involved bring a wealth of experience to their work as governors from a wide range of backgrounds, and that they are, in general, very experienced in governing body work, too, predominantly, but not exclusively, relating to Catholic schools.

It is of interest to know how foundation governors came to be appointed to their roles, because whoever has major responsibility in this area is, in consequence, likely to be in a good position to exercise considerable indirect influence on governing bodies. There appear to be several possibilities: they might have been invited by someone who was a trustee or a trustees' representative, or they might have responded to an advertisement. Alternatively, they might have been approached by someone local, such as a head, parish priest or another governor.

Only three respondents had been asked directly by a trustee. Of the remainder, fourteen were asked by another governor, twelve by the head, twenty-five by the parish priest, and five by some other unspecified person. Four respondents did not reply.

There are two ways of interpreting these figures. One conclusion might be that, despite its reputation for being a centralized, autocratic organization, the English Catholic Church has, in practice, devolved the appointment of its key representatives in schools to the localities served by those schools. The other would be that the dominant influence remains that of the clergy.

Ninety-two respondents think their work is of value to the school and only one positively said that it is not. The reasons given for this by the former were predictably very varied. The most frequent is a connection between the professional experience of the respondent and the needs of the school: bankers and accountants think they help with their school's financial affairs, and those with building experience, with the maintenance of the fabric. Other areas of expertise cited include health and safety, the law, and education in a context outside the school of which the respondent is a governor. This occurs twenty-seven times. The description being a 'critical friend' of the school is used nine times.[23]

The respondent who thinks his work is not of value to the school

---

[23.] 'Critical friend' is an expression that has come into vogue in the last decade. It seeks to describe a governor as someone who is fundamentally supportive of the school, but who nevertheless remains dispassionate enough to ask demanding and searching questions about its performance.

said 'The role of the governing body appears to be to rubber stamp the headteacher's decisions. Whilst we may debate the issues I have never known us to refuse to endorse her preferred options.' He later added 'I cannot say I get any great rewards from being a governor. The frustrations are that in spite of all the time spent carrying out the role I don't feel I have any great influence on the running of the school.'

In this context, references to issues that relate to the religious character of the school are infrequent and occur just seven times. One respondent says he has a 'continuing desire to contribute to the building up of the faith'. The second, an LA governor, refers to 'serving the RC Church'. The third, a parent of two children with additional educational needs, cites a 'strong belief in Catholic education'. The fifth says she sees her school as part of the mission of the Church and that she provides a link between the school, the church and the parish. The sixth judges her role as supporting and promoting the ethos of the school, and the last that she assists the head and staff 'to resist pressure to implement initiatives that could be regarded as undermining a Catholic vision of education'. One movingly said, 'I have a vested interest in everything the school achieves, as I am entrusting my most valuable assets: my children.' One enigmatically commented 'As a Catholic I can voice my concerns about topics that relate to Catholic secondary schools and offer support e.g. the current "strangulation" of the interview procedure for admissions by the bishops.'

The overwhelming majority of my respondents do not report that the Catholic or religious character of the school particularly interests them. Typical of the comments made are: 'helping the school my children attend'; 'the challenge of managing change as a governor, defining the governor's role in my own mind'; 'building relationships with senior management team'; 'curriculum and assessment'; 'I wished to do something to contribute and don't fancy standing behind a stall at fairs'; 'I have an administrative background in sport and thought this was something I could do.'

Just fifteen make specific reference to the Catholic or religious character of the school, double the number reported above who think their work was of value to the school because of its religious character. The comments include matters such as 'continued involvement in the life of the Catholic school'; 'fostering the Catholic ethos'; 'serving the school and faith'; 'an opportunity to contribute to the educational and spiritual needs of our children'; 'the opportunity it gives to evangelise'; 'watching the children grow in faith as well as being educated'. Other comments could be

taken to imply an interest in the issue, but are not explicit –
'helping to develop the philosophy of the school'; 'I try to encourage links between the school and parents and between school and
parish'; 'seeing us succeed in our goals'; and 'helping in the good
liaison with the excellent LEA and Diocese'.

Conclusion

Women are well represented in this survey compared with the
older studies of Streatfield and Jeffries, Keys and Fernandes and
Deem et al. A very recent survey carried out by Dean et al. might
indicate that there has been a shift during the last decade, and that
women may be much more likely to be found on school governing
bodies than before. If this is so, the position I have reported may
not be as favourable as it originally seemed. In the light of the very
limited field explored by Dean, however, it would be unwise to
draw any but the most tentative of conclusions until much more
evidence is available. Nevertheless, a finding that a little over half
my respondents were women does appear to be satisfactory.

On the other hand, on the evidence put before me, in Catholic
schools women are making a major and positive contribution to
the work of the governing bodies on which they serve, in contrast
to the picture painted by Deem et al. Power is not concentrated in
the hands of white males.

The ethnic make up of the sample that completed my questionnaire is better than that in the last reported general survey.
Nevertheless, the cohort is predominantly middle-aged and white.
No diocese is monitoring the ethnic make up of its governing
bodies, and, as a result, none of the diocesan directors had more
than a shadowy notion of how many foundation governors from
ethnic minorities had been appointed.

The need to reflect on this is highlighted by the findings of
Grace, particularly in the light of the rapidly changing character of
many Catholic school rolls at the present time. Governing bodies
are ideally placed to play a significant part in addressing the underachievement of ethnic minority pupils. New initiatives therefore
seem called for to try to involve parents as governors who are newly
arrived from European Economic Community countries, as well as
from those who have been here for some time and originated in
the Philippines and West Indies.

Members are well qualified academically, and many have
substantial experience of school governance, not only in the

school they are serving as recorded in this survey, but in others. They overwhelmingly think their work to be of value to the school, and would seek reappointment when their term of office expires, but they do not describe their interest as particularly linked to its religious character. A very large majority of the foundation governors was approached to serve either by the local parish priest or by the head. This practice raises the issue of how the process will be managed as the number of parish clergy continues to fall.

Chapter 5

The Bishop

Introduction

In Chapter 1, I have described how, since even before the restoration of the hierarchy in the middle of the nineteenth century, the Catholic bishops of England and Wales have regarded the provision of schools as of overriding importance to their work of evangelization[1] and catechesis.[2] One of the major areas of enquiry covered by my research was to see how the relationship between bishop and school governor was standing up in the face of the pressure all schools are now under from powerful secular educational agencies. I have reviewed the loss of power by LEAs, but have demonstrated that, after a brief and, perhaps, half-hearted attempt to devolve significant responsibilities to governing bodies, the state has taken to itself the effective levers of control over what schools do and how they do it.

I have explained that the Catholic Church in general, and the bishops of England and Wales in particular, have a clear and forcefully articulated view of the nature and purpose of Catholic schools, and that this appears to be increasingly at odds with that of the state. Yet, despite their important role as chief pastor of their flock, in the eyes of the Church, bishops appear to be left with only symbolic power in their schools as a result of the legislative activity of the state over a long period.

So how do governors of Catholic schools view their bishop? The picture that is painted, even by foundation governors, whose

[1] A word used to describe bringing the Christian message to those who do not adhere to the Christian faith.
[2] The instruction of those who are already members of the Catholic Church.

personal representative they are supposed to be, and, indeed, by whom they are appointed, is that he is a remote figure. If governors' perceptions of the personal interest of their bishops accurately reflect the bishops' views of the schools' continuing significance and importance in their work, there does seem to have been a change in recent years.

The Views of the Governors

The questionnaire provided the basis for this part of the enquiry by asking if a commissioning service had been arranged for governors when they took up office. This is a religious ceremony, the purpose of which is to attempt to make clear the relationship between governors, and, of course, in particular, foundation governors, and the bishop, and to emphasize the concept of community. The details of the ceremony understandably vary from diocese to diocese, but the consistent theme is to inform governors of the nature and purpose of the school which they have been appointed or elected to govern, and to seek a declaration from the foundation governors that they will discharge their duties in such a way as to uphold and develop the school's distinctive religious character. These ceremonies commonly, though not invariably, involve the bishop in his cathedral and occur at the time when the foundation governors are being (re)appointed, though it is customary to invite all governors, whatever their category, and their families. Sometimes the occasion is used to present a certificate of appointment to the foundation governors. Only a little more than a tenth (10.1 per cent) of respondents thought their diocese had arranged such a ceremony, whilst over two-thirds (70.7 per cent) said it had not, and almost a fifth (18.2 per cent) did not know. Given the nature and purpose of these events, it might be expected that the awareness of foundation governors might be somewhat greater than that of other categories of governor, and this was, indeed, so: about a sixth (14.5 per cent) said there had been a service, but still over two-thirds (67.7 per cent) said there had not and, again, almost a fifth (17.7 per cent) did not know.[3] When it came to the actual event, a little over a twentieth (6.1 per cent) of respondents, and just under a tenth (9.7 per cent) of foundation governors reported that they had attended.

[3] Statisticians reading this book will wish to know that the data were subjected to chi-squared testing. The results showed that foundation governors as a group were no more aware of these ceremonies than non-foundation governors.

The chair of Our Lady's thought that the ceremony he had attended was valuable because he felt he had received 'an element of appreciation' and it was good to meet the bishop. Although it had established a relationship, it was, perhaps inevitably, not a deep one. He would have welcomed his bishop's involvement in a seminar or conference on religious teaching. He did not take away from the event any feeling that, as a foundation governor, he was personally involved in the bishop's mission, rather that he was working on behalf of the Church in general.

His colleague, the parent foundation governor, did not know whether the diocese had arranged a commissioning ceremony at the time of her appointment. Although she had been a governor for only a short time, it was clear from her answers that the bishop did not feature prominently in her perception of the work, nor did she refer to any examples of his involvement in the school during the time her children had been pupils there.

The chair of St Joseph's had a view that differed in some respects from the one that has just been described. Her diocese does not currently arrange commissioning ceremonies, though the diocesan director has the concept under consideration. She regards herself as a representative of the diocese and of the Catholic Church, and the bishop appears not to feature in her work. In her case, it is the high-profile diocesan director who is the face of the diocese, though she does recognize him as the representative of the bishop. Of the bishop, she said, with a laugh: 'I do not think he knows who I am.' An almost identical view was taken by the governor of St Edmund's, in the same diocese, who said the school saw the bishop 'only very rarely'.

The LA governor of English Martyrs thought that people in the school 'do not know him', since the bishop's visits are so rare.

The chair of Corpus Christi described the involvement of her bishop in celebrating the completion of a building project in a way which demonstrates very sharply why the personal interest of bishops remains so important:

> I said 'I'm going to have a big opening ceremony for this ... we've been talking about raising the profile of the school in the town, we'll invite the bishop.' [My colleagues] said 'He won't come,' and I said 'He won't come if we don't ask him.' So I wrote to the bishop, but I have to admit I was put out. His secretary phoned the parish priest and said 'Yes, he'll come.' They never wrote back to me, which annoyed me, but anyway, yes, he could come, but he could come only on a specific date and I would be away on holiday on that date ... I said 'If that's the only date the bishop can come, he can come

and open the place, he can manage without me'. And then I said 'Right, we've got the bishop coming; we'll invite the MP, we'll invite the town mayor, we'll invite the director of the diocesan schools' commission', and they all came. Apparently it was a brilliant day ... everyone said it was fabulous ... The bishop was wonderful. He was only in the school for an hour and a quarter, [but] he went round every classroom, he looked at the extensions, he blessed the building, he sat in the hall and talked to the children, had a little buffet and then he left ... They said it was delightful. It's the first time since my eldest daughter was five that we've had the bishop come to the school. My daughter's now about thirty-four ... It was all over the papers and on local radio, so in terms of relationship with the diocese and the schools' commission, yes, that was very good, but that was possibly a one-off.

This is a very interesting vignette for a number of reasons. First, despite all the actions of the state to marginalize the trustees of church schools, which I have described in earlier chapters, if this community is in any way typical of English Catholic schools, it is to the bishop they principally wish to turn when they have something to celebrate, and not, say, the MP, the education portfolio holder of the LA or its director of children's services. There seems to be, therefore, a huge reservoir of good will available to the Church if it has the ability and desire to make use of it. What stands out equally clearly is that effective communication is vital. The way the event is described identifies it as a considerable success, but it was not overwhelmingly so. Although the chair of governors initiated the invitation, she seems to have been sidelined thereafter. Not only was she excluded at the preparatory stage, but, on her account, no one took the trouble to write to her afterwards either to thank her for facilitating the event, to express regret that she was unable to be present, or to register any view about the work of the school or the contribution of the governors to its success. If this is right, it seems a curious oversight, in all the circumstances.

The governor of Holy Cross, which serves a community largely comprising commuters, did not know whether there had been a commissioning ceremony at the time of her appointment. She did not regard herself as a representative of the bishop or part of his evangelizing team, though she then did remark that:

I can say from a personal point of view I do want to promote Catholicism. I want it to remain a Catholic school ... I want people to be pro-active in the Church. I would love it if they turned up every Sunday, once a month or once every term – the parents ... I actually do evangelize in my own way, not necessarily confidently ... but people know I go to church and I want them to know.

The elected teacher governor of Sacred Heart was not aware of any contact between the bishop and the school. He had heard that the bishop was a sick man and that others were having to undertake some, at least, of his duties.

These brief snapshots appear to indicate that the schools concerned see little of their bishops. When the point is put to them, the foundation governors do not believe they have a personal relationship with their bishop, nor do they see themselves as his representative in their roles as governors. On the other hand, the good that can come from contact with the bishop is vividly displayed in one of the extracts quoted.

The Diocesan Directors

I put this picture to the diocesan directors I interviewed. There was a fascinating geographical divergence of view, with those in one part of the country taking a starkly different one from that of their governors, and emphasizing strongly a continuity of approach with that of bishops of previous generations.

The diocesan director for Glastonbury was learning to work with a new bishop who was, in his words, 'finding his way'. He believed the bishop liked going into schools but he was unsure about how important he regarded governing bodies.

In his view, only a minority of foundation governors saw themselves as agents of the bishop. The majority were what he described as 'good, solid people'. His diocese had arranged commissioning services for governors in the past. The cathedral had turned out to be an unsatisfactory location to suit all parts of the diocese, so later 'we had them spread around a bit, but I don't know that the attendance was any better'. The liturgy was a Mass or part of a Mass and was:

> the chance for the bishop to talk directly to a large group of governors about their work, to encourage them, keep their spirits up, that kind of thing ... It wasn't an instructional liturgy in that sense. It was the kind of exercise by which you're encouraging governors to feel part of a special body giving service to the Church.

He expressed concern at the low rate of awareness of and attendance at commissioning ceremonies reported in my survey, but added 'whatever you do you won't get everyone in the same place at the same time'. The director for Much Wenlock expressed the view that his bishop had:

> a reputation for being very strong pastorally and for getting out into the community in the parishes, and I'd be surprised if our foundation governors were not familiar with what he stands for, if not necessarily having a direct knowledge from having met [him]. But he is not remote. The bishop is particularly keen to be close to the whole of the diocese.

He agreed that a personal relationship between the bishop and governors was a significant one, and needed 'to be even tighter than it is at the moment'. At the time of my survey, the strategy here was to build up the relationship by involving the bishop in in-service training courses, which were being delivered by a consortium of dioceses. This was partly for local, pragmatic reasons, but also because of a conviction that the diocese should be seen to recognize the corporate nature of governing bodies, with local authority and elected members included who might very well not be members of the Catholic Church, and for whom a Catholic liturgy might not be wholly appropriate. The concept of a commissioning ceremony was being explored, however.

The director for Athelney was equally adamant. This exchange was particularly interesting because one of the governors I had interviewed had been critical of the remoteness of this bishop, and a pertinent extract from the interview, in which it is alleged that no bishop had visited the school for almost thirty years, has already been included earlier in this chapter. When I suggested that bishops were perceived to be shadowy, the reply was:

> No no no! He has a high local profile within the diocese and gets out and about a lot ... He is extremely charismatic and connects well with people. He welcomes, he's invited to go, and wherever possible he tries to go. That's definitely not the case here. He's not a shadowy figure at all. He's good for the diocese and good for the Church in the diocese.

Again, at the time of my survey, no commissioning services were being held, though they had in the past. It was the intention to re-introduce them, but time pressures within the Commission had interfered with their development. The director for Lacock had this to say:

That wouldn't reflect our situation. He frequently visits. He does all of the confirmations himself on weekday evenings, so three nights a week he's in a different parish. He never celebrates Mass in the Cathedral apart from Christmas and Easter. It's in a different parish in the diocese, so he's very well known. He visits our schools frequently and it would be an unusual month if he wasn't in probably eight or nine of our schools. He would know all our heads personally. He won't know all the foundation governors, obviously, but he'll know a lot of them, and more importantly they all know him. So we're very blessed with that, and at governor seminars and suchlike he would often pop in. And where we've got particular issues, he makes a point of being in the schools [that are involved].

No commissioning services were held here, and none were planned because of the perceived special nature of the diocese. Nor were there annual conferences which the bishop attended. These were regarded, in the particular context of this diocese, merely as playing lip-service to the issue of relationships. On the other hand, individual foundation governors are commissioned here in their parishes when they are appointed, in the same way as newly appointed heads and deputies. The director accepted that such ceremonies did not involve the bishop, and were dependant on the goodwill of the parish priest, which was not always forthcoming.

A rather more cautious view was put by the Director of Tewkesbury, who tended to approve of his bishop's remoteness:

I think if people are foundation governors then they will see the bishop from time to time, because he's quite strict with himself over the question of visitations and, when he does visitations, he does get into the school, so they do get to see him from time to time. But I would have to say on educational matters the bishop is somewhat shadowy and I would want to keep him there actually. In point of fact if he gets too involved then at the end of the day it's very difficult to ensure that these things are being done in a legal, proper fashion rather than just acting on a whim. It is not expected that the bishop will know much about education law or about all the papers from the Department, and the rights and responsibilities of governing bodies, teachers, non-teaching staff and so on. So I like to keep my bishop certainly at arm's length from what's happening in the schools and I deal with these things myself. After all, that's what I'm paid for.

As to the perceptions of foundation governors about their relationship with the bishop, he continued:

> I would have said there would be quite mixed reactions from
> governing body to governing body and from governor to governor
> [on that point]. Certainly we make it very clear that it's the bishop
> that appoints them in the first place. I write the letters, but the
> letters of appointment are on behalf of the bishop, so from that
> point of view I don't see how they can escape the fact that they are
> in some sense agents of the bishop, which is the point that is made
> and is driven home quite strongly. But I do have to say that some of
> our governors, particularly with any legal background, tend to be
> quite difficult to call to order in doing the will of the trustees. They
> will interpret for themselves what they think is their role and respon-
> sibility and it becomes something of a tense situation when I have to,
> on behalf of the bishop, bring them to some sort of understanding
> that they're not there just to do as they please, even in the best inter-
> ests of the school. They have to [have] regard to the policies of the
> diocese, which are the bishop's own policies.

I asked him for examples, and he cited admissions and appointments:

> We do have one or two quite strange and bizarre, idiosyncratic
> governing bodies who operate all sorts of dodges round the corner
> in order to ensure that they admit who they want to admit ... [and]
> we've had a few struggles with one or two governing bodies over
> whether or not they will appoint or not appoint ... Sometimes it's
> really been quite extraordinary the choices they have made. But at
> the end of the day, since they are the ones who decide, and not the
> diocese or LA, we have to live with those problems and try and sort
> them out later if we possibly can.

A similar note of caution was expressed by the Director of Tintern
diocese, though here the claim was, as elsewhere, that the bishop
was far from remote:

> No, absolutely not. But knowing the bishop creates other issues. For
> example, our bishop is very pro-active. Every term I have a list of
> schools he plans to visit and the schools he's going to for interviews
> with the children, so he's very education-centred in that way, and I
> brief him on matters of education. Now the nuts and bolts I would-
> n't say give him great joy, but the going to the schools does ... When
> he visits schools, the governors aren't always invited to those visits.
> I'm trying to say to heads 'this is an opportunity for governors to see
> their bishop in their school's setting', but I wouldn't say there was

any governor in our diocese ... who would say they didn't know him. I think we have two schools he hasn't visited, but they're on the list and most of our schools he's been to more than once. And the reason he hasn't been to the two is that they've had a change of head, that kind of thing. So they would know him, they would feel free to write to him, and this is the downside. They would sometimes see him as the point of contact to deal with day-to-day issues ... because he is a very friendly outgoing person and so he sometimes gets caught up in the issues that schools are dealing with that would normally go to the chair of governors or the director.

Only Tintern was holding a commissioning ceremony at the time of my investigation, and even here things were not running smoothly. Some years before, there had been an attendance estimated at ninety per cent. This had fallen on the last occasion to sixty per cent, even though the venue, time, and day of the week were unchanged. The decline was attributed to changes in society in general and to changed perceptions in the diocese itself:

The mentality has moved on since then in terms of how much time we can give to these things. Over four years, I just think in general terms the time commitments of people have possibly changed, or was it that when we didn't have a bishop, and it was also my first year in post, I really rallied the crowds? Whereas now, things are ticking along and they see the bishop so frequently and often informally. Does making the effort mean as much?

Conclusion

There appears to be a conflict between the perceptions of governors and diocesan directors about the locus of the bishop in matters pertaining to Catholic schools. Governors see him as shadowy and remote. Directors, with one exception, think he has a high profile. Only in one diocese is there an ongoing attempt to bring together all governors. In two others, previous endeavours of this kind had been allowed to lapse. In all the dioceses consulted, except one, there was interest in the concept and a declared intention to explore it further. The evidence casts interesting light on the contemporary interplay of relationships between the various power centres that are involved with Catholic schools.

I have already argued, in Chapter 3, that the LA has been substantially marginalized, and that governors do not so much govern as manage their schools within parameters tightly drawn and controlled by the state. I have also described how the Catholic

Church sees its schools in an entirely different context: as part of its mission to evangelize. In this context the Church is not particularly, or at all, interested in the school as a vehicle for the delivery of the National Curriculum and the attainment of targets at the various national key stages, but in the creation of communities of faith, where the activity of central importance is the much quoted synthesis of culture and faith, and faith and life. This entails, above all, the transmission of values for living rather than knowledge. In this regard, the policy objectives of the Church have remained unchanged since at least the early decades of the nineteenth century. Foundation governors certainly do have legal responsibilities placed upon them to maintain the Catholic character of the school. The position of the other governors is not so clear-cut. Whilst heads and elected staff governors will have similar responsibilities through the employment law channel, the legal position of elected parent, sponsor and LA governors in this regard is, at best, obscure.

Against this background, the position of the bishop appears critical. In practice, he retains significant residual powers. He is initially responsible for proposing to establish a new Catholic school, and, though he has no power to close a school, he has the authority to withdraw its Catholic mandate. He is responsible for the appointment and dismissal of foundation governors. But, as far as the day-to-day running of schools is concerned, the legislative changes of the last thirty years have in practice removed him as a power centre in favour of the governors. His power in this context is symbolic only. Power to manage is unequivocally in the hands of the governors.

There is a manifest lack of convergence here which makes the way in which the bishop is perceived by governors, particularly those appointed by him, crucial to the smooth running of relationships between the Church and its schools. If schools form such an important part of the Church's missionary work, one corollary that seems to follow is that those who are, by law, charged with responsibility for delivering this need to be seen to be recognized as important contributors by the bishop. On the basis of the evidence that has emerged during this study, such efforts as are being made in this direction, as described by governors, do not seem to be particularly successful. There is a very great difference in perceptions at diocesan level. It seems important that this dichotomy be examined, perhaps diocese by diocese, in an attempt to find where the truth lies.

The point was well made by two diocesan directors that the

bishop should not become involved in the minutiae of day-to-day administration. Bishops are very busy people, and the contemporary education system is complex, not least in terms of the law. They need the support and advice of experts. Nevertheless, there is a role to be played here as the head of the Catholic community which appears, at least in some instances, to be unfilled, according to the governors who have taken part in my study. How it should be filled is another matter, but there does seem to be a place for a commissioning ceremony involving the bishop himself, a regular programme of visits to schools to which governors are invited, and the attendance of the bishop at conferences of teachers and governors so that he can affirm them by taking a personal interest in the work, sharing in its joys and frustrations, helping to remind them all the time of their dual responsibilities, and above all, establishing himself as the spiritual leader of his flock. At the moment, foundation governors do not, by and large, see themselves as personal representatives of the bishop, helping him in one of his essential tasks.

This is not to deny the difficulties involved in persuading people to avail themselves of the opportunities that are on offer. But, if steps are not taken to address the issue, it is arguable that governors, exposed to an ever-growing secular agenda, will increasingly use their legal powers to weaken the contribution to the work of the Church that they were originally established to fulfil. This could at best, lead to an acceleration of the trends already noted by Arthur towards the dual function school identified by McLaughlin, and cited by Arthur.[4] This is found where a single institution carries on, at one and the same time, two entirely separate activities: religious education, worship, and related matters such as support for charities, going on retreats and things of a similar nature; and the provision of a 'secular curriculum' which comprises the major part of its work, to which are added free-standing sporting and cultural activities. In this model, 'The Catholic ethos of the school is seen as something additional.'[5] At worst, it could produce further acrimonious and damaging litigation.

[4.] Arthur, *The Ebbing Tide, Policy and Principles of Catholic Education*, p. 227.
[5.] Ibid.

Chapter 6

The Partners: Diocese and Local Authority

Introduction

In Chapter 5, I showed that even the foundation governors of Catholic schools think their bishop is remote. Though there are exceptions, my enquiries pointed up the degree to which governors find the influence that both their diocese in particular, and the Catholic Church in general, have in their affairs, is similarly distant. The issue is not straightforward, and is multi-faceted, and, it has to be said, not all dioceses are seen in this light. As we shall see, some diocesan directors seem to have established a pivotal role in the affairs of their schools, but otherwise the diocese generally assumes a high profile only when a headteacher needs to be appointed.

For the rest of the time, many governing bodies seem to rely heavily on any priest, or member of a religious order, who happens to be one of their number, not only to provide the link between diocese and school, but also to discharge the governing body's duties in respect of religious education and worship. Whilst, on the one hand, priestly influence signals continuity with past tradition, the way this is exercised marks a profound change in the way Catholic schools are governed. In this regard, it seems that the affairs of some governing bodies are now much more compartmentalized, with religious education, worship and ethos in one compartment, presided over by a priest, and the rest of the enterprise: buildings, finance and the 'secular' curriculum in another, presided over by one or more lay experts: the dual function school of McLaughlin again: a single institution conducting two separate activities within itself.

I have drawn attention, in Chapter 2, to a number of documents emanating from the Sacred Congregation for Catholic Education and the Catholic Education Service in this country which stress that Catholic schools should be communities where faith, culture and life are brought into harmony, and all the different aspects of human knowledge, through the subjects taught, are integrated in the light of the Gospel; where religious education is the foundation of the entire educational process; and where the schools' values and beliefs inspire and draw together every aspect of the life of the school. According to this vision of the educational process, there is no place for compartmentalization or fragmentation in a Catholic school. *The Common Good in Education*, in particular, gives specific and detailed advice to governing bodies about a range of issues to which they should have regard if they are to reflect what the Church expects of them. The challenge that is presented by current practice is therefore twofold: first, to ensure that a Catholic school's distinctive character informs all its activities; and second, to ensure security for the school's religious character. This will be particularly important in the future, when priests are no longer available to recommend foundation governors, oversee religious education and the ethos of the school, and to act as a conduit for the passage of information between school and diocese.

The Historical Context

In justifying this proposition, I refer to Chapter 1, in which I described how, for most of the twentieth century, a typical Catholic primary school managing body in England comprised six members, four of whom were appointed by the trustees. For much of this period there was no shortage of clergy, and most religious orders were buoyant. It was therefore logistically easy for a parish priest effectively to oversee the affairs of his school. Even though, in theory, the LEA was responsible for the secular curriculum, the reality was that, so long as a scandal of William Tyndale proportions was avoided, schools could more or less pursue ends of their own choosing. These were the days before Ofsted, when decades could elapse between visits by His / Her Majesty's Inspectors. In any event, HMI Reports on individual schools were confidential and there was no such thing as a formally designated 'failing school'. An adverse report did not, therefore, produce the public odium that befalls a school requiring 'special measures' today.

Furthermore, many LEAs either did not have inspectorates at all, being content, instead, with advisers; or, if they did, used them in a very small number of specialist areas, commonly only physical education and home economics. These cadres, with the exception of the London County Council (later to be the Inner London Education Authority) Inspectorate, were generally not highly regarded by schools. The Kent LEA, where I worked in the early 1970s, had just two primary phase inspectors who had oversight of, and were required by the County Education Officer supposedly to inspect and report on, every two years, over seven hundred primary schools, as well as having secondary specialist responsibilities: clearly an impossible task. In these circumstances diocesan control and influence was a reality in all of its schools. The position in the secondary sector was not dissimilar. Here, the governing body of a voluntary-aided school was always responsible for the whole of its curriculum. The practice with regard to inspections was identical to the one that obtained for primary schools. Additionally, there were, in those days, no annually published 'league tables' of pupil performance at GCSE, AS and A2 levels. Though a typical secondary body had ten foundation governors, a combination of a large foundation majority (seven or eight) over the only other constituent – the LEA – a ready supply of priests and religious, and the practice of appointing a small number of specialist clergy to multiple governorships, ensured that clerical control was as much a reality in the secondary sector as it was in the primary.

This culture is described by Hornsby-Smith, who, in surveying a number of what he classified as injustices that might be found in Catholic schools, included situations 'wherever a parish priest has an automatic or dominant control of school managers'.[1] Later, he argued that '[T]he present structures of advice and decision-making on educational matters in the church in this country are inadequate and need reform.'[2] In particular, he cited disaffection with the processes for appointing school governors and managers, and the lack of opportunities they gave for parents to be involved.[3]

The Diocese

My route into this area of enquiry was to ask, in the questionnaire, about the respondents' experience of diocesan-provided in-service training. I have already dealt with the matter of initial commissioning ceremonies. Once governors have been appointed and are in office, the issue of in-service training and support becomes

---

[1] Hornsby-Smith, *Catholic Education: The Unobtrusive Partner*, p. 40.
[2] Ibid., p. 124.
[3] Ibid., p. 127.

important. The Catholic national and diocesan discourse and formal policy is that aided school governors' responsibilities are different from those of community schools' governors in terms of the appointment of staff, the admission of pupils, the conduct of the curriculum, the control of the buildings and, of course, with respect to RE, worship and the ethos of the school. In the light of this, it seems reasonable to expect that diocesan authorities would make a substantial investment of time and resources in these areas in order to ensure that all governors had comprehensive and accurate information about them.

In fact, less than half my respondents (47.5 per cent) thought the diocese ran courses on the appointment of staff; whilst a little over ten per cent (11.1 per cent) said it did not, and over a third (38.4 per cent) did not know. The figures for foundation governors closely mirrored the overall return: 48.4 per cent thought there was diocesan provision, whilst 12.9 per cent thought there was not, and 37.1 per cent did not know.

Rather more than half (52.5 per cent) of respondents thought there was diocesan provision in the matter of the admission of pupils, a little more than a tenth (11.1 per cent) said there was not, and about a third (34.3 per cent) did not know. The corresponding figures for foundation governors were virtually identical: 51.6 per cent thought there was diocesan provision, 12.9 per cent thought there was not, and 35.5 per cent did not know. With regard to curriculum policy other than RE, less than a third (30.3 per cent) thought the diocese provided support, about a sixth (16.2 per cent) thought it did not, and nearly a half (46.5 per cent) did not know. The foundation governor returns were, again, virtually identical: 30.6 per cent thought there was diocesan training, 17.7 per cent thought there was not, and 43.5 per cent did not know.

As to buildings matters, less than half (43.3 per cent) of respondents thought the diocese provided training, rather less than a sixth (15.2 per cent) thought it did not, and over a third (38.4 per cent) did not know. The foundation governor return in this instance was slightly different: 38.7 per cent of respondents thought the diocese provided training, 14.5 per cent thought it did not, and 43.5 per cent did not know.

It might be expected that awareness of diocesan support of RE and the ethos of the Catholic school would be significantly greater than in the areas just described but this proved not to be so. Only just over a half (56.6 per cent) thought that such provision was made in respect of RE. Whilst the number who thought there was not was very small (6.1 per cent), as many as a third (33.3 per cent) did not know. The foundation percentages are again almost identical: 54.8 per cent thought the diocese provided support, 6.5 per cent thought it did not, and 35.5 per cent did not know.

Perhaps unsurprisingly, the views about training in the matter of the distinctive nature of the school were almost the same. Just over a half (56.6 per cent) of the total thought there was a diocesan offer, one twentieth (5.1 per cent) thought there was not, and rather more than a third (35.4 per cent) did not know. The foundation returns were very similar.

As with the matter of the commissioning service, whilst knowledge of provision is one thing, actual attendance is another. Those who were aware of it were asked if they had attended any diocesan training since their appointment or reappointment. Only a little over half – 53.3 per cent – had, a little more than a quarter (26.3 per cent) had not, and a fifth (20.2 per cent) either gave no answer or, in the case of one foundation governor, added that (s)he was unsure. The corresponding figures for foundation governors were slightly different: rather more (58.1 per cent), had attended, rather fewer (19.4 per cent), had not, and rather more (22.6 per cent) either gave no answer or said they were unsure.

This means that, in five defining areas of activity: the appointment of staff; the admission of pupils; the conduct of the curriculum; the control of the buildings; and RE, worship and ethos; nearly half the Catholic school governors who took part in my survey were not being trained by the diocese – the organization that might be expected to have the requisite expertise.

Briefing Meetings

The provision of courses and conferences is, of course, not the only way that dioceses and LAs pass on the necessary information, advice and skills training to governors. Briefing meetings, either on a regular or ad hoc basis, are now a common vehicle for the transmission of up-to-date information on local and / or national matters. Here, almost two thirds (60.6 per cent) thought the diocese provided briefings, whilst a third (30.3 per cent) thought it did not. Just under ten per cent either did not know or failed to reply. The responses of foundation governors were almost identical. As to attendance, more than a third (37.4 per cent) had attended no diocesan briefing sessions within the twelve-month period before the survey, about a sixth (16.2 per cent) had attended one, 3 per cent had attended two, about a tenth (9.1

per cent) had attended three and a third (34.3 per cent) provided
no answer. The returns for foundation governors were again
almost identical. It seems then that less than a third of the respondents had attended any diocesan briefing during the year before
they responded to the questionnaire. Again, therefore, there is a
lacuna in the information chain which, taken with the low take-
up of formal diocesan training to which attention has just been
drawn, might indicate that the majority of governors lack
adequate knowledge.

Catholic Newspapers and Journals

One final potential source of information about Catholic education was investigated. The Catholic Church in England and Wales
is very well served by newspapers and journals of one sort or
another. The main ones are the weekly *Catholic Herald, Catholic
Times, Tablet* and *Universe* and the monthly *Pastoral Review.* There
was another influential monthly called *Briefing,* which was the official journal of the Bishops' Conference of England and Wales, but
this was discontinued during the course of my research. In
February 2009 a Bishops' Conference newsletter was reinstated.
Initially a monthly, publication soon became more erratic, but in
its new format it has regularly featured items relating to Catholic
education, many of which would be useful to school governors in
their work. It seems to have no specific title.

Respondents were asked if they had read any articles about
education in any of them during the previous twelve months.
Almost a half (47.5 per cent) had read something in *Briefing,* whilst
nearly two fifths (38.4 per cent) had not. A significant percentage
(14.2 per cent) failed to answer. The corresponding figures for
foundation governors were, perhaps surprisingly, somewhat different: fewer (41.9 per cent) had read something and more (43.5 per
cent) had not. As to the *Catholic Herald,* less than a sixth (15.2 per
cent) had read something, but almost a third (62.6 per cent) had
not. Over a fifth (22.2 per cent) did not reply. The foundation
governor figures were 12.9 per cent, 61.3 per cent and 25.8 per
cent. The usefulness of the *Catholic Times* and the *Pastoral Review*
seems negligible. Only four per cent had read anything in the
former, and three per cent in the latter. The *Tablet* was markedly
more successful. Here, over a quarter (27.3 per cent) overall had
come across an educational article. This weekly was even more
successful with foundation governors, having reached exactly a

third of them. Finally, 14.1 per cent of respondents said they had seen something in the *Universe*.

These figures suggest that only one periodical was managing to communicate reasonably effectively with Catholic school governors on educational matters: *Briefing*, the very one the bishops decided should cease publication. The only other journal to make much impact was the *Tablet*. It is to be hoped that the new bishops' conference newsletter is as successful in the education field as was *Briefing*.

The Role of Clergy

I investigated the relationship between dioceses and governing bodies in my programme of interviews.

One reason the diocese seems remote to governors is that there is an understandable tendency to see the priest or member of a religious order as the expert on matters to do with religious education, worship and ethos. This means that the other governors do not get involved and do not, therefore, form the personal links and contacts with diocesan officers that would almost inevitably promote a sense of community. The chair of Our Lady's put it this way:

> I suppose I have a much more close relationship with the state through the LA than I do with the diocese itself. There are certain times when the diocese comes into a leading role, like the recruitment of a new headteacher where they play a big part. They helped with the interviews and helped to put a lot of the structure and the process together. But after that it's a much more backroom part they play, whereas the LA come in a lot and help the new headteacher into their position, they help with the school improvement plan, and provide a much bigger service than the diocese would. We ensure the local priest is a governor, and that brings in the diocesan element into the school. He is the vice chairman. He's got that diocesan view. He can put it forward and if there's anything we need to do for the diocese, that's our link and our route. If we want anything specifically in [the diocese], they're very good at giving advice if we need it.

His foundation governor colleague expressed much the same, but put it more graphically:

> We tend to do our bishopy things and diocesan things via our priest, so in the meetings we say, 'You'll do that won't you, you'll make that

call?' and he does that and links back, because he obviously knows
the people. It's part of his job. I know the headteacher has good
links with the diocese because it comes up in meetings, phone calls
she's had or things that have happened. On the governing body we
have Sr....so we've got another religiousy person there, and we have
Fr.... who's the assistant priest, so they've got links with the diocese
anyway. From my viewpoint, I don't have all that much personal
contact. We just delegate to people who know more about it. If you
had a financial thing going on and you had someone on the board
who was an accountant, you would trust him there, knowing more.
They know more, they're linked to that . . . That would be their thing
because we all have our strengths.

These comments again seem to confirm the existence of
McLaughlin's dual function school, a concept that is not endorsed
in the documents emanating from the Sacred Congregation and
the English and Welsh Bishops' Conference that have been examined in Chapter 2. They may also underline the consequences of
the low take-up of diocesan in-service training to which attention
was drawn earlier in this chapter.

   The chair of St Joseph's had a very different experience. She
described her relationship with the diocese as:

   very, very good. All the heads meet once a term with the director. I
   have a good relationship with him because I had a couple of issues
   I had to go to him directly about and he's been very supportive . . .
   If I have an issue I'll ring him or email him and either he or his assistant will get back to me, so they're very, very good. The assistant is
   always on our panel when we're doing senior posts.

However:

   The diocese provides regular briefings for headteachers, but not for
   governors as far as I know. The LA does it. [Our relationship with
   the LA] is close. They have a governing unit you can ring up and
   they know who you are and because of the kind of governor I am I
   try and do as much with the LA as I can, so when anything happens
   I tend to go [there]. When you have a group of governors that
   always attends functions, they tend to know who you are.

The LA governor from St Edmund's was highly critical of the parish
priest's lack of involvement in her school. Here, however a member
of a female religious congregation, who is also the parish organist,
stepped into the breach as chair of governors and is in a prime position to say to the parish priest 'This is what we have been doing, this

is how we wish to continue.' Relationships between the diocese and the school seemed problematic. There had been a dispute over the appointment of a previous head, and by the time of my survey, a situation had arisen where all the foundation governors except two were employed at the school. This meant, according to my respondent, that, given the indifference of the parish priest, and his lack of involvement in the school's business, the governing body was failing to act as a 'critical friend'. In her view, it was incapable of doing so. 'When you either work there or whatever, you won't speak your mind on occasion, because you're either worried about your children, or worried about your job.' She had raised the issue with the diocesan director, but nothing had been done.

The parish priest is the link governor for RE, but, she continued, 'In the last two-and-a-half years since he started with the school, I've only got one report [from him]. If we were doing English or something, we would go in every term.' The chair, to whom reference has already been made, had two major concerns: that the governing body had allowed the head too much latitude in 'put[ting] her stamp on the school', and that it would be without an effective leader when either the order moved her on, or she wished to retire.

She had concerns with the service provided by the LA. She thought the relationship with the school was 'quite good'; a situation she attributed to the fact that she personally knew quite a few officers there:

> They do respond quite quickly, but they do not always know what they're doing. For instance, one gentleman came to give us a talk about self-assessment, and admitted he hadn't done the course to enable him to do a self-evaluation plan. He'd got the scheme from another LA but it hadn't been tweaked so that it matched a school in [this one].

She thought there was a lack of understanding about the differences between Catholic schools and others amongst LA staff. The LA had recently failed an Ofsted inspection and many staff were new because there had been a great turnover.

There were serious relationship problems at Corpus Christi, already referred to in the previous chapter, which had had its first visit from the bishop for almost thirty years: although things at the time of my enquiry were said by the chair to be:

> as cordial as [they've] ever been. There have been occasions in the past when the antagonism between the parish priest and the head,

well, you could perceive it. It was tangible. The two establishments barely coincided. An example: we've recently had a new notice board put up in the hall of the church. I asked the parish priest if we could have a section of this for notices, and he said 'Why?' And things happen at church. They're not mentioned in the parish bulletin, even though every Friday morning Father goes up to the school and the school secretary types the parish bulletin. There's never any mention in it of anything going on in the school.

Perhaps unsurprisingly, she described relationships between the governing body and the diocese as 'non existent'.

The foundation governor from Holy Cross, who believed her governing body was effectively run by a small caucus from which she was excluded, thought that the head's relationship with the diocese was good. She added, however, that she was not aware the governing body shared this closeness.

She had only recently been appointed to the curriculum committee where a document from the LA had been discussed that described what curriculum governors were meant to do. She admitted to being 'horrified to think we don't do anything like that at all'. She continued 'I don't think the governors have been trained at all in any particular region.' She added that a decision had been taken to put this right. In answer to a question about whether they would turn to the LA or the diocese, she said it could be either, and the decision would depend on the availability of funds. I expressed surprise that the diocese would make a charge.

> If it's free, why aren't we utilising it? Why isn't the diocese putting out what they want us to do, helping us? We get so many forms to fill in or questionnaires from [the LA].

In summary, she thought the relationship between the head and the diocese was a good one, but the governing body did not seek support from the diocese and therefore that relationship was not a close one.

The elected teacher governor from Sacred Heart saw the chair, a priest, as being the dynamic link with the diocese. He was highly critical, overall, of the way the governing body had operated, describing it as 'a nodding shop' whose function was to endorse the actions of the head. The chair was, however, trying to make it more of a monitoring body, in the light of an impending visit from Ofsted. He was not aware of any working relationship between the governing body and the diocese, but:

> We are bombarded with bits of information from the LA and diocese, and frankly myself and the other teacher [governor] have other things to do. We could go on courses and things ... but we've got families, so it's something we don't feel overly interested in.

The comments of the LA governor from English Martyrs perhaps best underline the complexity of the issue. Here, the parish priest is a governor (though not the chair), goes into the school regularly, and provides a weekly Mass in the church for the juniors. He (the LA governor) was unsure both about whether the school prepared children for their First Holy Communion, and about the extent to which the governing body monitored the religious education and ethos of the school. He had been on diocesan training, and said a diocesan adviser had been to the school 'to do whole governing body training in how to be a Catholic governor'. In comparing the school's relationship with the diocese and LA, he continued:

> I've been on the Council for yonks, so I tend to see it that way. I think it would be true to say the school relies more heavily on the Authority to provide general support and assistance, and would turn to the diocese in two areas. One is when we want to raise funds, because capital funding has to go to the diocese, and when it comes to matters of religious ... for instance, the admissions policy had to be cleared with the diocese as well as with the authority. So it's areas like that. We were told in no uncertain terms that our policy, which said that priority would be given to regular attenders at [our parish], had to be re-written to allow for this other parish ... so the diocese was slapping our wrist.

This is an extremely illuminating comment, coming, as it does, from a Catholic who has many years experience of education as a local authority elected member. He appeared uncertain about a number of matters to do with the religious life of the school, despite, or perhaps because of, the parish priest's involvement. I draw attention to the sole example he gave of a religious issue which brought the school into contact with the diocese: an apparent disagreement about the admissions policy, a matter in which, legally, the diocese had, at that time, no locus.

I discussed the issue with the diocesan directors, and the overwhelming response was that what we are now seeing is a profound change in the way the clergy view their role in the schools. There were very differing views, however, on whether priests should still

serve on governing bodies or not. The director for Glastonbury
said at once:

> There are a number of priests who do not want the responsibility of
> going to all the meetings, and all the bureaucracy involved in being
> a governor of any school, and a number of clergy who are not really
> interested in it, and therefore shy off from it, and let others get on
> with it. This is causing difficulties. Lay governors feel that the pres-
> ence of the Church, as the person with a collar on, or in a habit, is
> quite important, and they feel the school is lacking something if it's
> not there. And even if we've got lay chaplains, they want priests
> around. It would be lovely to think that every school would have a
> priest on the governing body ... but it's going to get harder ... They
> don't mind going into the school, though some of them find that
> very hard, even though the head is trying to involve them.

I asked him if he thought bishops should put more pressure on them.

> It would work with some, but there are some who are no good at that
> kind of work, and are not suited to it, though they're nice people.
> There has to be a fair amount of training for them.

The director for Much Wenlock was far more sanguine about the
position, both as to principles and the consequent practicalities.
The issue of training arose again:

> Perhaps traditionally there was an expectation amongst the local
> clergy that they would automatically go onto the governing body,
> and might automatically assume the throne as chair of governors,
> perhaps forgetting the precise nature of the legal position of a
> governing body ... However, it is highly desirable that there are
> strong links between the respective parts of a parish – the parish
> church, the priest, the school, the home. Without those parts
> working together, the sum of the parts is not as effective as it should
> be, so therefore I think it is preferable – and that's where I would lay
> the emphasis now – that the parish priest should be in membership
> of the governing body.
>
> If one takes account of all the demands on local clergy now, and
> the declining numbers of clergy, it's becoming difficult for them
> always to take up positions on what might be a whole plethora of
> governing bodies in the area that they're now serving. If they're not
> on the governing body, there should nevertheless be regular contact
> with the school, because we have some sad situations where there is
> a breakdown in the relationship, and the priest might pull out of the
> governing body, or in extremis, not be associated at all with the
> school.

He then went on to summarize, very neatly, how far, at least in his diocese, change had swept through the schools, and what the challenge was for the future:

> Now, how do we get round that? I think by ensuring that the foundation governors who are appointed recognize fully what their role is ... and it's drawn through their appointment by the bishop ... It is they, the foundation governors, who carry what might have been seen as the role of the priest in the past. They carry the responsibility for ensuring that the traditions, the character, the ethos of the school, the mission of the Church in its practical expression in the diocese, is carried out at school level.

I put it to him that this implied that foundation governors are ready, willing and able to assume the kind of role that priests had exercised before. He replied:

> They should be. Whether they always are is a different matter. So, in the primary sector, in appointing them ... we look to the local parish priest for nominations, for confirmation that the person is a fit person to undertake the responsibility, and that forms a key part of the [bishop] agreeing, or otherwise, the appointment. In the secondary schools, it had been the tradition, until most recently, for the chair of governors of the secondary school to indicate who he/she would wish to re-nominate, or to make new nominations, but we will then consult the dean within whose deanery the secondary school is set.[4] That's step one. Step two is for us to build up the ... training for foundation governors and the briefing that they would be given at the outset of their assuming responsibilities. So the theory is great. They should carry out the role as the guardians of the diocese's interests in the schools. Do they always? Not necessarily. Should they? Of course they should, and it's down to us to improve the quality of the training they receive. They certainly, in the formation that they're given at the outset of their period of office, are given information about what their role is, and beyond that it's down to us, it is incumbent upon us to ensure that they get good quality training.

Thus, again, the centrality of the issue of training arises, as a significant challenge for the future. He went on to describe steps that had already been put in place to begin to address the issue.

[4.] A deanery is a collection of parishes in a discrete geographical area which is overseen by one the parish priests who is designated dean by the bishop.

Athelney diocese had much the same experience as Glastonbury and Much Wenlock:

> What you're tending to find is not necessarily now an assumption that [the parish priest] will take the chair of governor role. This will now be a lay person. I think it's very important to have priestly representation ... but not necessarily as chair of governors. This is good, because sometimes, in difficult pastoral situations, it allows the priest to act in a pastoral role, and I think that's important. There are very few places where people say they're not bothered one way or the other whether the local parish priest is [on the governing body]. I think there's an expectation of them forming that important relationship with the parish in the sacramental life of the school, and particularly making sure that there's a coherence between the parents' and the child's experience of the sacraments together.

Things could not be more different in Lacock:

> We've encouraged parish priests not to be chairs of governors [and now the chair is occupied by] a tiny minority. One of the reasons is conflict of interest. The first priority is chaplaincy and pastoral support. I still sit in on many governors' meetings where there's a deference, be it [with regard to] the opening prayer or a religious issue. It's getting less and less so.
>
> An increasing number of our priests aren't foundation governors. A fifth of our schools don't have a priest who's a member of the governing body. It tends to be the view of the priests that they don't like the bureaucracy. We've encouraged them not to be, and it works well, I think, so they go in in a pastoral role. A growing number of our priests are looking after more and more parishes. It's not unusual for a priest to look after three parishes, with, possibly, three schools.

I asked him how, in this situation, the diocese handled the traditional priestly function of identifying and nominating potential foundation governors. Did it have a policy?

> It does ... No one can be appointed as a foundation governor unless they've a signed statement of support from a parish priest. We've some foundation governors who are not Catholic, which might be quite unusual ...We haven't got many. In those cases where non-Catholics have been appointed, they tend to be active in the life of the local parish.

This does seem very unusual, and indeed its legality is open to question. No other diocese reported the appointment of non-Catholics to these posts.

Tewkesbury diocese also has a policy on priestly involvement, which to all intents is the same as that of Lacock, but without any suggestion that non-Catholics are foundation governors:

> We have a fairly firm rule that the chair [and vice chair] of governors should not be a priest or religious, [but] we have one or two people who buck the trend on that. When it happens, I would say it does cause no end of trouble, because there tends to be a disabling of the rest of the governing body across the board in relation to the school … But I think the governing body, the foundation governors particularly, would tend to follow the priest's lead, and leave him to worry about things like ethos and RE … Most of the clergy don't want to be chair or vice chair if they possibly can … because the chair of governors now is quite an onerous task. But also they are very much seized of the idea that there are immediate conflicts of interest which may occur, particularly over discipline and grievance procedures, or complaints. It's better for them to step back out of the situation … So I think many of them don't particularly want to do that anyway.

I asked how the diocese was preparing to meet the impending fall in the numbers of clergy. The issue of training arose immediately:

> In our training in the diocese we make sure that it's very clearly understood that the foundation governors, particularly, have a responsibility for the Catholic ethos of the school, and that they, as the corporate body, should be taking a fairly strong lead under their chairman. Even if there is a priest there, they need to have accord between themselves about the direction in which the school is going, as part and parcel of what they're there for in the first place. But certainly, in the training, we point out very clearly that it's the foundation governors' responsibility to make this their own, priest or no priest.

The picture is rather different in Tintern, where the director described a diocese in transition. Yet again, the centrality of training arose:

> When I came into the work [the situation was very much that] if there were priests or religious on the governing body, they took responsibility for the … RE inspection, the RE curriculum, standards in RE, ethos, and any of those difficult questions linked to the

recruitment of staff, Catholicity, and so on ... I felt we should address it, particularly as we all know that there's going to be, and is, a shortage of priests and religious. So one of the strategies was to put on training for governors, both at school and diocesan level, in different venues, on those issues.

I would say across the diocese there are governors now who have taken on the suggestions that we've made, like having a nominated governor as well as Father X or Sister Y who will take responsibility for the Catholic life of the school, for religious education. Don't always rely on the parish priest. That's improved the situation, but it hasn't addressed the whole [of it]. The other side is that we have some very strong characters in some of our priests and religious, who believe it's their domain, and would be the first to respond on these issues, and would not find it helpful for the lay members of the governing body to be giving what they believe to be a diocesan view. So, I think there are two strands.

The Local Authority

I have dealt with the governors' perceptions of the provision of diocesan in-service training, and the extent to which governors avail themselves of it. I now move to the position of the LA in this area.

Respondents to the questionnaire were asked if their LA provided training in those areas of activity that were particular to voluntary aided schools and therefore differentiated them from community ones: the appointment of teaching staff, the admission of pupils to Catholic schools, curriculum policy and buildings matters. It was assumed that, for all practical purposes, LA support and training with regard to RE was confined to matters related to the Agreed Syllabus.

As many as two-thirds (66.7 per cent) thought that training was given in the matter of staff appointments and only a tiny proportion (2 per cent) thought it was not, whilst a little over a quarter (26.3 per cent) did not know. The foundation figures were almost identical. As to pupil admissions, a fifth (21.2 per cent) thought the LA provided training, whilst over a third (35.4 per cent) did not, and a further third (36.4 per cent) did not know. The foundation figures here were slightly different: whilst rather more (22.6 per cent), thought the LA provided training and did not (37.1 per cent), fewer were unsure (32.3 per cent). On curriculum policy, well over two-thirds (70.7 per cent) said the LA provided support, whilst, again, only a minute proportion (2 per cent) thought it did not. However, almost a quarter (24.2 per cent) were unsure. The foundation returns were slightly different: two-thirds (66.1 per cent) thought there was LA training, and rather more than in the general return (3.2 per cent) thought there was not, or were unsure (27.4 per cent). Finally, on buildings matters, rather more than a half (54.5 per cent) reported that there was LA training, whilst almost a tenth (8.1 per cent) said there was not, and almost a third (32.3 per cent) were unsure. The corresponding foundation figures were 50 per cent, 9.7 per cent and 33.9 per cent.

More than half (55.6 per cent) of respondents had attended an LA course, and almost a quarter (24.2 per cent) had not. The number who did not reply to this question was high: 20.2 per cent. The foundation governor figures were very similar.

A very high proportion (81.8 per cent) reported that their LA provided regular briefings for governors compared with only 4 per cent who said it did not. Rather more than a tenth (12.1 per cent) did not know. The corresponding foundation figures were virtually the same. Almost a third (31.3 per cent) had not attended any of these briefing sessions in the previous twelve months, almost a fifth (19.2 per cent, and 17.2 per cent) had attended one or two sessions and 5.1 per cent three, 3 per cent four and 4 per cent more than four. The failure to reply rate was high here: a fifth (20.2 per cent). The foundation figures were somewhat different: about a quarter (25.8 per cent) had attended none, another quarter (24.2 per cent) one, less than a fifth (17.2 per cent) two, 3.2 per cent three, 4.8 per cent four and 1.6 per cent more than four. There was, again, a high incidence of failure to reply (22.6 per cent).

Comparing these data with those given earlier in the chapter about diocesan provision of training and briefing sessions, it appears that there is greater – sometimes much greater – awareness of LA activity than diocesan except in the area of pupil admissions. As to attendance, a little over half the respondents had attended training by both providers, but attendance at LA briefings was much higher (about 48 per cent) than diocesan (about 28 per cent).

Summary

Two major themes emerge from these data. The first is this: as I have stated in Chapter 2, the formal position of the Catholic Church is that 'Christ is the foundation of the whole educational enterprise in a Catholic school', and the school's task is to provide 'a synthesis of culture and faith, and a synthesis of faith and life' by 'integrating all the different aspects of human knowledge, through the subjects taught, in the light of the Gospel'.[5] 'The living presence of Jesus' must influence the entire life of the school community.[6] This, as we shall see later, is colloquially referred to by one of the diocesan directors as 'the Brighton Rock approach', where the defining characteristic of the school permeates its entire being. Yet the evidence seems to suggest that what may be emerging is a strong contradiction: McLaughlin's dual function school, to which reference was made on p. 122.

This model takes us back to the early nineteenth-century Irish system, to which reference was made in Chapter 1, and which was, at that time, supported by the English Catholic community, but rejected because of opposition from the dominant Protestant churches. Has the wheel turned full circle, and has the time now arrived when this model needs to be re-examined?

The second major theme, which is at least in part connected to the first, is the potential for the distinctive nature of the Catholic school, at least as it is currently conceived by the Congregation of Catholic Education and the Conference of English and Welsh Bishops, to be diluted to the point where Catholic schools are indistinguishable from any other: the final exhaustion of Grace's 'spiritual capital'.

The position of priests and professed religious in Catholic schools is clearly a major issue here. Three factors are creating a trend which leads in a single direction: the first is the decline in numbers, which inevitably will lead to a commensurate decline in influence. The second is the changing notion of the priestly role in governance to one of pastoral care, against which some functions of governance are seen to militate. The third is the increasing reluctance amongst priests to commit time and energy to the ever-growing demands and complexities of governing schools. All these point to a sharp reduction in the influence of clergy in the lives of Catholic schools.

The problem here is that, if Catholic school governing bodies are relying on clergy to act as the essential link between the Church (in the form of the diocese) and the school, and to discharge some of their most significant functions in terms of religious education and worship, and clergy are increasingly unable or unwilling to shoulder this burden, the stewardship of the school's distinctive nature seems likely to be put at risk.

5. *The Catholic School,* pp. 14–15.
6. *Lay Catholics in Schools: Witnesses to Faith,* pp. 12–13.

Before reflecting on the evidence that has already been cited earlier in this chapter, it is worthy of note that, throughout this entire study, not a single person referred to any of the work of the Congregation for Catholic Education, and only one – the diocesan director for Tewkesbury – cited one of the Bishops' Conference documents.

It is arguable that to expect busy governors to be aware of these texts, some of which make for difficult reading, is unrealistic, and that what one should be looking for is the mediation of diocesan experts through the in-service training route. But it is at this point that further incongruity is manifest through the evidence. If a comparison is made of the responses about governors' awareness of, and participation in, in-service provision, the results demonstrate conclusively that LAs appear to be more effective deliverers than dioceses in key areas of Catholic school activity: Unless, therefore, some agreement has been reached between dioceses and LAs about the nature and content of the support that is offered to Catholic school governors in these central areas of Catholic school activity and dioceses are confident about that support, these findings will be of concern to those working in diocesan offices.

Another surprising omission in the interviews was the absence of almost any reference to the contribution that permanent deacons and lay chaplains, both growth areas in the Catholic Church, might make to this situation. The office of permanent deacon is a very ancient one, but fell into disuse over a long period in the Dark and Middle Ages, to be revived in 1967 following a decision of the Second Vatican Council. By 2005 there were almost eight hundred permanent deacons in England and Wales, with many more in training.[7] Permanent deacons have a general remit to assist bishops in their work, but this notion does not yet seem to have extended to educational matters.

The position of lay chaplains seems even more unsatisfactory. For whilst there is a consensus about the role of permanent deacons and their training can only take place in a seminary, and is therefore directly under the control of the bishops, there is no similar consensus about the role of school chaplains, nor is there any agreed training programme for them.[8] Whether or how they might be harnessed in this regard are matters that have yet to be addressed. Within the terms of this study, it is clear, on the basis of the evidence I have obtained, that whilst some continuity can still

[7.] Sidleka, *The Permanent Diaconate in the UK and Ireland – an overview.*
[8.] A seminary is a training college for priests.

be discerned in the role of clergy and professed religious, strong
incongruities are manifest in the way Catholic school governing
bodies discharge their functions in matters that are central to their
identity. The manner in which these changes are being managed,
or perhaps, more accurately, not managed, appears to be creating
a situation where future challenges to the control of the Church,
through the bishops, seem more, rather than less, likely. Many
governors are not only not being trained in their responsibilities by
the Church, they are also much more likely to receive the information they need from the LA. As we shall see, there is evidence
that an LA can not only be ignorant of, or indifferent to the
Church's views, but actively hostile to them.

Chapter 7

Catholic School Governors at Work: Curriculum Issues

Introduction

Can there be a Catholic School Curriculum? asks Arthur in a report from the Centre for Research and Development in Catholic Education at London University.[1] The answer, succinctly provided by his co-author Walsh, is 'And why ever not?'[2] Nevertheless, the authors point out that for many years now, there has been pressure from a number of secular sources to homogenize the school curriculum. Catholic authorities have made sporadic efforts to counter this trend, with varying degrees of success. Walsh very rightly claims 'Curriculum is the school's core mission, the medium and the substance of its teaching and learning.'[3] The report quotes one school case study. My study aimed to look more widely at what the position was in Catholic schools in England and Wales.

The School Development / Improvement Plan

Respondents were asked about their involvement in drawing up the school's development / improvement plan. They were given a series of options to choose from. Almost half – 40.4 per cent – said the governing body had approved a draft prepared by the staff and submitted by the head, whilst about a fifth (21.2 per cent) claimed a group of governors had worked on it, and another fifth (20.2 per cent) said the whole of the governing body had drafted and agreed it. 15.2 per cent did not know how the development plan had been

[1] Arthur et al., *Can there be a Catholic School Curriculum?* p. 1.
[2] Ibid., p. 31.
[3] Ibid.

prepared. Of the foundation governors, rather fewer (34.4 per cent) said the governing body had approved a draft prepared by the staff and submitted by the head, whilst a fifth thought a group of governors had worked on it (20.3 per cent) and another fifth (21.9 per cent) said the whole governing body had done so. More (18.8 per cent) did not know.[4]

Given that the development or improvement plan is, arguably, the single most important document to be produced by a school, setting out, as it does, its aims and objectives over a three- or four-year period, it is surprising that almost half the governors who took part in the survey think their governing body is not actively involved in the detail of its preparation. These findings reinforce the proposal I have already advanced in Chapter 6 that what we see here is a change with potentially far-reaching challenges for Catholic schools. This development or improvement plan, one of two documents that crucially define the nature and purpose of a school, and therefore with whose content the governing body might be expected to be deeply involved, effectively rests in the hands of the teachers. The other, the mission statement, will be fully examined in the next chapter.

The Curriculum

The curriculum is a matter on which the Catholic Church both as a whole, through the publications of the Sacred Congregation, and within England and Wales, through the Bishops' Conference, has a definite and clearly stated view, as we have seen earlier, in Chapter 2. At the same time, Catholic school governing bodies have a duty, under secular law, to see that the requirements of the National Curriculum are met in full, and that, in particular, they have regard to, whilst not being compelled to accept, the curriculum policy of their LA. Both governors and teachers are busy people. Furthermore, a significant and growing percentage of teachers in Catholic schools, particularly at secondary level, are not Catholic. The CES Digest of 2009 Census Data puts this at 29.4 per cent in maintained primary and 53.5 per cent in maintained secondaries.[5] How do they, governors and teachers alike, reconcile the

---

[4.] Applying the chi-squared test to these data again shows no association between foundation governors and others at the five per cent level.

[5.] Catholic Education Service for England and Wales, *Digest of 2009 Census Data for Schools and Colleges*, p. 20. The accuracy of these statistics has been called into

demands of the Catholic Church, on the one hand, with those of
the state, on the other, in those areas which are sometimes loosely
referred to as the 'secular curriculum'? Are they, indeed, aware of
the official view of the Catholic Church? Is the curriculum offered
by the school an indivisible, seamless robe, or does it, in reality,
comprise two parts: a secular offer which is largely indistinguishable from that of any other school, with distinctive RE stuck on
with Sellotape?

Respondents were therefore asked how much of their LA's
curriculum policy for subjects other than RE they had adopted.
Over a tenth (11.1 per cent) said they had adopted all of it,
between a third and a half (39.4 per cent) most of it, and only ten
per cent half or less. A third (32.3 per cent) said they did not know.
The position with regard to foundation governors was somewhat
different. Here, less than a tenth (7.8 per cent) thought their
school had adopted all of the LA's policy, but nearly the same
proportion (40.6 per cent) thought they had adopted most of it.
Rather more (12.5 per cent) thought they had adopted half or less,
and rather fewer than a third (29.7 per cent) did not know.

Major issues appear to emerge as a result of this. However the
statistics are viewed, it is clear that half the respondents think their
school has adopted the majority of their LA's curriculum policy.
Only a very small minority – less than ten per cent – confidently
assert that they have adopted either very little or none. In the light
of this finding, one is bound to wonder about the extent to which
anything at all distinctively Catholic characterizes what is being
taught in fields such as geography, history, English or science, to
name but four subject areas at random, in ways envisaged by the
Sacred Congregation; whether, indeed, the schools are 'centre(s)
in which a specific concept of the world, of man and of history is
developed and conveyed'[6] and whether there is the genuine
synthesis between culture and faith called for in *The Catholic School
on the Threshold of the Third Millennium.*[7]

Here was clearly an issue to be followed up in the programme of
interviews with individual governors.

---

question by A. E. C. W. Spencer, a former statistical adviser to the Catholic
Education Council.

[6.] *The Catholic School,* p. 7.

[7.] *The Catholic School on the Threshold of the Third Millennium,* para. 14.

SATs, SATs, SATs[8]

This was the despairing response of the governor of Our Lady's when we started to discuss the curriculum in her school.

I wanted to explore further the dichotomy between the Church's view of a Catholic school, which might loosely be defined as the unitary view, and McLaughlin's dual function school. I put to all the governors I interviewed the two basic approaches and asked them which they preferred. There was a fascinating variety of views.

The chair of Our Lady's initially seemed unsure: 'I think everything we try to deliver has a Catholic aspect. Even when they're doing religious education they do discuss other religions, but always from a Catholic point of view. Obviously mathematics is rather more difficult to bring into the equation.'

But when I asked him how the governing body could be confident that the class teachers were actually doing what it thought they were, his answer had two facets:

> Governors are attached to a subject. They go in once a term to see a class in operation. Having appointed what we consider to be an extremely good Catholic headteacher, quite a lot of that ethos is delivered through her. We would rather expect that. In our discussions with her and her reports we would expect that to come across.

The problem here is clearly that if governors are unaware of what to look for, almost total responsibility devolves to the head. Furthermore, when I asked if she reported on the matter in her termly reports the reply was:

> Yes she does. It doesn't actually come across 'how is the mission statement being carried out?' but I think if there was a shortfall, she would be aware and would tell us. If teachers were doing something not in accord, we would find out. And certainly because we've got other Catholic members of staff on the governing body we would quickly be aware if there were difficulties.

---

8. SATs is the acronym for Standard Attainment Tests, which were originally required by law to be taken by all pupils unless they are individually and specifically exempted, at the ages of seven, eleven and fourteen. The regime has been considerably modified over the years. The subjects covered are English, maths and science.

I ended this part of the interview by putting to him the definition of a school governor as 'an agent of the state at a distance'. His reply beautifully encapsulated the dilemma:

> I don't think of myself as that at all. I regard myself very much as a foundation governor looking after a Catholic school on behalf of the diocese, but obviously implementing what the state is putting down with regard to the curriculum.

His colleague, whom I quoted at the beginning of this chapter, saw the matter in, as it were, basic and routine pedagogical terms:

> You can either keep things separate or you can try and make things as cross-curricular as possible. So, for example, with literacy, you don't have to keep that within the literacy hour ... that will come into science and history and everything, and you have to keep that in mind when you're planning what you're teaching ... It's not one or the other, it's a balance of both. If you're doing algebra, it's not really going to concern geography or history or English or RE. But where there are opportunities to link different subjects, whether it's RE, science or PE, that's what you should be doing.

I asked her how, as a governor, she could be satisfied that things in this regard were as they should be in the school. Her answer initially echoed that of the chairman:

> I couldn't answer that question, but the headteacher looks at planning on a weekly basis and she will check that things are as they should be, and since she is in constant communication with the LA I would imagine and trust that things are OK, and also because we get good SATs results you have to be covering everything.

I put it to her that it sounded as if the governors were very heavily reliant on the head.

> But we question a lot, so it's not a case of assuming it's been done ... but we don't see schemes of work.

I asked if she thought governors should.

> That depends on how well the indicators are of how well the school's doing. I think that if the school is doing a very, very good job and educating the children in the whole sense, I don't think we necessarily need to see the nitty-gritty. You'd go down that avenue if things weren't right.

That obviously again led to the question as to how governors would know. Her reply was that Ofsted would pick out what had not been done. I pointed out that Ofsted would not pick up the fact that a particular curriculum area was unsatisfactory from a Catholic point of view, and that the S.48 inspectors would not concern themselves with 'secular' subjects.[9] We left the matter there.

In that it appears to negate the whole rationale for the existence of Catholic schools, a very surprising view was taken by the chair of St Joseph's:

> All children should be taught the same. The difference is obviously when you're doing RE. I have four children. My two oldest [who she said elsewhere in the interview were 'naturally brighter children'] went to the [non-Catholic] grammar school ... I always believe you're taught at home. I'm not bothered about the influence of the Catholic school because I know they've got the foundation already from the very beginning ... I think, yes, all the other curriculum should be the same, but the RE bit should be more based on Christianity.

I asked how children get on in the school who might come from less supportive home backgrounds.

> I don't think there's a problem, I think they get on fine. They follow the same kind of thing: to love your neighbour. They all have the same kind of RE, and because of the type of parish we come from, most of the people who live in the parish are strong Catholics, so you find everybody will be in church.

When I asked if she perceived any tension between the Church's view of education and that of the state she said:

> No, I wouldn't say that. Our school educates the whole child to a certain extent. Because of the climate we live in, it is about league tables ... You want your school to be top of the [LA].

Later, however, in reply to a related question, she said:

> At the end of the day, you have to look at the individual child. You may have ... a child at Y6 who achieves level 3. That's an achievement for the child and the teacher. League tables are for selling your school.

[9.] This refers to the inspection of RE and worship by diocesan inspectors as part of, but distinct from, the inspection of the rest of the school's activities by Ofsted-appointed inspectors.

I asked if the governing body ever discussed this kind of issue.

> I would say no. The problem with that kind of discussion is that we
> have to set targets for the following year, so we have that discussion
> then in the sense that the LA will give us a target, and it's up to the
> governing body whether we accept it or not.

I made further efforts to attempt to clarify matters, but without
success.

The Catholic LA governor of English Martyrs recognized a
distinctive Catholic element to the curriculum, but in somewhat
narrow terms:

> I have always defended Catholic education on the ground that there
> is a distinctive Catholic view of things other than just religion. I'm
> not sure about Catholic maths, but certainly I'd say it's important to
> have a Catholic slant to science, but that's more secondary than
> primary ... Our understanding of the Reformation clearly requires
> a Catholic approach ... look what happened to the Martyrs.
> Nowadays, St Thomas More is seen as a hero, but when I was a kid
> he was still seen as a bit of a suspicious character. That would also
> apply to literature. There are elements in literature which, as a
> Catholic, I would have a different view over ... many non-Christians,
> atheists and agnostics ... I'm not sure about Catholic geography or
> Catholic maths. Science, history and literature there are Catholic
> concerns that we are right to make sure our children understand.
> And sex, obviously.

The non-Catholic LA governor of St Edmund's was one of those
who had reported that her school had adopted the whole of the
LA's curriculum policy. She said that every policy within the school
had been copied from another source, and it worried her that this
seemed to indicate the school did not have a mind of its own, whilst
recognizing there was little value in seeking to re-invent the wheel:

> I was looking at some of the project work they were doing in the
> infants school. They'd been out looking at trees and drawing them.
> Then they were doing from the Gospels (sic) that this is part of the
> Garden of Eden with the apple, and bringing the scriptures alive,
> like that ... Faith as well is just looking at a picture and perhaps
> looking at the beauty and the good art, and this is a gift from God.

She initially said she was unsure whether this approach to the
curriculum went all the way through the school, but at a later stage
in the interview was much more positive:

> I am hoping now that this is something we have asked the teachers
> to take on board. I would say the majority of them have done, and
> can see that it's good practice. We were having an Ofsted coming up
> and we thought it would be a good thing to make sure that they did.
> I hope it's not going to fade. It has been good.

It seemed from what she said that there had been some reluctance
on the part of the head to go along with this, but it had been made
plain that this was what was required.

This was an interesting reply, because elsewhere, this governor
had complained that many of the foundation governors were
employed at the school and were unwilling to rock the boat on
controversial matters. I put this to her. She answered by saying that
the group was easily led, and on this occasion had been prepared
to support the chairman (a nun) rather than the head. There was
to be a discussion about it at a forthcoming meeting.

The chairman of Corpus Christi, which had adopted most of
its LA's curriculum policy, thought her school 'does give things
a Catholic stance', but this quickly became centred on sex
education:

> They certainly look at geography and science as the miracles of
> God's creation, and [through] geography they're very aware of
> peoples in other lands and all being part of God's creation and one
> family... They do not do sex education. I did talk to the head about
> that during [the] year and she's not happy with any of the sex educa-
> tion programmes that she's seen ... even the Catholic ones.

I tried again, by asking how governors knew that the curriculum
was being delivered from a Catholic point of view, and it immediately became clear they did not:

> I suppose I'm not speaking for the governing body, I'm speaking for
> myself ... and maybe I've been too gullible in accepting what I've
> been told. We get bits of paper ... at the beginning of each term, a
> little booklet on what is to be taught in the different classes and it
> reads very well. Now whether what is on paper and what takes place
> in the classroom are the same thing I don't know, short of going
> into a classroom and disrupting everybody ... I haven't got round
> that one yet.

The foundation governor from Holy Cross saw problems:

> I think it would be hard to do it in our school because of the teach-
> ers [the majority are not Catholic]. I don't know if it's the right way,
> to be honest. I'd have to think about that.

I quoted to her the views expressed in *The Religious Dimension of
Education in a Catholic School*, and asked her if anything like this had
been discussed by the governing body. She said it had not.

The elected teacher governor of Sacred Heart is a science
teacher, which explains how he

> can talk about the science department, most of whom are Irish or
> Catholic. Over half the department are biologists as well, so when it
> comes to talking about things like evolution, it is something they
> would mention – 'this is the view of the scientist, this is the view
> perhaps of other people. The Catholic Church is fully OK with the
> way we think evolution has occurred.' I don't know ... I think it's
> down to the individual teacher. There's nothing where anybody
> would, or the head, would say 'This is the way, focus there ...' We
> all, as form tutors, have to teach citizenship. I think that could be
> used a bit more in talking about morality-type issues. I know that
> people who are not Catholics teach it in the school and don't want
> to be bothered with the Catholic ethos at all. They're often very
> moral people and talk about citizenship in a moral sense rather than
> a Christian type sense.

Linked with this is the issue of whether Catholic school governors
discern any tension between the requirements of the state with
regard to the National Curriculum and what they perceive to be
the Church's requirements, matters that have been examined in
Chapters 2 and 3.

The parent foundation governor of Our Lady's was confident
there was no difficulty but, with one exception, the examples she
gave could have applied to any school:

> We're quite lucky in that we agree that SATs are not the be-all and
> end-all, that it's ... the experience that the children have at the
> school that's important. But the school I'm a governor at, we ensure
> that the quality of the teaching is good [but with] the broadness you
> used to think was linked to going to primary school. At primary you
> had all these fantastic things – you might go for a walk, do pond-
> dipping, and sports day, and various concerts, and days when you
> were just practising all day ... We have a good structure of teaching,
> so the SATs results are also good. But ... we can still do those other

things because all those other things are important to the education of the whole child instead of just sticking them with work, work, work.

The chair of St Joseph's agreed that the school should educate the whole child, but gave very few examples of how they set about it. Her comments, indeed, almost exclusively surrounded the need to be seen to be performing well in the league tables.

I asked her if the governing body ever discussed the issue, but she said it did not. Rather, the discussions they did have were confined, according to her, to whether to accept the LA's targets for the following year. She volunteered that the head had put what she described as 'strong' teachers into year 6.[10]

I tried to open up this issue once more, but after stressing that 'at the end of the day you have to look at the individual child' her comments were exclusively about SATs and league tables.

The LA governor from English Martyrs had no doubt about what his school's job was:

> The critical Catholic parent in [this borough] would much rather we concentrated on getting the kids good results so they can get to good schools and good universities ... [The parents] veer towards [the view that] the school's job is to ensure the kids do well financially, academically etc. rather than that the duty of the school is to ensure that they're lovely, well brought up, pleasant people. Not that they shouldn't be pleasant people.

A different view was expressed by the LA governor from St Edmund's:

> I do in a way agree that exams aren't everything. I think it is important to build the child as a whole to make them a model citizen, and to be good ... I think moral education is very important. I wonder at the government filling so much of the day up. We've got to have the literacy hour, we've got to have this, we've got to have that, that the teachers perhaps would like to spend more time on religion and do not have time because they have so many other commitments.

It was clear from other comments made by this governor that relationships within the governing body were not easy. She and the

---

[10.] This refers to the year group that is required to take the standard attainment tests at the primary stage and whose performance is therefore critical to the school's position in the league tables.

chair appear to have one view about the direction in which the school should be going, which is very much along the lines laid down by the previous head, whilst the other governors – employees working at the school, and the new head – have an opposing view which, by implication, is more concerned with conforming to the LA norms.

The chair of Corpus Christi said: 'The matter has never been discussed.' It seems, however, that the emphasis on SATs and league tables, that has been noted elsewhere, is not in evidence here.

Holy Cross uses its two form-entry to stream.

> We've got a top and a bottom, and within those groups they're split as well ... God help the poor child who is at the bottom of the class and is feeling the pressure of not being able to understand.

Contrary to what one might expect, however, she asserted that the overriding priority at this school is to 'address the less able ... we don't touch anything for the more able'. She was aware of 'terrible tension to perform and meet these statistics'.

The teacher governor at Sacred Heart began by restricting his answer to his direct experience as a science teacher, and his comments have already been quoted (p. 151).

Conclusion

Many governing bodies have adopted much of their LA's curriculum policies, apparently with little reflection as to the implications of what they have done. Some of those I interviewed seem clear that their governing body has given the matter no discussion; some have, as individuals, given little or no thought to it; others appear to take the view that a distinctive Catholic perspective may apply to some parts of the curriculum; yet others take the view that it is a matter for the individual teacher to determine. One chair goes so far as to deny that the Catholic school curriculum should be different from that of any other school, in contradiction of everything promulgated be the Congregation for Catholic Education and the Catholic Bishops' Conference. What is conspicuously lacking throughout the responses is a coherent understanding of the curriculum as envisaged by the Congregation. This could well mean that the majority of what pupils are taught in Catholic schools is indistinguishable from what those attending other maintained schools are taught. This appears to signal an incongruity with regard to the expectations of the Church authorities. It certainly poses a challenge to them.

The position, viewed in the round, appears to confirm the conclusions of previous chapters of this study and those of Grace and McLaughlin, which have already been cited. These are that the spiritual capital of Catholic schooling may be in decline, and that one manifestation of this decline is the emergence of the dual function school: a school carrying on two separate functions at one and the same time. Given the interplay of the various partners: trustees, governors, LAs, it seems inevitable that the vision of Catholic schools as communities of faith, which provide a unique synthesis of culture and faith, and of faith and life, will become increasingly opaque. There are two linked aspects to the concept of the challenge here: on the one hand, the challenge is to the Church to accept and respond to the concept of the dual function school. On the other, if it fails to do so, it is likely to find itself open to increased challenge from its schools as its formal position is seen to be increasingly out of touch with the realities that governors find themselves grappling with in their day-to-day activities.

Chapter 8

Managing and Monitoring the Ethos
The Role of Catholic School Governing Bodies

Introduction

For many members of the Catholic community, what defines a Catholic school is not so much its academic strengths and weaknesses as its ethos. I therefore decided to ask those I interviewed what they understood by the term. I quoted an experience I had in 1982 when, as a newly appointed diocesan director, I met the head of a flagship ILEA girls' comprehensive school at a conference. She said something along these lines:

> I am an atheist, but I believe in many of the things you pride yourselves on: fairness, justice, equality, and so on. So what is it that is so special about your schools? Why don't you close them down, leave education to the state, do your thing in Sunday schools, and save yourselves a lot of money and effort?

I struggled to produce a reply, and am not sure that I even convinced myself, let alone her. In order to come to grips with this issue, however, it is first necessary to consider the connected one of the mission statement.

The Mission Statement

It was expected that all Catholic schools would have a mission statement of one kind or another. The governors' involvement in its compilation, together with the school development plan, was considered to be a suitable indicator of the governing body's active involvement in setting and monitoring the ethos of the school. As to the mission statement, almost all (98.4 per cent) of my respondents reported that their school had one. Only one person failed to answer the question. It seems reasonable, in the circumstances, to regard this as an oversight and to conclude that the true figure is 100 per cent.

Respondents were then asked about the governing body's contribution to drawing it up. About a quarter (26.3 per cent) said they approved a draft prepared by staff and submitted by the head, a little under a third (31.3 per cent) said that a group of governors worked on it with the head and that the governing body approved the final draft, whilst a fifth (20.2 per cent) said that the whole of the governing body was involved in drafting and agreeing it. A sixth (15.2 per cent) did not know what had happened.

The foundation figures were, in one respect, startling different. Only 10.1 per cent of the respondents thought the whole governing body had been involved, compared with the percentage in the whole survey. It is not clear what conclusion might be drawn from this. One possible explanation is that foundation governors have a different view from others either of the nature of a mission statement or of its significance to the life of the school. If you see it as a paper exercise, with marginal relevance to how the school actually conducts itself, you may perhaps be more likely to misunderstand what is involved in the process. Be that as it may, what is clear is that only about half of those who took part in the survey thought they had played some active part in the preparation of the statement. If it is accepted that a school's mission statement is the foundation stone on which the whole edifice of a school as learning community is constructed (including the development plan, which was examined in the previous chapter), this proportion seems low.

School Ethos

The difficulty in defining a school's ethos was rehearsed by McLaughlin in 2005.[1] In the course of his review, he approves the distinction made by Donnelly in his survey of two Northern Ireland schools (one a Catholic primary and one a grant-maintained-integrated), between what he defines as a positivist viewpoint, which comprises 'the expressed wishes of those who command authority within an organization', and an anti-positivist one, which is the 'process of social interaction', experienced by those who are

---

[1.] McLaughlan, *The Educative Importance of Ethos.*

members of it, within the organization itself.[2] How useful this might be is questionable: it seems that a governing body's view could be at one and the same time both anti-positivist, viewed by the diocese or the Sacred Congregation, and positivist when viewed by the staff of the school.

McLaughlin points to the large variety of features through which ethos may be identified. I have already referred to six specific ingredients that are claimed to make up the Catholic 'school climate' in *The Religious Dimension of Education in a Catholic School*. McLaughlin does not mention this source, but cites Scottish, Irish, and Church of England initiatives. The Scottish one includes twelve, the Irish twenty-one, and the Church of England no fewer than twenty-four, but unfortunately he does not tell us what they are.[3]

He draws attention to the 'clear resonances between the notion of an ethos and Bourdieu's notion of a "habitus": the deep structured cultural dispositions within a community or an institution'.[4] He argues that no attempt should be made to identify a single definition of the concept, but nevertheless proposes that 'At the most general level, an ethos can be regarded as the prevalent or characteristic tone, spirit or sentiment informing an identifiable entity involving human life and interaction.'[5] This is not too far from the *Chambers Dictionary* definition of 'the distinctive habitual character and disposition of an individual, group, race, etc.'.

For Hornsby-Smith, the defining characteristic of a Catholic school is its religious socialization of pupils: their 'introduction ... to the essential articles of religious faith and the norms of religious worship', which brings into play the interdependent contributions of various agencies and institutions, including the parish and Catholic teachers.[6]

Sullivan examines ideas influencing the practice of Catholic schools, and concludes that 'It is communion with Christ that is meant to give all the various activities of school a coherence and their special religious tone.'[7] In particular, 'Catholic perspectives should permeate the curriculum ... [and] priority should be given to fostering of personal prayer and public worship' and 'The

[2] Donnelly, *In pursuit of school ethos*, pp. 136–7.
[3] McLaughlin, *The Educative Importance of Ethos*, p. 309.
[4] Ibid., p. 314.
[5] Ibid., p. 311.
[6] Hornsby Smith, *Catholic Education: The Unobtrusive Partner*, p. 113.
[7] Sullivan, *Catholic Schools in Contention*, p. 177.

gospel should be brought to bear on all aspects of school life.'[8] He endorses Courteney Murray's (1994) view that 'Christian theology is the architectonic science that furnishes the basic postulates of the theory of Christian education, specifies its objectives [and] invests the whole process with a distinctive atmosphere.'[9]

Sullivan returned to the issue in 2001 when he argued that Catholic schools need to be both distinctive, which he defined as faithful to tradition, and inclusive, that is, liberal and progressive. This they can achieve by adopting what he describes as a 'living tradition', a process whereby they draw on the strengths of tradition, but interpret them in the light of contemporary circumstances.[10]

In Sullivan's analysis, the Catholic view of education shares many features with a broad Christian approach to belief in God, the divinity of Christ, and the work of the Holy Spirit, but it has a particular conviction of the prominence given to the papacy and the universality of the Church. He identifies three key themes in the Vatican texts that have been examined in Chapter 2: the autonomy of various branches of knowledge, the need for the integral development of the human person, and also for a synthesis of faith and culture.[11] He approves the claim made in *Signposts and Homecomings* that what makes Catholic education distinctive is that all activities – curriculum, syllabus, discipline, systems of rewards and punishments, worship, relationships and catechesis – have a 'special perspective which is derived from communion with Christ'.[12] He identifies four ways in which Catholic education may be said to differ from other interpretations: the importance of conscience; the central role of religious education; a specific understanding of the human person, its origin and destiny, incorporating the view of life as a gift, the existence of sin, and the need for obedience and faithfulness; and the concept of vocation.[13]

Pring quotes Rutter in defining ethos in terms of the values, aims, attitudes and procedures of a school which interrelate and which remain a relatively permanent feature of the school.[14] 'To get at the ethos of the school', Pring says, 'you need to examine the various stable procedures through which the business is conducted

[8.] Ibid., pp. 97, 109.
[9.] Ibid., p. 124.
[10.] Sullivan, *Catholic Education: Distinctive and Inclusive*.
[11.] Ibid., pp. 76ff.
[12.] Konstant, *Signposts and Homecomings*, p. 87.
[13.] Ibid., p. 108.
[14.] Rutter et al., *Fifteen Thousand Hours*, pp. 182ff.

towards individuals and their work, towards the community as a whole and towards those outside the school.'[15]

In the light of this, how might one expect those intimately connected with Catholic schools to describe their ethos? Difficult though McLaughlin may have found the concept, many Catholics think they know what they mean, and it is this evidence, unreflective or undeveloped as it might be, with which researchers have to deal.

The first ingredient would seem to be, without much argument, that religious belief and the practice that springs from it have the defining significance. Commentators might go from a foundational claim of this kind in a number of directions: one might be to describe the school as a worshipping community, with an emphasis on liturgies, and the development of private prayer amongst both pupils and staff. Associated with this might be the provision of a chapel or prayer room and religious artefacts of various kinds. Another might be the extent to which the whole of the taught curriculum is influenced by the conviction that all knowledge and truth come from God. A third might concern itself with relationships, both within the school and with the wider community, through, for example, charitable activities.

The problem with this last approach is that, as has already been demonstrated, these concerns are no longer, if, indeed they ever were, exclusive characteristics of Christian communities, so unless they are firmly attached by the school to its religious nature, they do not assist the argument. Such an attachment might be achieved by explicit reference to the two great commandments to love God and one's neighbour (Matt. 22:37–9), or the Beatitudes (Matt. 5:3–10), or to what are frequently referred to as 'Gospel values', though these would need to be defined.

Because of the difficulties associated with the subject matter, and its importance to the study as a whole, I thought it might be of interest to show, in some of the examples, how my respondents' comments developed as the interviews progressed.

The foundation governor of Our Lady's, who had, herself, attended, and later taught in, non-Catholic primary schools, and whose insights were, accordingly particularly interesting, said that, in her view, there is a difference between what she described as 'mainstream' and Catholic schools:

People who don't know about Catholic schools assume that it's Catholic religion and you just doing Mass or whatever. But the

[15.] Pring, *Implications of the Changing Values and Ethical Standards of Society*, p. 20.

> whole feel of a Catholic school is different because of the Catholic
> ethos, and the caring ... and trying to follow the Catholic way of life
> as well...the people who are sending their children to you are
> backing [you] up already by sending their children there ... It's not
> just the Catholic religion, it's a way of life.

As we shall see, unlike many of the other governors I interviewed,
there is a complete absence, here, of any reference to the externals: statues, bibles, crucifixes and the like. But what she eventually
arrived at appears to describe a situation where there are close
links between the local Catholic community and its school, and
where there is an attempt to follow through the requirements that
arise from the religious belief of the parents. That said, there is
nothing in her comments about the school itself as a worshipping
community, or about the encouragement of the children in their
own faith-development. Nor is there is any suggestion that the
curriculum might be distinctive.

The chair of St Joseph's soon experienced the same difficulty in
describing the Catholic ethos of her school, but the starting point
was completely different. A stranger coming into it would immediately be conscious of the ethos:

> because the first thing you would see is a statue of the Virgin Mary,
> and the bible would be open, and the children would be ... you
> would know it's a Catholic school, definitely, because as soon as you
> entered the hall that's the first thing you would see, and then there
> are statues all over the school ... I don't know what it is, but you can
> just tell. Maybe it's because I'm a Catholic and you are kind of
> looking for signs.

Relationships within the school were part of its ethos, and she also
referred to the school's annual Christmas and Easter productions,
together with the active role in the school of the parish clergy.

The initial response concerned itself exclusively with externals,
and, as with the first governor, there was no specific reference to
the school as a community of faith or to the encouragement of
children on their personal journeys. There was no comment at all
about curricular issues, but this was hardly surprising, as this was
the governor who was emphatic, at another point in the interview,
that all children, in whatever type of school, should be taught the
same curriculum, except for RE.

The LA governor of English Martyrs thought the school had a
special ethos, which he initially ascribed to a factor relating to a
practice of the school rather than anything else:

There is a school Mass in the church every week that the juniors attend. The parish priest is closely involved with the school and goes in regularly. He's a governor ... There are visible signs round the school. Otherwise ... I dunno. It doesn't hide the fact it's Catholic, and there's its name, of course.

If this description of the school is accurate, its distinctive ethos is, then, confined largely to a number of artefacts that adorn the premises.

The LA governor from St Edmund's was sure her school had a special ethos:

Yes ... We do nurture the children to be brought up in the Catholic faith and be good citizens ... in pursuit of the Gospel message. The staff, as well as the parents, are committed to the journey of faith, if you like, by baptism, etc, and attending church. The priest does come in and takes services within the school. When it was fifty years old we actually had a room built that's our own little chapel, as it were, and it's a quiet room for the children to sit [in]. We try to build on the foundations of the faith that are started in the home, and we try to bring it on and also we do invite parents in, and we do invite them to Masses and everything.

This appears to echo the position at Our Lady's: the school and the Catholic families are working together in nurturing the faith of the pupils. There are references to the Gospel message, though this is undefined, and the concept of both staff and pupils being on a journey of faith. It is notable that this, most articulate description so far, comes from a governor who is not, herself, a Catholic. Nevertheless, there is no comment about curricular issues at this point in the discourse, though later, when discussing the curriculum, she indicated that attempts were made to deliver it against a religious background. It is interesting that she did not identify this as a contributory factor to the school's ethos.

At Corpus Christi a very interesting mixture emerged:

The children are delightful. They're polite, they're open, they're friendly, they're chatty. If someone turns up at the school, the children will go and talk to them ... The children are involved in charitable things such as fundraising during Lent ... They're very aware of the need in the world. The ethos of the school seems good, but it seems separate from the church. The children occasionally are taken down to the church and some do the readings and they sing a few hymns, or Father goes up to school and says Mass in the school hall and that's as far as it goes.

> I think the way the children treat each other, the way they greet visitors and the courtesy and consideration they show, that to me reflects the caring love of neighbour ethos. This sounds awful, but I'm not so sure about the staff. They do tend to shout a lot and criticize. The children speaking to each other are lovely ... There is a caring atmosphere among the children. Lovely. And also, I have to say, the support staff.

What, therefore, seems to be described here is a school where the externals are in place, and, as at English Martyrs, there is, as it were, an external religious practice. There is no view expressed about the centrality of Christ in the school's work, or of anything that might be derived from such an understanding, such as (as we have seen previously) the school being a specific way of life, or nurturing the faith of the pupils.

It was not easy to get a clear picture of the position at Holy Cross. The governor thought her school had a special ethos, but, when asked to define it, said briefly that 'it's one that's kind of emerged over the years'. When pressed, she continued:

> I would say it's a special school, and I think it's mainly down to the headteacher, because she's kind of unforgettable, really, and that's the way she greets you, and she's enthusiastic, and she clearly wears her religion. You know that she's a Christian, and you know that's what she practises. And whilst she is tolerant of all other areas, and so are we, she wants it to be a Catholic school.

The next question was, obviously, how one would know she was a Catholic Christian, and the answer was 'From what she said.' I tried again, by asking what were the sorts of things that would manifest this, and we immediately entered the area of the caring community:

> It is a very caring school ... You walk in the door, and there's a picture of Our Lady, and we have a picture of the bishop, and we've got crosses around, but on the whole the school is just a very friendly school ... I don't know how to define it necessarily. I'd love to say it's because we're Catholics, but I don't think it is. I think it's probably a combination of many things.

Once more, we see that the only clearly articulated characteristic is the artefacts. The children are happy, but the governor does not think this springs from the Catholic nature of the school. She appeared to attribute the strength of the school's ethos to the example set by the head and the number of priests from the parish who were able to go into it. There was no reference to a community of faith, nor to the role of the school in nurturing the faith of the pupils.

The elected teacher governor from Sacred Heart thought it had a distinct ethos, but not of a Catholic, or even a religious character. When asked to describe it, he said it was:

> Calm, disciplined. The thing is, I think a lot of our parents think the school is great because of its reputation, and what their perceptions and expectations are of the school.

By 'reputation', he said he meant its academic standing in the community. There is a perception that the school is a shouting environment. The new head has taken a stand against this, and, in this governor's view, standards of discipline have deteriorated as a result, because the pupils are no longer frightened of the staff.

I put it to him that the impression I had formed in the light of his comment was that parents chose the school because it was very successful academically rather than because it was Catholic, but he was adamant that this was an over-simplification:

> No, I think it's a mixture. But it's something the parents in this borough don't need to think about, because it just so happens that it's a Catholic school which is the best in the borough.

In the light of this, I asked him how the school's Catholic character manifested itself to the boys and parents. He said:

> I'm not really sure how parents perceive it, to be honest. We go to Mass every once in a while, we start lessons with prayers, or are supposed to. That's something that's going to be pressed more and more this year.

I asked him to explain 'supposed to'.

> It's not adhered to much by the staff. If you want to do it, you do it, if you don't, you don't.

He then went on to say that the school employed a chaplain and that ...

> The RE department are stuck away ... no, not stuck away, but they're in the farthest reaches of the school, for historic reasons. They've got a prayer room up there and they run SVP societies, and

a prayer group, and that sort of thing.[16] Every message that goes home has a message from the chaplain ... We do a sponsored walk for charity once a year. All those sorts of things. The priests are for ever coming in ... We've had nuns teaching in the school. We're next to the church, so the parish priest, who's chair of governors, comes in all the time. People see clergy walking in and out.

I said that these things did not seem to impact much on the life of the school. He agreed:

I wouldn't have thought so ... There's a certain hard core that gets involved in all this sort of thing and often will get involved with the RE department because of the individual teachers in the RE department that they get on well with, not necessarily because they are overly spiritual.

Despite that, however,

Someone who is more articulate than me ... would be able to argue strongly and effectively that the school does come across as being very Catholic in its ethos ... I feel its quite a Catholic type of school because I'm a Catholic myself. [The pupils go on retreats] and some of the teachers are involved in the deanery for confirmation. The kids will see, in certain parishes, that the teachers who teach them every day are also doing that, so they can see it's living outside their school premises. The thing is this seems like a fantastic school if you want to do things that get you in the limelight. For instance, one of our kids was chosen to receive Holy Communion from the Pope. That sort of thing seems to happen quite a lot here ... Every single classroom has got a crucifix in. All their planners have got a number of different prayers, and history about the different saints ... Plus everybody does GCSE in RE.

It appears from this that at least three, if not four, contrasting concepts of ethos are struggling to co-exist at this school: the first celebrates academic and sporting excellence. It is underpinned by a strict dress code, a climate of fear generated at least in part by what is described 'a shouting sort of environment', and externally imposed discipline. One consequence of this is that one of the most senior members of staff, as well as the governor being interviewed, have judged the school unacceptable for their own children. The second is perhaps best described as the official line,

---

[16.] SVP is the Society of St Vincent de Paul, an organization that brings practical help to the poor.

whereby all lessons are supposed to start with prayer, the school goes to Mass 'every once in a while', messages from the school always contain input from the chaplain, every classroom has a crucifix, the pupils' planners contain prayers and details of the lives of saints, and there are charitable activities and a prayer group. The third is the de facto situation in which the teacher governor describes the 'RE department are stuck away ... no, not stuck away, but they're in the farthest reaches of the school', where things are done to ' get you into the limelight', where the policy of starting each lesson with prayer is ignored by staff at will. The fourth might be described as the new ethos, not fully articulated by the governor, which the new head is trying to introduce. To what extent this has been discussed or endorsed by the governing body was not revealed, but it does entail a reduction in the incidence of shouting, and has already had a deleterious effect on discipline, in the view of the governor whom I interviewed. How, or perhaps whether, all this fits together into a harmonious whole, and how the new head is faring were not, unfortunately, the subject of my study.

The Views of the Diocesan Directors

In the light of this, it was imperative to ask the diocesan directors what they were looking for when they wanted to evaluate the distinctive Catholic ethos of their school. The replies were very different and, perhaps understandably, more precisely articulated. The diocesan director for Glastonbury went straight the point:.

> I've always said that the strongest pressure on the students is peer pressure. We've got to be a bit careful about bringing things down from the top ... It's too easy to say 'We're Catholic and therefore we're special.' [What I look for is] first, how they treat each other: staff and staff, and staff and pupils. And awareness of the Lord. In some schools now, chapels are quite important places and some have Reservation of the Blessed Sacrament. Even where they don't, it's a special place and it's not just used for public celebrations, but for private prayer. That's really important.

I put it to him that very few primary schools could run to a chapel.

> No, but very often the ones I do know have a space for private prayer, whether it's a corner of the library or a corner of a class-room.

He played down the importance of religious artefacts, on the ground that, after a time they are 'just part of the furniture'. Similarly, retreats and pilgrimages 'are powerful at the time, [but] I'm not sure yet how long-term effective they are', and there is usually a committed teacher behind most charitable activities, without the influence of whom interest amongst pupils will fade.

In summary, for him, the crucial element in defining a Catholic school with a living ethos is the life of prayer of the people in it.

> You can get a good non-faith school where they are very caring for each other. It's not the fact that they're caring for each other that's important, it's the reason why they do that, and that's what it's got to be founded on.

The Director for the Diocese of Much Wenlock prefaced his answer with comments that would have been recognized by the governors I had interviewed, but then quickly moved, to a limited degree, into territory similar to that of his colleague in Glastonbury:

> I could go into a Catholic school and recognize it as a Catholic school, not just by the physical, external manifestations of what might be regarded as Catholic, but by the sense that the school is firstly clear in its mission statement that it is a Christian, Catholic establishment, that there is a clarity about the way in which the school will operate and manage not only issues of excellence in academic terms, which is perfectly right and proper, but excellence in the way in which it will pursue with parents the responsibility of trying to assist in the formation of children in the broadest of senses. The whole being is important, the individuality of the pupil is important. You can turn round and say: 'In the best of schools that should be the case '... so what else? ... It should be evident in the way it goes about it's day-to-day expression of the purpose of the Church, the purpose of trying to assist young people in their formation to find God through Christ, the way in which it will live its life in practice in the school against the Gospel values ... The effective Catholic school should in its admissions policy be looking to be inclusive of the whole Catholic community. If, having served the whole of the Catholic community's needs, it will go further and not be picky. We know some Catholic schools are very picky in their admissions ... [and] may well be flying in the face of what should be the proper practice of admissions into a Catholic school, where we're looking to serve the whole community.

A great deal of work has been done on this issue by the Schools' Commission in the Diocese of Athelney, but in such a way that it is not possible to quote from it without revealing its identity. In general terms, however, the concept of ethos has been analysed in considerable detail, and schools have been invited to reflect on a number of issues that would help them identify the extent to which they meet what the bishop considers to be of central significance. Amongst these is the development of the spiritual life, through liturgy and prayer, of both pupils and staff. The director had this to say:

> OK, so what's the Catholic ethos? The answer was always 'Well, you can't put your finger on it, but it's there.' I'm terribly sorry, if Ofsted has taught us to be able to put our finger on what is good teaching and learning, to develop a language and vocabulary so that we can talk about it, and through that process raise the quality of teaching and learning in our schools, coach people, mentor people, develop people, my argument is you can do exactly the same for the Catholicity of the school, because if you can't find the language to describe the provision in the school that ensures Catholicity developing well, the outcomes that are achieved through that Catholic ethos, then how on earth can you induct people into it, enable them to engage in it, to commit to it, to celebrate it, and to promote it? So there has to be an understanding of what it is we provide, and what are the outcomes that are distinctive from our absolutely outstanding community schools.

The director for the Diocese of Lacock said he would be distressed if the ethos wasn't explicit and implicit. In his schools, all the staff, both teaching and non-teaching are encouraged, and offered the opportunity, to take an active role in the ministry of the school, and he had gone to great lengths to see that this was a reality, as the following extracts from his interview amply demonstrate. His vision in large measure mirrored that of the director for Glastonbury in its emphasis on prayer, but he started with artefacts:

> I'd be horrified if I went into one of our schools now and within the first five yards I didn't know it was Lent. I'd expect to see Lent and I would [see it] ... It would say 'Welcome to so-and-so school as we journey through Lent towards Easter', primary and secondary. I'd expect to know from the way I was greeted by the secretary or the admin. staff I was in a Catholic school ... We have an annual secretaries' conference ... because we regard them as fulfilling one of the most Christian ministries ever: the ministry of welcome ... We also have a programme for our support staff ... So it's right the way through – it's the old Brighton rock stuff, isn't it? But it's there in people's understanding. We haven't just focused on governors in

terms of understanding the explicit nature of Catholic schools, we've tried to get in at every level.

I'd expect all the meetings to begin with prayer. I'd expect governors' meetings to have a reflective element to them, not just a quick Hail Mary or Our Father tagged on to the front of it. I'd expect every school and governing body to use our diocesan prayer book ... Every foundation governor has a copy of that ... But we say in addition to that, let's have a daily prayer so that, in the course of a two year period, every one of our schools is prayed for, and if we know there's a school with a particular need, we make sure that school is represented in there ... So ... conferences, seminars, meetings for all members of staff are always on an underlying Catholic theology, so irrespective of who's in our schools, the roots would always be embedded in a strong Catholic theology.

The Director of Tewkesbury covered ground that the governors I interviewed would recognize, but like his colleagues elsewhere, prayer was central. He prefaced his remarks by saying that some of the things he would look for

would not necessarily be of themselves alone Catholic, but still, nevertheless, I think they contribute to the general scheme of things. I like to see that the pupils in the schools are orderly, respectful, relatively obedient to instruction and organization, that they are working hard at achieving, that they are in an atmosphere where prayer is not unusual, it's accepted as part and parcel of the daily routine, and that they not only submit to it, but as far as possible, are showing some sense of participating in it. I would like to see the ethos also working the other way round, insofar as the teachers are respectful of their pupils, where discipline is very clear and very clearly understood, but nonetheless, if sanctions have to be applied, they don't in any way degrade or denigrate the pupils themselves ... There'll be signs that this is a Catholic school, that the crucifix, statue of the patron saint of the school, or whatever it may be, are in evidence ... There must be visible signs that this place is a holy place, that it's a place where anybody who comes in will be made to feel welcome.

The director for the Diocese of Tintern was less prescriptive, saying that what was important was

to see that what is actually said about the school by the head, the governors, the parish priest is linked to relationships, the prayer life of the school, the opportunities for all of the students and all of the families within the community to have the best experience of both an education and a religious education; of their spiritual life happening, and not just talked about but lived out. So when I hear and read something like; 'The ethos of this school is positive' and then I have an issue to deal with like the exclusion of a pupil, or something to do with admissions, where the process has not been fair, that for me is how I judge the school. So, is what is put down as policy and the vision of the school actually happening?

I walk into this school where the mission of this school is welcoming and I'm sat outside the office for an hour waiting for somebody to deal with an issue, and observe during that time that I'm not the only one; children are spoken to and dealt with in a way that isn't appropriate; the telephone is answered in a way that isn't helpful; and things occur, where we're looking at standards, and I'm thinking particularly of secondary schools now, where public accountability with examination results makes me question 'Are we as inclusive as we might be?'

I suggested that any of that would apply just as readily to a community school. He answered by providing a negative example:

It would. But when I go in, perhaps on an in-service day, or I go to a governors' meeting, and there is no focus on using, or having, a little liturgy, or even a prayer which would make me think 'well, I could be anywhere'; When I walk into a school and they're talking about plans for the next academic year, or I trawl through governors' minutes and I see that nothing in terms of the spiritual life or the spiritual opportunity for those pupils is even mentioned [I would have concerns].

Managing and Monitoring ethos

On the evidence available to me, described in Chapter 6, it seems that governors are happy to allow clergy or members of religious orders to act as the link between school and diocese, where the latter are members of a governing body. Education law in England has, for many years now, placed responsibility for the entire conduct of voluntary aided schools wholly on the shoulders of governing bodies. How, in practice, is this working in matters of religious education and worship? Is this again an area into which lay governors are nervous of being seen to intrude, or is change either occurring or discernibly in the wings? If so, to what extent may the new order present a challenge to the Church?

The Governors' Views

The chairman of Our Lady's said his governing body had six committees: Finance, Health and Safety, which took in buildings as well; Curriculum; Admissions; Personnel; and Disciplinary. The last Ofsted report had spoken very highly of the school's Catholic ethos. I asked him how they kept the spirituality of the school under review. He said.

> It stems from the mission statement, which clearly states that Christianity runs throughout the school and throughout the teaching, and throughout relationships, and throughout the community. It's there – implicit in everything that one does.

When I asked him how he knew that the aspirations of the mission statement were being put into practice, he said the governors would expect the headteacher (who is also the school's RE co-ordinator) to tell them in her termly report. Her role in this matter seemed pivotal:

> Quite a lot of that ethos is delivered through her. We would rather expect that, and that it would come across in our discussions with her and in her reports. It doesn't actually come across 'How is the mission statement being carried into practice?' but I think if there were a shortfall, she would be aware of it and tell us. If teachers were doing things not in accord [with it] we would find out. And certainly, because we've got other Catholic members of staff on the governing body, we would quickly be aware if there were difficulties.

The governors monitored RE by means of an annual report from the head.

His colleague agreed with him, but gave more detail about the osmotic process by which the mission statement and ethos fed into the day-to-day work of the school:

> We were discussing last Christmas's play, a lovely play, absolutely fantastic. The children were excellent; the teachers had put in lots of time. But you walked away from it thinking: 'and the moral was?' ... because it wasn't a nativity play, it was a bit vague. So we said, even on that level, can we make sure that, this Christmas, what goes into the performance represents what the school stands for and represents?

She went on to say that the school's Catholic ethos informed all the work of the governing body, and was in everyone's minds. When I asked her how she knew she said:

> Because if, sometimes, you lose your way and forget about it ... somebody will remind [you] about it, especially if you've got things like finance and stuff like that where you can get lost ... and start going off at tangents.

When I asked for examples of how this worked in practice, what emerged was a picture of a school serving a close-knit community where there was a vision of the role of the school that was shared by clergy, governors, teachers, parents and others:

> We have input from the diocese, we have the priest come in, various people. We even have parishioners who have no children at the school – they may be retired – who listen to readers. There's that sort of link with the wider community ... parents, people whose children went there who've grown up, they still want to do something for the school.

In the particular circumstances of this school, perhaps the monitoring mechanism that has evolved here, although it may appear loose, in textbook terms, is exactly what is needed, and the governors are right to be confident that all is as it should be. Greater formality may be unnecessary. On the other hand, if the concept of ethos is never explicitly discussed, how can its effectiveness or appropriateness be evaluated?

The chairman of St Joseph's said that there, too, the governing body did not have a committee keeping the ethos of the school under review, but a link governor for RE, who was employed in the school as a member of the support staff. Link governors are required to visit the school once a term. The practice had been that their reports would be either oral or written, but Ofsted requirements had persuaded them to require only written reports, so that evidence was available. I put it to her that the emphasis of her work would be RE and assemblies, and she agreed. I tried to bring the discussion back to wider questions of ethos, by raising the issue of relationships, but the reply immediately referred, briefly, to assemblies and then went on to the nativity play, class Masses, and the imposition of ashes on Ash Wednesday.

If there is any active monitoring of the ethos at this school, it was not easy to discern how it was done, other than that, as in the case of Our Lady's, the school is extremely popular with the Catholic community (it is over-subscribed by Catholic children), and has very close links with the parish – it is physically next door to the church, and the clergy visit regularly.

The governor from English Martyrs started with an uncertain reply, and then, as at St Joseph's, went on to talk about something else:

> I suppose the answer is 'yes'. I'm not sure. We start the meeting with prayers. The religious curriculum is something we discuss. In fact we nearly came to blows a couple of years ago over the sex curriculum … It's not a major issue, and you occasionally get letters from parents complaining. The sex one is an example, or whether there is enough firm Christian, Opus Dei-type teaching … I've been on the governing body fifteen years, and there have been three or four issues in that time, so they're not coming up every week, but it's there in the background.[17]

I asked if his answer implied there was not much positive involvement of the governing body in monitoring the RE and ethos. He did not agree:

> I have difficulty in giving you chapter and verse of what we've done, and how we've done it, My feeling is we're aware of it, and we take note of it, but it's not something that is … I suppose 'cos my main area is finance, I care about the budget.

Later he volunteered that a scheme of link governors is in operation and that there is a governor responsible for RE. Link governors report to the governing body after their visits. This is only one way in which the governing body keeps the affairs of the school under review. There is also a curriculum committee that 'is more concerned with policy than its application'. I asked him if this committee kept under review the RE syllabus, but he answered by talking about a decision to change the maths books.

St Edmund's has a committee structure that is similar to that of Our Lady's, so there is, again, no group looking systematically at RE and ethos. There had been one, instigated by the former head whose departure this governor so regretted. It had been discontinued at the behest of the new head, who had argued that, as the school was Catholic, and seen to be running satisfactorily, it was

---

17. This is a reference to an organization within the Catholic Church which is regarded by its opponents as being traditional and out of touch with modern life, a view implicitly supported by this governor, who goes on to say, at this point, 'You'll gather I'm a liberal Catholic.'

unnecessary to have a committee or individual governor for this purpose. Religion, according to the new head, 'was taught within the school day in, day out . . . we need other things to focus on than that'.

The parish priest was the link governor for RE, but, as already reported, had submitted only one post-visit report in two years instead of, as in other curriculum areas, one each term. In her view, the RE and ethos of the school were not, now, being monitored.

Things seemed even more problematic at Corpus Christi, where, according to the chair, nothing was being properly monitored. She was fearful about what would be the outcome of the next visit from Ofsted.

A monitoring committee exists at Holy Cross because, although the school had received a glowing report from Ofsted, one of the areas noted as in need of improvement was the monitoring role of the governors. It was not easy to discern what the precise arrangements were, but there seems, now, to be a freestanding committee responsible for RE and ethos which reports to the monitoring committee.

I have already recorded that the teacher governor of Sacred Heart sees his governing body in similar terms to that of Corpus Christi: 'a nodding shop', but despite the school's size and location, there are resonances of the way Our Lady's and St Joseph's operate:

> They use the word 'monitor', and, because Ofsted are due to come in . . . the chairman has been pressing to make it more of a monitoring body. We've had inset from the LA about how we do that, but it's not overly clear. Perhaps I'm jaded, but it seems that a lot of it is just lip-service.
>
> The chairman [the parish priest] . . . knows what's going on. He speaks to a lot of people, some of whom are parents, and he will get a feel for the way it is. He speaks to members of staff. He is somebody who is trying to make it more of a monitoring body. He also knows the headteacher has got to get things done, and as long as he's not going totally against his own view, I don't think he's going to push it.

I asked if there was, as in a number of Catholic secondary schools, a sub-committee dealing with ethos.

> No, as far as I'm aware we haven't got that. I think, generally speaking, that someone who is more articulate than me, is more of a

politician than me, they would be able to argue strongly and effectively that the school does come across as being very Catholic in its
ethos ... I just don't know.

The Views of Diocesan Directors

The Director of Glastonbury affirmed what appeared to be the
approach to monitoring at Our Lady's, and had manifest sympathy
with the burden facing secondary governors:

> In a small primary school in a village like this, I can remember
> saying to an Ofsted inspector 'You know straightaway what's going
> on. You get the feedback.' Much more difficult in secondary
> schools, where you have hundreds of pupils, and it's very hard for
> the governors to spend time in the school, because they're working.
> It is difficult enough to get them to give up the time to come to
> meetings. They haven't the time to come into school and see what
> it's like and observing and watching and being around.

In the light of the information that had emerged from the governors, the increased emphasis placed by Ofsted on the monitoring
activities of governors, and the significance of ethos in the perceptions of many, I asked him if he thought a dedicated committee was
a useful arrangement. He had reservations:

> It could be if you get the right people. You need people who have
> the time and the information and the ability to absorb the impres-
> sion of what's going on.

Because of this reservation, I asked if there was anything a diocese
might do to assist governing bodies. The issue of training quickly
arose:

> We have the RE inspectorate that covers things like ethos, and they
> try to talk to governors about what's going on, but that's post
> factum, as it were. If we're going to ask people to become governors
> of a school, we've got to train them.

The director for Much Wenlock was very much more confident
about the ability and willingness of his governors to make a strong
contribution in this area: 'My experience here is that there is quite
outstanding commitment on the part of governors.'
Since this response appeared to be so much at odds with what I
had been told in Glastonbury, I asked him how they worked.

By forming an acceptable practice with the headteacher of having
permission to come into the school, not in an interfering sense, but
looking to assist, and play a role in the school from the inside as well
as just turning up to one or two governing body meetings a term . . .
They take an active part in the debates that take place within the
governing body, and call for reports rather than just waiting for the
head to hand them down.

This is a diocese where responsibility for RE rests with a separate
diocesan department. The training issue emerged again. He said
he was aware it ran programmes for governors to assist them in
understanding and knowledge of what the RE curriculum is and
added: 'There is an intimacy about the diocese's involvement with
the schools that might not be apparent elsewhere.'

The director in Athelney agreed that, in his experience, governors' monitoring of RE and ethos could be hit and miss. Yet again,
training was raised:

Yes. I think if you look at schools generally you will see a whole range
of ability on the part of the governors. We do training on strategy
roles and responsibilities, and we say in a Catholic school you have
a dual responsibility. One is for the quality of the education
provided in the school, and the standards achieved, and the other
one is that you secure the character of the school as a Catholic
school. In training, we focus on those two responsibilities, and look
at what they mean.

This director took issue with the notion of a dedicated committee
to oversee the ethos:

The danger of that is that you marginalize that aspect of the life of
a school and take it away from leadership and management, take it
away from teaching and learning, take it away from the curriculum
by definition . . . I don't think they should be separated off, because
when you're asking about how effective the leadership and management of the school is, it's in terms of its being a Catholic school, so
you're asking about that, not necessarily separating things off . . . if
you start creating committees like that, somehow or other, the
people that monitor that bit are the parish priest or people who are
seen as particularly local Catholic worthies . . . I wouldn't encourage
that because I would say it is a corporate responsibility. You all hold
responsibility for the life of the school.

The director for Lacock had found that the monitoring of his schools' ethos was problematic, and here, again, the issue of training emerged:

> I would say that's one of the weakest areas of governance – the lack of monitoring of the Catholic life of the school. Where you have good heads, or good heads of RE, or good RE teachers, or good parish priests, it would happen, but we found it was a huge area of concern. People taking it for granted in some places, and in other places it's not [as] important [as] standards.

He had decided the only solution was to institute a formal diocesan review, rooted in the experience of the foundation governors:

> The first question is 'To what extent is the Catholic ethos known, celebrated, and monitored?' Foundation governors are asked that question, so they're all involved in articulating the response. The review is very rigorous, and people are asked how they assess and monitor, so that's tightened things up a bit. It's still not as good as it should be ... The self-evaluation form under the S.48 inspection arrangements is strong on the Catholic life of the school, so that's good.[18]

I asked how a primary school would go about it. 'through the head-teacher's report. One of the areas would always be the Catholic life of the school'. I said that governors have to know what questions to ask.

> They've been encouraged to ask the right questions, both through communications, our website, and seminars. If you go on our website, you'll find a liturgy audit which we've briefed governors on. That's available. But very much, I suppose, the headteacher's report and the sef.[19] And the sef increasingly now because it has to be updated every year. It gives us a wonderful opportunity to make sure that that is happening on an annual cycle ... The bishop has said he will keep schools open only if they are vibrant Catholic communities serving the mission of the Church in education. We need [the schools] as mission, and therefore the Catholic life has to be to the fore.

[18.] This refers to the statutory provision for the religious education and worship of denominational schools to be inspected as part of, but distinct from, the Ofsted inspection process.

[19.] This is an acronym for the self-evaluation form, a document schools are required to complete as part of the Ofsted inspection process. Its content and purpose are self-explanatory.

The director for Tewkesbury was as sanguine as his colleague in Much Wenlock:

> I think in the main it is addressed. Again, it may be addressed very largely by the clergy, raising the situation where they're on the governing body, sometimes positively, sometimes negatively, but at the end of the day, I do think it's being addressed on a fairly regular basis through the year. I wouldn't say it figures at every governing body meeting. I do read all the governing body minutes ... and I do find areas where these things are being addressed, either through RE, or through the general behaviour policies in the school, or when the time comes round for them to re-examine the mission statement, they are dealing with this, and getting to grips with it. It depends on the governing body. Some of them will go into it in some detail, some will touch on it, and either hand it over to somebody else, like the parish priest, to sort out, or just put into place something that looks OK and then move on quickly to something else.

I asked what happened if he found a school was not reviewing its mission statement on an annual basis. Would he write, or phone?

> Oh no! I do better than that. I would send one of my advisers in to find out what the health of the nation is, and raise the issue that way. I find that when dealing with things of that nature, the personal contact is a great deal better than writing letters ... I'm trying as far as possible to persuade people that this is the way they should be going rather than instructing them.

I wondered if the problem was more a secondary one than primary.

> I wouldn't say that it was ... Most of our secondary schools take this extraordinarily seriously. Primary schools tend to work on the assumption that all this works by osmosis. It's therefore to a certain extent a given which you're living with all the time, and perhaps don't begin to extrapolate from the practice to see if the principles are all secure behind it, and whether those principles are clear enough from what's going in the life of the school. So, sometimes primaries need a little bit of help in that direction.

The Director of Tintern, like his colleague in Tewkesbury, reads all the minutes of governors' meetings, except for two schools that decline to send them. The knowledge that he gleans from this, together with information that comes in as a result of visits from his team of advisers, assures him that most schools are keeping questions relating to the ethos under regular review. He was able to quote an instance when a head, in his report, had misled the governing body on a related matter. This had led to a prompt intervention by the diocesan office to rectify the situation.

Conclusion

A number of important issues arise from these data. The first is, very obviously, that there appears to be no consensus as to what constitutes a Catholic ethos in a school. Furthermore, there appears to be a significant disjuncture between the views of the diocesan directors on the one hand, and the governors who were interviewed, on the other.

The key ingredient for the diocesan directors was, without question, prayer. After a brief comment on relationships, the director for Glastonbury identified the life of prayer practised by both pupils and staff as the defining feature of a Catholic school; he did not put much, if any, weight on the importance of artefacts, pilgrimages, and charitable activities. The director for Much Wenlock may be prepared to give some recognition to what he described as 'external manifestations', but for him the essential characteristics are the process of working with parents to help their children find God through Christ, and the living out of gospel values, of which he identified forgiveness and reconciliation, and a just admissions policy. In Athelney the concept was to help develop the spiritual lives of both pupils and staff through liturgy and prayer. The schools in Lacock are expected not only to mark their distinctiveness by means of displays, but also through the practice of prayer. The director for Tewkesbury had perhaps the most comprehensive overview, which encompassed a number of factors including an explicit mission statement, the practice of Gospel values and artefacts, but, here again, 'Prayer is not unusual, it's accepted as part and parcel of the daily routine.' Finally, the director for Athelney expects to see evidence of prayer linked with the day-to-day activities of his schools, both as they concern pupils and adults.

There did not seem to be any similar identifiable common theme running through the responses of governors. The emphasis on prayer is largely lacking, though it might perhaps be implied in some of them.

Absent from both sets of responses is any acknowledgement that the taught curriculum may have any connexion with, influence, or be influenced by, the school's ethos. In the light of the frequently expressed view that there is no such thing as a value-free 'secular' curriculum, and the corollary that this makes the provision of a separate schools system essential, this is interesting.

It is also notable that there is, with two exceptions, not a single reference to any of the work done by either the Sacred Congregation, the Catholic Education Service or the Bishops' Conference in this field. Whilst this might not be surprising for the governors, busy people as they generally are, they did not manifest any awareness of any mediating activity that their dioceses might have carried out in the way of conferences or courses on what must be a matter of central significance for anyone involved with Catholic schools. The director for Tewkesbury referred to courses which draw on *Evaluating the Distinctive Nature of a Catholic School,* and the director for Athelney referred to a document prepared in his diocese covering this ground very comprehensively, and usefully drawing on a large number of both English and Roman sources. Two governors did refer to training provided by their diocese. One implied that the initiative had to come from the governing body to make a specific request. If this is an accurate account of the position, the obvious difficulty with it is that it is not easy to ask for training in a deficiency of which you are unaware. The other cited specifically diocesan training in school discipline and the introduction of a new workforce agreement.

The final comment on the data is that there appear to be schools where the governors interviewed experience difficulty in identifying what is distinctive about the ingredients of a positive Catholic ethos. I refer in particular to the quoted examples of the apparent denigration of pupils by teachers who shout at them and what seems to be the fiercely competitive ethic at the Sacred Heart school. Whether this has arisen because of an unrepresentative account on the part of the governor who spoke to me, or the situations described really do exist cannot be judged.

At Corpus Christi, although the externals are there, the school appears to be isolated from the parish, and the chair has reservations about the way the conduct of the teachers is undermining its ethos. The chair of St Joseph's began by defining ethos in terms of externals, but then went on to refer to it in a way which would not find favour in the Diocese of Athelney: 'I don't know what it is, but you can just tell.' At Holy Cross the externals and the commitment of the parish priest are again relied on, together with the example of the headteacher. Only the non-Catholic LA governor from St Edmund's spoke in terms which might be said to relate directly to the documents I have cited, by referring to things such as nurturing the children to be brought up in the Catholic faith, the gospel message, and the journey of faith, though even here the chapel that has been built is described as 'a quiet room for the children to sit in.' rather than a place for private prayer.

The governor from Our Lady's again speaks in very general terms about the ethos of the school, and much of what she says applies to any well-run school. Unlike St Edmund's, however, there are no tensions that might adversely affect relationships, and the school is described as being an effective part of the local Catholic community. But it has to be said that, overall, there is a lack of specificity.

Several schools referred to the active involvement of a local priest, and the presence of statues and other artefacts was clearly of major significance. In only two instances – St Edmund's and Our Lady's – did the concept of a faith community arise. In the case of Our Lady's even this was not straightforward, because what the governor was proposing did not refer to the school itself as a community, but as an adjunct to the local faith community. It was possible to discern warm, co-operative and caring communities of children in most of the schools, but there are suggestions that this does not always apply as far as the adults are concerned.

In summary, what is presented is very largely non-specific, in that what was described might apply to any school, except for what might be classified as the externals: the statues, the crucifixes, and the pictures of the pope, and what was done to the school through the involvement of local clergy. What appears to be strikingly absent is any specific reference to the school as a community of faith at which Christ is the centre.

The findings of this part of the research are, perhaps, the most important to emerge. During the short lifetime of the project, the climate of opinion with regard to church schools in England and Wales appears to have become much more hostile. At least partly because of the principal recommendation of the *Dearing Report* that one hundred new Church of England secondary schools be established for which there is no evidence of denominational need, it may be increasingly necessary for the Catholic church to be able to justify the continued existence of its schools in its own terms. Pring has warned the churches that they 'must be aware of many of the legitimate concerns' of their opponents.[20] These may be said, essentially, to be that they are using their voluntary-aided status,

[20] Pring, *Faith Schools: Have they a place in the Comprehensive System?*

with the consequent facility for each governing body to control its school's pupil admissions, to indulge in covert social (and therefore academic) selection. Whilst this comment was made in the context of secondary education, it is equally valid in the primary sector. If one of Grace's central propositions is that Catholic schools were established with a strong spiritual ethos by priests and members of religious orders, the evidence of this chapter seems to support his view that this spiritual capital may be running out, not only in the inner-city secondary schools that were the subject of his research, but in both primary and secondary schools throughout the land.[21] In terms of this study, what seems to be evident is that the schools are living through a period of significant change which could lead to early challenge, not only from within the system itself, as governors and individual schools choose to exercise their powers in ways which may not be palatable to the trustees, but from without, as the state further inhibits what remains of their freedoms.

Only two schools amongst those whose governors I interviewed have a formal monitoring committee for ethos. One, Holy Cross, had introduced it as a result of adverse Ofsted comment. There seems to be a separate RE or ethos subcommittee reporting to it. The other is English Martyrs, but here the governor was unsure what the procedures were. He said there is a system of link governors, with one covering RE, that the governing body do discuss the religious curriculum, and there is a curriculum committee, but it was, again, not clear whether any active monitoring takes place.

Our Lady's, St Joseph's and Sacred Heart seem to rely on an approach which appears to be based on a conviction that, if anything is amiss, the governors will hear about it somehow. Someone from the diocese had visited Our Lady's, presumably to carry out some sort of review or inspection, though the purpose of the visit and its outcome were not specifically put to me. The governors of this school rely on the head's periodic reports to assure themselves that all is well. One issue of contention – the teaching of other faiths – had conspicuously not been discussed by the governors. The chairman believed this was a requirement of the National curriculum and the LA.

St Joseph's and St Edmund's both have a link governor. In the case of the former, this was a member of the school support staff, and it was not clear whether her terms of reference embrace

---

[21.] Grace, *Catholic Schools, Mission, Markets and Morality.*

questions of ethos or were restricted to RE and worship. As to the latter, this was the parish priest, who was said not to be discharging his responsibilities in a satisfactory manner. According to the chairman at Corpus Christi, nothing was monitored by the governors.

The views of the diocesan directors are mixed. On the one hand, the Director of Much Wenlock, who is in personal touch with an impressive proportion of his schools, thinks his governing bodies are carrying out their monitoring functions well. In similar vein, the director for Tewkesbury thought that, in the main, the task was being undertaken, albeit very largely, still by the clergy. The overall picture in Tintern is the same, though here there was no specific reference to the contribution clergy make. On the other hand, in Athelney the matter was said to be hit and miss, and in Lacock problematic. The director for Glastonbury was the only one to differentiate between the primary and secondary sectors: he was supportive of the approach that seemed to have been adopted at two of the primary schools: governing bodies effectively monitor the ethos via the community. He recognized a problem in the secondary sector. The one consistent theme that ran through the diocesan directors' comments was a recognition that this was an area where they needed to be developing programmes of support and training.

There is here, again, then, a disjuncture between what the governors are saying and what is the reported experience of the diocesan directors. If it is true that, until the changes of the 1980s, control of a Catholic school's ethos was in the hands of the Church, through the all-pervading influence of the parish priest, a process of change is now under way. This has been brought about by both legislative requirements and demographic change in the form of the decline in the number of clergy.

Chapter 9

Governors, Trustees and Some Sensitive Issues

Senior Staff Appointments

Three questions were asked which touch on areas where tensions could again arise between governors and trustees. The first raised the issue of senior staff appointments.

This is a matter which has been investigated and commented on by Howson for many years, and his criticism of the bishops and dioceses for allowing what he sees as an unacceptable situation to persist, with no apparent acknowledgement or remedial action, has frequently been scathing. The overall figures since the surveys began do, indeed, make depressing reading: with very few exceptions, the trend has been one way – an inexorable rise in the number of Catholic school headships that have to be re-advertised. His report for 2009–10 was, however, more optimistic, and he had this to say:

> A recurring theme throughout these annual reports has been the relative difficulty faith schools, and especially Roman Catholic schools, have experienced in recruiting new headteachers. That theme can be reprised again this year, albeit with some signs of improvement ... Local authorities who failed to ensure succession planning to the degree that some diocese (sic) have done over the past decade would have been subject to intense public scrutiny, not to mention concerns over the waste of public money involved in the advertisement process ... especially if temporary replacements recruited through agencies come with an even higher price tag than a permanent appointment.[1]

The improvement noted on that occasion proved, unfortunately,

[1] Howson, J. and Springade, A., *The State of the Labour Market for Senior Staff in Schools in England and Wales 2009–2010*, pp. 134–5.

to be short-lived. The 2011 Report found 'a staggering turnaround for Catholic schools from their best year since 1998–99 to their worst on record'.[2] The official response to the 2011 Report was curious. The chairman of the Catholic Education Service was quoted in *The Tablet* as claiming that 'Governors now are much more discerning than they would have been a long time ago ... [They] are much more professional in the way they seek these posts to be filled so that makes them a little bit more fussy ... and quite rightly.'[3] Unfortunately, this claim is not supported by any empirical evidence.

Since my research was concerned, amongst other things, with two issues: the on-going relationship between trustees and governors and the extent to which Catholic schools' spiritual capital was becoming exhausted, it seemed important to ask governors whether they thought there were any circumstances in which they would be prepared to appoint a non-Catholic to a headship, deputy headship or the headship of the RE department. As many as 41.4 per cent said there were, 51.5 per cent said there were not and 7 per cent did not know. The foundation figures were 41.3 per cent, 55.6 per cent and 3.2 per cent. In other words, almost half the governors surveyed would be prepared to go against national policy in a crucial area of staff appointments in certain circumstances. I now examine the responses. They are grouped according to what appeared to be the reasons offered.

An Appointment of Last Resort

Categorizing the responses has required the exercise of some judgement, and the outcome cannot be claimed to be precise. There was a degree of overlapping. This is why the numbers in the following sections do not equate with the summaries given above. However, seven governors appeared to say they would be prepared to appoint a non-Catholic to a headship, deputy headship or the headship of an RE department if repeated attempts to secure a suitable Catholic had failed. Six were male; the female was a head-teacher governor, who did not make it clear whether her reply was made as a general principle or applied only to the possible

[2] Howson, J. and Springade, A., *26th Annual Survey of senior staff appointments in schools across England and Wales*, p. 19.
[3] Bishop Malcolm McMahon, quoted in *The Tablet*, London, 15 January 2011, p. 31.

appointment of a deputy to her. The governors concerned were all older than forty-one and had experience ranging from less than one to nineteen years. Four would make only an acting appointment, to give themselves the opportunity to try again for a Catholic at a later date, one would consider a non-Catholic only if the other most senior post holder was Catholic, and two would be prepared to make an unconditional appointment in these circumstances.

In addition, four said they would be prepared to make an appointment of this nature because of the known difficulty of appointing Catholics, but did not go so far as to say they would defer such a move until all other options had been explored.

Appointment to Particular Posts

Twelve differentiated according to the post in question. They were evenly split between men and women and, again, the length of experience seemed to have no bearing, ranging, as it did, from one year to eighteen. Five of the twelve were in the forty-one to fifty age bracket, with one aged thirty-one to forty, and the remainder evenly spread between fifty-one and seventy plus. Nine of the twelve would be open to appointing a non-Catholic deputy; one would not appoint a non-Catholic head of RE, two would be less likely to do so, and one was unsure. Two would never appoint a non-Catholic head, but two would be prepared to do so, and three would appoint to either a headship or deputy headship.

A Liberal Response

The third group took a more liberal view and seemed prepared to contemplate the appointment of non-Catholics to these posts even if Catholic applicants were available. Twenty-eight respondents made comments of this nature, and of these, seventeen were women. It is perhaps of interest that they included nine who had served for one year or less. This raises the question as to whether longer service might lead to a modification of view, or whether what we see is a shift in the perceptions of the most recently appointed / elected governors. In opposition to the former hypothesis, the group also included five governors with between ten and nineteen years' service.

One would require the candidate to be a 'highly competent, spiritually aware member' of the Church of England; another 'a practising Christian from a Protestant Church', and yet others 'practising Christians'. Many, however, were unspecific, and simply referred to the need to appoint 'the best qualified or 'most suitable' candidate.

My subsequent interviews with governors did not add anything of significance to what had emerged in the questionnaire returns. The issue was, however, of such importance that I did raise it with the diocesan directors.

Reactions of Diocesan Directors

The Director of Glastonbury confirmed that the issue had arisen in his diocese:

> We've had problems. People want to appoint a senior team who are not Catholics ... But I can see it coming, unfortunately, because we don't have a sufficient quality of our own leadership to fill the posts, and that is very difficult, because you've got to fill the posts somehow.

The Director of Much Wenlock had again experienced the problem:

> First and foremost, we want, if at all possible, high quality educationists who are practising Catholics, who are able to lead our schools ... but there are exceptions. Four schools that have struggled have used the device of changing some of the deputy positions to assistant headships where there isn't that absolute requirement.

He went on to give an example of a non-Catholic being appointed. Governors had tried and failed to appoint a Catholic. He had therefore obtained the bishop's approval to the appointment. He said that the diocese would always take a pragmatic stance to the particular circumstances of an individual case. A completely different approach is taken in Athelney. I suggested that governors' views on policies relating to reserved appointments were beginning to become diluted.[4] His response was short and to the point: 'Not in this diocese!' I asked him if his position was secure.

---

4. Reserved appointment is the technical term applied to the ring-fencing of senior teaching posts in Catholic schools for members of the Catholic Church.

We've never shifted yet, and I would ask the fundamental question the bishop asks: 'What right have you to lead a faith community?' Because, if you're a faith community, where the fundamental core purpose is to pass on the faith, if you haven't got it, I really don't know how you can properly begin to understand the model ... God will solve the problem. The Church has lasted 2000 years. We're looking into the supply of school places. We have, for example, one school that has no Catholic children in the community. That school has changed its character and is now a community school.[5] That reduces the need for one Catholic head. Federating schools, working collaboratively, all these options enable you to put very strong Catholic leadership at the head of the school.

The director for Lacock said he saw the appointment of Catholics to posts such as essential. I asked him what would happen if a governing body reminded him that, in education law, they had the power to decide who was, and who was not, appointed:

In the appropriate way we'd tell them where to go. We wouldn't threaten them obviously, but ... The question does come up quite often. Especially when we're struggling to appoint, some governors will say this, but they back off when told this is the policy of the Bishops' Conference of England and Wales. We've not had a problem. No, no!

The director for Tewkesbury had the same view, and also echoed the thinking of the director for Athelney. He thought

governors are relatively understanding of the fact that to appoint a non-Catholic to a headship, deputy headship or head of RE would not only be very much against diocesan policy, but when [it's] explained to them [they] do begin to realize that it doesn't make a great deal of sense how you can have people who do not subscribe to and live out the faith instructing others and providing an example of how the faith is lived.

The director for Tintern sensed a growing problem here:

What I've found is not a vast number, but the numbers are growing, of individuals and governing bodies, and, in some cases, headteachers if it's a deputy headship, questioning the policy. Last term I had

[5] A legal term. A school's character is made up of a number of ingredients, one of which is whether it is voluntary aided (this usually means in the ownership of a religious denomination, livery company or other educational charity), community (owned by an LA), or one of a number of other categories. The point being made here is that the diocese, having no further use for it, has sold it to the LA.

a situation where an officer from an LA questioned the policy, [taking] the lead from a questioning governor ... If it hadn't been for the fact that the person chose not to [go through with the application], I think we could have had a test case ... What we've got now is a great move across the diocese, particularly in the primary schools, to assistant heads, because we don't have that as a reserved post ... So our next group of leaders is diminished ... We've got a mentality which is 'fix the problem now, and we'll worry about that later, because I might not even be here.' We have the hierarchy sympathising with people who are trying to recruit, and by sympathising are being interpreted as condoning what they're trying to do, which is quite an interesting dimension. But the whole business of reserved posts is getting more and more difficult to contain.

What is notable about these data is that no one in the field, despite the recent suggestion by the chairman of the Catholic Education Service, denies there is a problem, be they external commentator, diocesan director, or governor of whatever category. On the one hand, there is a national policy promulgated by the Bishops' Conference, and on the other, governing bodies implementing it as best they can, and with apparent varying degrees of difficulty. In the middle there are the diocesan directors, doing their best to hold the ring. Their problem appears to be compounded by the bishops themselves, who seem to have adopted, pragmatically, a different (and more liberal) approach to Catholic independent schools. The same liberality, in regard to headship, has been shown in at least one maintained school. The dichotomy is eloquently described by the directors for Athelney and Tewkesbury. At deputy head level, several of those interviewed described the adoption of a procedural device that will get a school over the immediate difficulty. This involves appointing an assistant head, for which there is no national policy restriction, instead of a deputy, for which there is. The problem with this is pointed out by the director for Tintern, who also draws attention to the incongruity that can arise when bishops, by expressing sympathy and concern for governors in their attempts to resolve these issues, are then interpreted as condoning breaches of the policy.

Specific mention of RE posts was not common, but all except one of those who raised the point were clear that the head of RE or RE Co-ordinator must be a Catholic. The one who was not (female aged seventy plus, with five years' experience) said she was not sure.

Governors, Teachers and Morality

The second question asked if governors thought Catholic teachers should still be required to be 'in good standing' with the Church. It is of interest that this was the issue on which respondents had, by far, most to say, and their views were expressed with more vehemence than on any other.

As an introduction to the topic, it is important to state what the position is. Almost all teachers are appointed to Catholic schools on a contract drafted by the Catholic Education Service which states: 'You are to have regard to the Catholic character of the school and not to do anything in any way detrimental or prejudicial to the interest of the same.' As far as it goes, there is nothing in employment law that is exceptionable about this. No employee may do anything detrimental or prejudicial to the interests of his employer without risking disciplinary action. The problem arises because this basic principle can be construed to mean that Catholic teachers working in Catholic schools can be expected, and required, to uphold the Church's moral teaching in their private lives.

The legal background to all this is now the Equality Act for 2010, which brought together the provisions relating to discrimination in a number of pieces of earlier legislation, particularly of an employment nature.

The new act prescribes a number of 'protected characteristics' and makes it illegal to treat an individual less favourably than someone else because of a protected characteristic. Thus, age, disability, sex, sexual orientation, marriage and civil partnerships, pregnancy, race and religion are all protected characteristics.

However, existing exemptions for schools with a religious character are retained. These are principally defined in sections 58 and 60 of the Education Standards and Framework Act of 1998. This means that the conduct of a teacher that is incompatible with the precepts of the Church, or which fails to uphold its tenets, may be taken into consideration in determining whether the teacher's employment should be terminated. However, in all this, an employer's actions have, according to the Act 'to be a proportionate means of achieving a legitimate aim'. There appears to be, therefore, every possibility of endless litigation about what is proportionate and what is not.

The matter is sensitive because adherence to the policy can obviously constrain governors in appointing staff. It can also cause staff in post to resign either freely or under pressure. It has, on more than one occasion, led to litigation. I have already cited one

important case which went to the High Court rather than the
Employment Tribunal (R. v the Trustees of the Diocese of
Southwark ex p. Kemmis-Betty).[6]

The picture that emerged from my research was that 56.6 per
cent of respondents thought the traditional standards of conduct
should continue to be applied, whilst 29.3 per cent did not, and
13.1 per cent did not know. The foundation governor response was
rather more clear-cut: 61.9 per cent were in favour of maintaining
the traditional stance, whilst only 23.8 per cent were not and 14.3
per cent did not know. Even so, it can be seen that more than one
third of foundation governors do not necessarily support the
orthodox position.[7]

Of the four heads who took part in my survey, just one, aged
forty-one to fifty, supported the traditional approach. She said: 'We
need to be seen to practise what we preach.' One who disagreed
made a number of interesting comments in support of her view,
including a reference to a practice that puzzles outsiders: the application of two entirely different systems of values depending on
whether the teachers are Catholics or not. She proposed that the
criterion to be used in dealing with difficult situations of this kind
was that of public knowledge. This is a view shared by others, and,
as we shall see, is very much in line with the contemporary thinking of a number of diocesan directors. The other head, who was
not in support of the traditional position, also female, aged forty-
one to fifty, had perhaps a more theological approach: 'Christ's
teaching is that we love our neighbours regardless. Our Lord was
friends with everyone. Who are we to judge?' The issue of judgement is, again, as we shall see, one that is exercising diocesan
authorities at the present time.

The head who said she was unsure, also female aged forty-one to
fifty, appeared not to wish to enquire into matters of this kind
when interviewing candidates: 'I would find it very difficult to
appoint staff if I looked into this when interviewing.'

The teacher governors were also divided, with two in favour of
the traditional policy, three against and one who did not know.
One of those in favour gave no reasons; the other echoed the views

---

[6.] R. v Trustees of the Roman Catholic Diocese of Southwark ex p. Kemmis-Betty
1990.
[7.] Chi-squared testing of these data leads to the conclusion that, at the five per
cent level, there is a significant relationship between the gender of governors
and their attitude to teachers' sexual morality. Women are far more likely to
question the official position than are men. There is, however, no association
between the age of governors and their views.

of the first head quoted above: 'I think we have an ideal role model to fulfil.' The first who did not support the traditional stance also put forward no reasons. The second wanted nothing to do with role models: 'Regardless of a teacher's personal life, their ability and professionalism is at the forefront. They should not be discriminated against because of their matrimonial situation or sexuality.' The third agreed: 'I don't think it affects their ability to do their job properly.' The teacher who did not know said she felt unable to comment as she was not a Catholic.

Seven LA governors supported the traditional position. Two adopted the role model stance, one with an interesting extension: 'I think irregular matrimonial situations, and the practising of homosexuality, are not good role models for children – nor indeed for Catholic parents of pupils.' A third thought these matters were bound to affect the ethos of the school, but did not elaborate. She added: 'I find difficulty dealing with this.' The issue of ethos was taken up by a fourth: 'The ethos of a Catholic school is strongly family based and directed by the Church's teachings. To that end the teaching staff are critical to the whole Catholic upbringing.' One governor who supported a stance based on the Church's teachings said: 'As a Catholic school we should reflect the values of the Church, not those of secular society.'

Others argued that the nature of teachers' private lives does not affect their professional competence or the ethos of the school. An Anglican commented: 'It is in this area that I am not in unity with the Catholic Church. I am a Christian ... and believe that God loves all of us regardless of our own matrimonial status or sexuality. Teachers in general should be appointed on ability first followed by strength of religion.'

Parent governor respondents' opinion was perhaps more clear-cut. Six supported the maintenance of a traditional approach, whilst three did not and one did not know. Views expressed by the first group appeared similar. One said: 'We belong to a community which has a current, official policy. We cannot with integrity appoint those in open opposition to such a policy.' Another was more laconic: 'If we Catholics can't adhere to our beliefs – God help us all!' A third appeared to take a similar line, but perhaps expressed it in a more balanced way: 'So little of society is based on "standards". It is fashionable to be deviant / different. In time the old values will return – they always do historically – and so we should not try to be "trendy" – but be steadfast in outlook. This is not to say we stick in the past but we do not have to go out on a limb simply to curry favour.'

Two parents differentiated between heterosexual and homosexual relationships. One had this to say: 'I agree they should not be in a practising homosexual relationship but feel it is the norm these days for heterosexuals to live together.' In similar vein, another said: 'Irregular matrimonial situations can occur for all manner of reasons, many not the fault of either party to the relationship. They can also be conducted in a caring Christian environment. Homosexuality, while practised by Christians, and not detracting from their faith in any way, is nevertheless unnatural and not appropriate for exposure or contact with impressionable young people in society in general and schools in particular.'

In opposition to this view, the governor who was uncertain said: 'I am a practising Catholic and believe that certain views should be upheld. However, homosexuality is an area that I have problems with accepting the view of the Church.'

One of the sponsor governors said he was in support of the traditional approach and added: 'I abhor the decline in standards and behaviour generally, with particular reference to homosexuals, especially in the Church.' The other did not support the traditional approach, but interestingly had the same worries about homosexuals.

The foundation governor responses revealed some misunderstandings about the situation. One said: 'I agree in principle. However, practice is more difficult and guidance may be needed from the parish priest or even the Bishop. I am divorced but "in good standing with the church". As I was divorced against my will, I would not like to think that I might be barred from being a Governor, when I could not control the divorce process. The divorce was not my choice.' Other respondents revealed the same misunderstanding about the position of divorcees.

The issue of school ethos predictably arose: 'It is the norm that teachers should be models for both pupils and the communities they serve. Therefore the Catholic faith makes explicit its values beliefs and ethos and so anyone wishing to work under its umbrella should follow the Catholic school's ethos.'

Similarly, the view of teachers as role models that has already been encountered featured in many foundation governor responses: 'Teachers are models for their pupils. It is important that there is consistency in what they teach and what they do in their own lives,' and 'Even more so today I want our children to be happy and at peace with God and themselves. I firmly believe in the Church's teachings on these matters – and after the fall-out of the

60s and 70s when a lot of teaching of the Church was watered down – we are left with many Catholics with an unreal or partial understanding of their faith. The examples set before the children are PARAMOUNT' are typical comments.

One thought that '[T]eachers provide an example to parents and pupils. Catholics teaching in Catholic schools should expect people to look on them as examples. Nevertheless, the application of these policies should be tempered by tolerance and understanding.'

The differentiation between marital status and homosexuality that has already been encountered recurred here: 'Sometimes circumstances may warrant someone being divorced, for example their husband / wife may have left them through no fault of their own. And they are still good Catholics. I do not think homosexuals should be employed in a Catholic school.'

Some saw the issue as a straightforward matter of authority: 'This is consistent with the directives and expectations placed on all Catholics by the Pope and it serves to give all children a clear understanding of what the Catholic Church is about.' Parental expectation was proposed by another: 'Parents ... really expect high moral standards from those involved in the care of their children.'

A number of foundation governors were unsure about their view on this whole matter. One expressed her uncertainty this way: 'What is important is the ability and willingness of the teachers to work with the Catholic ethos of the school. Any irregularities of private life should not intrude into professional behaviour and teaching.' Another pointed out that '[i]n secondary schools there are many non- Catholic staff. Some of them may not be so scrutinized.' A third was uncertain of the legal position: 'What questions are or are not allowed to be asked at interviews?' Another in the same age group had the same difficulty, which she expressed in a long exposition of her doubts:

> It is not so much that these standards are not relevant, but I think it inappropriate to make judgements about individuals' particular circumstances. Logically we would have to consider disciplinary action against members of staff who fell into the above situations if we were to use such factors as reasons for disqualifying new applicants. Honesty about individuals' situations and dedication to supporting the school's mission statement would be more important to me. I think we might hit problems with employment law. I don't see that it is the governing body's role to judge how far a candidate is 'living in sin'.

A similar reservation was expressed: '[T]he gospel values are in direct contrast to the values of a secular society. Should we appoint a person who is in good standing and then encounters difficulties in their marriage and / or ...? Then pastoral support should be forthcoming.'

The range of views amongst those foundation governors who were unable to support the traditional approach was equally diverse and passionately expressed. Some objected on principle:

> They [the requirements] are quite outrageous and totally at vari- ance with contemporary understandings of human dignity. They also inevitably seem to provide support for the homophobic senti- ments often found in schools of all types. Isn't it interesting that 'good standing' is all about sexuality as you describe it above? How ludicrous that the two should be equated!

Others linked principle with pragmatic or theological considera- tions, or the view that has already encountered that the overriding consideration for governors is the basic pedagogic professionalism of the teachers with whom they have to deal. The need to differ- entiate between private-life situations and those which might be causing public scandal also arose. 'I have no personal problems with persons in the above matrimonial situation being teachers provided they keep their private lives private', was the view expressed by one. She continued:

> Their life experiences may prove useful when dealing with the wide variety of lives children come from these days. They should be open- minded but remain moral and prudent. The universal Church should be there for everyone just as Christ intended. Their lives may be strengthened from contact with a Catholic school. We must look at how they live, not just what has happened to them. If we don't we can't accept Mary the Mother of God – Mary Magdalene etc.

Others took the practical approach: 'So-called irregular relation- ships are becoming the norm. Teacher recruitment is difficult enough.' Again, 'A school is a professional organization and a teacher should be judged by his / her professionalism, not personal life unless scandal were to be given or a child put at risk – and this would apply in any school, not just a Catholic one.' A third commented:

> If the person believes in the basis of the Catholic religion – this is important. There are many married or heterosexual people who are

baptized Catholics but do not practise or do not believe in Catholicism. Others may also have done things not recognized / approved of by the Catholic Church, but not as obvious. How can I judge?

Echoing the governor whose protest about the restricted view of acceptable conduct was reported above, another asked: 'As long as they foster a true Catholic ethos in the school who are we to judge or condemn and why is it that the only weaknesses mentioned are of a sexual nature? Is it acceptable to be a drunk or dishonest?'

The Views of Diocesan Directors

This was a matter on which there was a greater congruence of views amongst the diocesan officers. The director for Glastonbury had this to say:

> You come up with the ideal of forgiveness, and the old-fashioned term of 'scandal'. Will it make a difference if they don't teach in the same school, live in the same area? What if they're youngsters living together because they're going to get married, but they're not married yet? There's a wide range of differences ... If they're good people, and are not just wife-swapping when they feel like it, it certainly colours the way I look at things. I can remember a case when a Catholic who'd got married in a Registry Office and then got a divorce could get married in our Church because he was techni- cally clear by our laws. He married a non-Catholic. At the same time, I was dealing with a case where a Catholic girl wanted to marry a non-Catholic who was not baptized, and therefore his Registry Office marriage was regarded as valid by the Church. But within six months he found her in bed with another man, and got a divorce, but I had to say: 'The law says you can't marry again.' It's difficult, but you have to go to first principles to understand why. It's not just a matter of personalities and the rest of it.
>
> I think it's going to get harder and harder. It's very difficult, now, to have enough confidence in your own vision and judgement. It doesn't automatically fit the normal standards, or whatever you like to call it. It's going to come down to a person's integrity, and that's very difficult to judge ... Somehow or other we've got to do our best to make sure that what goes on inside the hearts of people is the same as what they say and what they do, and that's a very, very diffi- cult thing to do.

I said this sounded an unattainable objective: in the eyes of the Church, everyone is a sinner.

But then you go back to the Gospels and say 'What would the Lord have done?' and that's when you come up with different answers.

These comments provide a vivid account of the sorts of issues that have to be evaluated by those who are responsible for making judgements on matters of teachers' sexual morality. In this instance, the diocesan director appears to be working on his own, with no external support, and he recognises his loneliness and personal difficulty in having to try to resolve situations that do not 'automatically fit the normal standards.' Implicitly, however, at the end of his response he seems to hint at a more liberal approach: 'But then you go back to the Gospels and ... that's when you come up with different answers.' In Much Wenlock:

> When it comes down to individuals who might find themselves in some difficulty over their personal life, I think the approach in this diocese is not to fall into the trap, and to try to persuade governing bodies not to fall into the trap, of being judgemental.

The details of each case are put to an expert moral theologian:

> who will always say 'What is the view of the local clergyman to whom this teacher would be known?' and if the local priest is able to say: 'this person, to the best of my knowledge, strives to do his or her best, and is trying to fulfil the life of a good Catholic, a good Christian,' then that's what will determine the judgement ... I think we would always be hesitant about making a judgement without full knowledge. Should we be trying to get that full knowledge? I don't know. It's an area where we are quite hesitant these days, but I believe we have a system which tries to be open, honest, non-judge-mental in the sense that there are others that might be able to exercise a degree of judgement. But I don't think any of us as human beings is in a final position where we should make a final judgement on someone. That's for some other body, person, or being, not us! ... I'm not going to make a judgement.
>
> I think I would say in short we are aware of the tensions, and we have played a part in trying to devise more sensitive guidelines. But each situation needs great sensitivity applied to it, and if it gets really difficult, then it's right that the governing body be guided away from prejudice into accepting advice from here, where we do have someone who can provide a consistency of approach.

Here, the diocesan director works as part of a team that involves the local priest and, if necessary, a moral theologian. There is a manifest reluctance to become involved, and a clearly expressed desire to put a reported situation in a broader context that resonates well with the Glastonbury question: 'What would the Lord have done?' In this diocese, advice has been prepared and guidelines issued.

A similar approach is taken in Athelney, though without the involvement of a moral theologian. Each case is examined on its individual merits:

> We try to give human, thoughtful, Christian advice. If the situation arose, you'd be asking whether they were intending to marry, is it causing any concern in the community? It's trying to respond to the individual situation, and giving thoughtful advice.

In Lacock the decision has been taken by the bishop that the greater scandal would be for a Catholic school to refuse to appoint, or seek to dismiss, Catholic teachers because of issues of sexual morality. Only where they were using their situation actively to oppose the Church's teaching would difficulty arise.

The director for Tewkesbury is

> very careful to talk to governors about not digging into people's private lives ... unless there's a very, very good reason to do so ... There are going to be circumstances where, if it becomes common knowledge that certain things are going on upon which the Church would frown, they'd need to refer that to me and we'd try and find a *modus operandi* to be able to deal with the situation. Nine times out of ten it does tend to work out very successfully...When it is carefully pointed out that what they are doing is in contravention of their contract, then they are helped to move somewhere else, gently and quietly.

The director here is required to operate on his own, without support, as in Glastonbury. Whilst in some respects there are features that are common to what has been seen before, in particular the degree of public knowledge attaching to the situation, this is the first reference to procedures to remove the teacher from a Catholic school.

The Director of Tintern believes his governors across the board:

> would be of the opinion that if you don't know about it, please don't ask the questions. If you don't know about it you don't have to do anything, and whose business is it anyway? We are not the moral police force of the diocese.

Pupil Admissions

The final question related to pupil admissions. This is an issue
which has been a matter of contention for a long time in the eyes
of a number of secular agencies, but is one that rarely generates
much in the way of major publicity, though difficulties do arise
from time to time. In 2010, indeed, the two London dioceses of
Southwark and Westminster used new powers to lodge objections
to the Schools' Adjudicator about the admissions policies of two of
their schools: Coloma Convent in Southwark and Cardinal
Vaughan in Westminster.

The question is complicated by the fact that, as has been shown
in Chapter 2, there appears to be a contradiction at the heart of
the Church's view about who Catholic schools are for and how
priorities are to be worked out. On the one hand, we have seen
that the view of the English Catholic Church, since the end of
penal times in the early nineteenth century, has been that the
provision of schools to serve the needs of the Catholic community
has been an overriding objective, and one that has been pursued
unstintingly ever since.

On the other hand, the Second Vatican Council, in *Gravissimum
Educationis,* urged Catholic schools to have special regard for
'those who are strangers to the gift of faith'.[8] The point was reiterated in *The Catholic School on the Threshold of the Third Millenium,*
which again proposed that the Catholic school 'is a school for all,
with special attention to those who are weakest', and adopted by
the English and Welsh bishops in *The Common Good in Education*
where they assert that 'Schools have to accept their responsibility
for the education of all, particularly the most disadvantaged in
society.'[9] How are governors, who are responsible for admissions,
to reconcile these two positions?

Perhaps, in days gone by, there was no difficulty. Non-Catholics
would not have been pressing for the admission of their children
in any numbers. An aunt of mine was appointed one of His
Majesty's Inspectors of Schools in 1948. Her second posting, in
1953, was to Liverpool, an LEA where many maintained schools
were Catholic-aided rather than county. She told me in conversa-
tion that, at that time, if she wanted examples of first-class
education she would never have turned to a Catholic school, all of

---

[8.] Abbott, W. M., *The Documents of Vatican II* (1966), p. 648.
[9.] *The Catholic school on the Threshold of the Third Millennium,* para. 15 and *The
Common Good in Education,* p. 14.

which, in her territory (Bootle to Southport), she described as, at best, 'third rate'. However, over the years, things changed and Catholic schools began to be regarded as desirable by parents, whether Catholic or not. In 1975 I was appointed to the staff of the Inner London Education Authority, and discovered that the diocesan authorities involved (Southwark and Westminster) had by that time agreed with the Authority that they would advise their schools not to accept non-Catholic pupils in order to avoid complaints from other schools that they had been 'poaching' pupils for whom appropriate provision had been made at county or Church of England schools.[10] This had become necessary because of the perception – later to be under-scored by the publication of 'league tables' – that Catholic schools were now delivering a quality of education that was better than other schools.

More recently, however, there have been claims, partly based on the sectarian problems that have been experienced in Northern Ireland and in parts of Birmingham, Bradford and Lancashire, that the religious exclusivity of Catholic schools is socially divisive and should be discontinued by requiring them to admit a quota of non-Catholic pupils. Such a proposal was made in the autumn of 2006 by the former Conservative Secretary of State for Education, Lord Baker. Controversy arose when the Labour government of the day signalled its intention to support the measure, only to subside when, equally suddenly, it changed its mind. Interestingly, the latest Catholic Education Service Data (for 2009) show that, as a national average, about twenty-five per cent is just about what is the size of the non-Catholic population of Catholic maintained primary and secondary rolls.[11]

There were, in addition, allegations that Catholic school governing bodies had been abusing their right to interview potential pupils to assess their commitment to the religious character of the school, in order to operate covert selection on the basis of academic ability. Though the right to interview was withdrawn in 2006, this particular difficulty has not gone away. The complaint is that certain very popular and over-subscribed schools are grading qualitatively the Catholic commitment of potential pupils by, for example, seeking information on the application form about both the parental and pupil involvement in the wider life of their local church. The argument runs that this enables the schools to give

[10] Storr C., 'The purpose of Catholic Schools', *The Tablet*, London, 28 October 2006.
[11] Catholic Education Service for England and Wales, *Digest of 2009 Census data for Schools and Colleges*, p. 10, but see note 5, p. 145.

preference to children from more privileged backgrounds, whose parents have the ability to meet such criteria as these, but who may live many miles from the school, over children living in close proximity, but from poorer, maybe single-parent, families who struggle to attend Mass weekly, let alone serve at the altar, sing in the choir or work for church charitable organizations.

Similar considerations apply to the few governing bodies that had begun to change their admissions policies in order to give priority to practising non-Catholic and even non-Christian children over non practising Catholics. Whilst it may appear that this type of policy might answer the accusation of religious exclusivity, it can open the door to the same charge that has been made in the preceding paragraph: the governing body is operating a different kind selection by giving preference to more socially acceptable non-Catholic children rather than to less desirable Catholics. These latter, having been baptized, ought, it is argued on the other side, to be given priority for admission to a Catholic school because attendance at a Catholic school will, in all probability, be their only contact with the Church during their formative years. Respondents were therefore asked if, were their school to be over-subscribed by Catholic pupils, there were any circumstances in which they would be prepared to admit non-Catholics in preference to Catholics.

It should be noted that, during the lifetime of my enquiry, the law changed to require schools to admit pupils, in certain circumstances (those with additional educational needs, or 'looked after' children), on the direction of the LA.[12] Where a respondent replied to this question in the affirmative and gave this as the only reason, the reply was changed to a negative for the purpose of the analysis.

The results were that 27.3 per cent would be prepared to admit non-Catholics to Catholics, 64.6 per cent would not, and 5.1 per cent did not know. The corresponding figures for foundation governors were rather different. Only 20.6 per cent would be prepared to admit non-Catholics whilst 69.8 per cent would not, and 3 per cent did not know. In the matter of pupil admissions, therefore, foundation governors appear likely to take a more orthodox line than their colleagues.[13]

[12.] The term 'looked after' was introduced by the Children Act 1989, and refers to children whose birth parents are unable to provide ongoing care. Children can either be looked after as a result of voluntary agreement by their parents or as a result of a care order.

[13.] The responses were again chi-squared tested, and show that, at the five per cent level, there is no significant relationship between either the age or the gender of the governors and their views on pupil admissions.

The reasons given show governors wrestling with a number of issues. One of the most common was that of siblings, and appeared ten times. Others were aware of the dilemma relating to the practising / non-practising debate: 'Where an applicant came from an accepted Christian background and was a regular church-goer and where it could be confirmed that the remaining Catholic applicants were not practising then I would consider admitting them to the school,' and again: 'My school is in this situation – I would still consider having a balance with some non-Catholic pupils. I'm concerned about the "exclusivity" of total Catholic pupil population in our schools.' Another appeared to suggest that illegal selection by academic ability is being practised: 'If actively practising pupils from other faiths expressing a clear desire for a faith-based education and if of a standard appropriate to the school made application they would be preferred to the many non-practising Catholics who attend church for a minimum period prior to application and then stop attending once admitted to the school.' Another foundation governor was even more radical: 'This is a dodgy one – but I would rather admit a child from a committed believing family (Christian, Muslim, Jewish, Hindu ... any) than a child from a family that has suddenly moved next door to the church and has started appearing at Mass.'

Respondents who would not give priority to non-Catholic pupils were not asked to elaborate on their reasoning, but one had this to say: 'Catholic pupils should always have priority to a Catholic education before non-Catholics. Catholic parents support the community, church and school, and it is their right to have their children educated in a Catholic school.' It seems from this survey that Catholic school governors, particularly foundation governors, are very substantially of the view that Catholic pupils should have priority in the matter of admission to Catholic schools, irrespective of the extent of their practice. Leaving aside the issue of pupils with additional educational needs, with respect to whom governing bodies may have no discretion, the main exception related to the admission of siblings. A few governors would give priority to children who were practising members of other Christian denominations or, indeed, of other religions. Although it is not relevant to this study, there was very little evidence of irregularities in the operation of admissions policies.

Conclusion

It is now almost fifty years since the opening of the Second Vatican
Council. Many serving head and deputy head teachers and school
governors have therefore grown to maturity in the post-Vatican II
Church, and during the legislative and social changes that have
been described earlier in this study. It is, therefore, hardly surprising to discover a plurality of views over issues that, before 1962 or
even 1980, rarely arose. There was then no shortage of Catholic
teachers to fill key posts in Catholic schools, or indeed any posts at
all in primary schools; there were no legal constraints on which
pupils could be admitted; and whilst employment legislation was in
its infancy, there was no strong challenge to the imposition of the
Church's views on sexual morality in its schools. The evidence
revealed by this study shows the extent to which governors are now
having to agonize over these matters.

The first key issue appears to be that there is a lack of debate
about what considerations are central to the future of Catholic
education. If this analysis is accepted, the second issue, which flows
directly from it, is who should be involved in drawing up the
agenda. The trustees, who initially established the schools, and still
own them, will, no doubt, wish to have a voice, but parish clergy,
governors, teachers, and present and future parents also have legitimate interests. A number of dioceses have either recently
organized, or are in the process of organizing, consultations on
their future parish structures in the light of the decline in the
number of clergy to serve them, so there is some experience in how
to manage arrangements of this kind.

The difference between the consultations that have recently
taken place and those that are now needed is that, since the difficulties facing the schools arise out of changes brought about by the
legislature, a response may need to be nationally, and not locally,
based if it is to be effective. It therefore appears sensible that it
should be organized by the Bishops' Conference, and be seen to
command the support of all the bishops, even if the logistics are
left to the Catholic Education Service. One benefit of an arrangement of this kind is that the bishops would be in a much better
position to assess the climate of Catholic opinion than they seem
to be now. A corollary would be that such knowledge ought to
strengthen their negotiating position in any future disputes that
may arise. As I have proposed in the immediately preceding para-
graphs, an informed debate seems desirable about what are the
essential characteristics of Catholic schools in the context of the

pressures they are likely to face in the immediate future and medium term. When I planned my study, three seemed relevant: pupil admissions, senior staff appointments, and the application of the Church's teaching on sexual morality to Catholics teaching in its schools.

I have drawn attention to the lack of convergence in the official documents about who the schools are for: are they for Catholic children, the children of the poor, or for those who have no faith? The clear perception of the governors who took part in my survey is that Catholic pupils should have precedence over others. This issue was put to the test unexpectedly in late 2006, when the Catholic community reacted vigorously to a proposal that they should all be required to admit a quota of non-Catholics. The speed and vehemence of the Catholic community's opposition took many, not least the politicians at the centre of the controversy, by surprise.

In the light of the hospitality provided by Catholic schools to immigrant children, particularly from the expanded European Union, it may be that pupil admissions ceases to be an area of contention, at least in the foreseeable future, though a number of secularists have the issue on their agendas. Be that as it may, on the evidence before me, trustees are unlikely to face major challenges from governing bodies in the matter, except perhaps in London. If further legislative curbs are sought, it seems they can be assured of strong support from governors and parents. To that extent, there seems a continuity of approach over the decades. The appointment of non-Catholics to senior teaching posts is a very different matter. Here, the evidence shows an incongruity: not only are almost half the governors prepared to make such an appointment, but opinion amongst diocesan directors, who are reflecting the views of their bishops, is similarly divided. This without question marks a major shift in custom and practice, and raises a number of issues. The first is, clearly, that if the appointment of a non-Catholic head is seen to be acceptable to at least one bishop, on what ground might other bishops now object if their governing bodies choose to follow this lead?

Second, how does a move of this nature, as the director for Athelney succinctly put it (see above pp. 186–7), sit alongside the concept of the school as a community of faith, when one of the most senior members of its teaching staff – perhaps, indeed, the most senior – does not share that belief system?

The position could be even more difficult than it might seem on the basis of the evidence provided by this study, which is concerned exclusively with maintained schools. A little-publicized fact is that several Catholic independent schools have non-Catholic heads, some of many years' standing. In each case, the bishop appears to have raised no objection to an appointment of this kind. These data appear to suggest a situation where one set of criteria applies to the independent sector, and an entirely different set applies to maintained schools.

The same arguments arise in respect of the headship of RE departments in secondary schools. Reference has been made to the practice of suppressing deputy headship posts, which national policy requires to be reserved for Catholics, in favour of assistant headships, which are not. Whilst this may solve the immediate problem for an individual school, a moment's reflection will indicate that all this does is to exacerbate the problem of headteacher recruitment in a few years' time, by reducing still further the already small pool of Catholic deputy heads. It is therefore no stable solution.

If the bishops wish to manage this situation, the available options appear limited: either there will have to be a shift in policy, or there will need to be, as suggested by one of the directors, acceptance of the concept of federation, or a number of schools will have to cease to be Catholic, either as a result of closure or transfer to another church body (and this may not necessarily be Christian), or the LA. Only the first of these options will avoid challenge, either from either governors or parents or both. Based on precedent, some of these challenges could result in litigation.

The first option, however, is not without its dangers. If it is to be successfully pursued, it will require a very careful examination of the whole of the philosophy that currently underpins the Catholic schools system, and a redefinition of what are to be regarded as the essential features of a Catholic school. Care will need to be taken to ensure that what Sullivan (2001) refers to as the integral approach does not over-dilute the distinctive character of the schools. Were this to happen, they could either become unacceptable to future generations of Catholic parents, or open themselves to attack from secularists, who will argue that there is so little difference between them and non-denominational schools that their continued public funding is no longer justified.

The final option would be a negotiated re-opening of the nineteenth-century Irish system, to which attention has been drawn at various points in the study. Whatever view one takes, it seems clear that an examination of the issues is required if it is to be managed rather than left to chance, with all the risks that the latter course would undoubtedly entail.

The position with regard to the standards of sexual morality expected of employees in Catholic schools is infinitely more complex. There are a number of difficulties and contradictions about contemporary practice. Though the contractual requirement is very broadly described, the only area of morality that appears to be caught is sexual morality. It is hardly surprising that those who are outside the Catholic education system find the situation baffling, and that Catholic teachers (particularly the young) are apprehensive about putting their careers at risk by seeking posts in Catholic schools which may open their private lives to unwelcome public scrutiny.

As with a number of other relevant matters, the position facing governors has changed significantly in recent years, and though schools with a religious character have been given some exemptions from the full rigours of recent anti-discrimination legislation, the courts have made it clear they are going to treat these very narrowly. Governing bodies will have to proceed with infinite caution. As I have already remarked, governors taking part in my survey had more to say about this than anything else, and the passion with which they express their views is manifest. As with the matter of ethos, however, there is a clear divide between them and the diocesan directors, who, for whatever reason, appear to adopt the more liberal approach, presumably with the full knowledge and assent of their bishops. If this correctly reports the national position, what we have here is an undoubted shift in the Church's formal position.

Chapter 10

The Governors, Spiritual Capital and the Future

I have several times cited Grace's proposition that Catholic schools are drawing on reserves of spiritual capital that have been invested by past generations and which, today, are not, being renewed.[1] The distinctive character of Catholic education, he argues, is becoming ever more dilute, and will disappear altogether unless steps are taken to rectify the situation.

One purpose of my study was to examine Grace's hypothesis by enquiring into the way in which a number of school governors set about their work. As a preliminary, the historical, ecclesiastical and social contexts were set. A number of incongruities were revealed, the principle one of which is the growing disjuncture between the Church's view of the nature and purpose of school education and that of the state. Governors sit uncomfortably in the middle. They are required, somehow, to work out, day by day, means that will seek to keep most of the constituencies involved: the diocese, the LA, the parish, the parents, the staff, and, not least, the pupils, happy for most of the time. It is, perhaps, a tribute to their good sense that so little in the way of challenge has arisen.

My study obtained the views of almost one hundred governors, followed up by interviews involving a representative sample of officials working at diocesan level. This is one of the few occasions on which facts and perceptions relating to Catholic school governors have been surveyed.

As with school governors in general, my sample was overwhelmingly white, middle-aged, and middle-class. Women were well represented, statistically, however, and appeared to be taking a full and active part in the work of their boards, not shunning office-holding, or being reluctant to challenge. Overall, those taking part in my study were very experienced, and thought their contribution

[1] Grace, G., *Catholic Schools, Mission, Markets and Morality.*

was of value to the school they served, though its religious nature was not a primary influence in persuading them to undertake the work.

Governors' relationships with their bishop and the diocese were examined. Legislative change has reduced bishops, very largely, to a symbolic role in their schools once they have appointed foundation governors. This has produced a situation in which Catholic education is locally configured, but no longer church-dominated.

Against such a background, as close a relationship as possible would seem to be a essential ingredient for the avoidance of misunderstanding, challenge and conflict. A lack of convergence is manifest here. The governors seem to regard their bishop as remote; the diocesan directors, very largely, some of them vehemently, appear to disagree. Two make the reasonable point that they are paid to do a difficult and technically challenging job, and it is in no one's interest to create situations where a bishop's well-meaning intervention could cause legal mayhem. Nevertheless there does appear to be an issue here that would benefit from review, even if a solution satisfactory to all parties is not easy to conceive.

McLaughlin's concept of the dual function school has been referred to on more than one occasion: the school that carries on two separate functions within itself. A school of this nature appears to be a contradiction in terms of the church documents I have cited. Much evidence that has emerged as part of my study tends to suggest, however, that the dual-function Catholic school is a living reality in many places. The consequence must be that the possibility of challenges between a diocese on the one hand and a governing body on the other are an ever-present fact of life, even though they lurk beneath the surface most of the time.

Many examples could be quoted: the tendency of governors to leave relationships with the diocese, and matters relating to religious education and worship to clergy or members of religious orders; the lack of knowledge governors appear to manifest about the Church's well-documented views on the nature and purpose of Catholic schools; the primacy of the LA's curriculum statements and in-service training facilities; the difficulty which many governors appear to have in defining what are the essential Catholic elements in the ethos of their school; and the absence of systematic monitoring or review arrangements.

Taken together, all this seems not only to underline McLaughlin's thesis, but also to support Grace's view that the inherited spiritual capital of the schools is being eroded or diluted. All

the governors taking part in the survey were asked to comment on
three problem areas: senior staff appointments, teachers' sexual
morality, and pupil admissions. In the first area, clear ambivalences
arose between the views of many governors and the stated national
policy. What is particularly interesting is that ambivalences also
exist at policy level. There appears not only to be a fairly widespread
acceptance of non-Catholic senior appointments in independent
schools, but one bishop has now conceded the principle in one of
his maintained schools. Because of the acute nature of this
problem, as registered by Howson in his various reports, challenges
seem inevitable. The present position seems untenable in the light
of very recent legislative change. Whilst education law may give
Catholic schools, along with other voluntary-aided schools that have
a religious character, a number of rights to help them secure that
character, the exercise of these rights, according to the Equality Act
2010, has to be 'a proportionate means of achieving a legitimate
aim'. The difficulty is that the more governing bodies and bishops
agree to appoint non-Catholics to such posts, the more difficult it
will be in the future to argue that the restrictive practice remains
proportionate in the light of a challenge. The position seems to
require resolution one way or the other.

There is also incongruity amongst governors about the extent
Catholic teachers should be expected to adhere to a standard of
sexual morality that has long been abandoned not only by the rest
of British society but also by many Catholics. The incongruity
exposed here is between the overwhelming diocesan view, which
has abandoned the traditional one, and the many governors who
still see teachers as essential role models, some for parents as well
as their pupils. One issue that emerged was that some governors
appear not to have an accurate notion of what is the official line on
divorce. This raises the more general question of training, to which
I will return.

The final matter was the admission of pupils. The incongruity at
policy level between the service role of Catholic schools in respect
of the poor and those without faith, on the one hand, and the long-
standing English and Welsh policy of a place in a Catholic school
for every Catholic child has been noted. There is no discernible
conflict between governors' views and that of the English and
Welsh bishops. I referred to the 2006 controversy. It is interesting
that those non-Catholics pressing for legal changes to be made to
admission arrangements appeared to be more in line with the
views expressed in *Gravissimum Educationis* than did the English
Catholic Church's spokesman.

The issue of training arose in my discussions time and again. There is no doubt that the diocesan and national officials see their future success in terms of the provision of greatly enhanced training opportunities. The problem here is simply put: even if all the resources in terms of manpower and facilities can be made available, how can there be confidence that busy governors will avail themselves of them? One contribution to the answer might be a re-examination by the bishops of the way they work, and a re-evaluation of the contribution of their schools to their evangelizing and catechetical work. It is one of the interesting features of recent English and Welsh social history that, as church congregations have dwindled, so church school rolls have increased. If governors can more easily see that their work is valued by their bishop, personally, they may be more prepared to avail themselves of training opportunities provided by the diocese.

The role of the permanent diaconate in Catholic educational matters appears to be one area that needs to be explored. Another that seems ripe for development relates to the ethos of Catholic schools. There is a manifest disjunction between the views of diocesan officials and governors about the essential features of a Catholic ethos. Allied to this, if it is right that the nature of the ethos is crucial to the identity of a Catholic school, it seems unsatisfactory that many of the monitoring arrangements seem rather haphazard.

Nevertheless, the diocesan directors are far from gloomy. The director for Glastonbury said:

> We go through cycles. Things do ... the Lord will look after us anyway ... Somehow or other, we've got to make [people] realize that there's more than technicalities in getting your headship qualification and the rest of it, and there's something about prayer and prayer life and inner spiritual strength that's got to be there. You can't tick boxes on that one. Was it St. Francis who said 'You've got to pray as if everything depended on the Lord, and work as if everything depended on you?' You've got to keep the two sides together, because if you only work as if everything depended on you, but you haven't got this other side to you, you're lopsided.

The director for Much Wenlock continued Grace's metaphor, but shared Glastonbury's confidence in the future:

> I understand the fear, and I understand the concern that there is a danger of this [the gradual loss of distinctiveness]. But the view of the trustees here, using the terminology of capital, [is that] our

schools are investing in people over whom it might appear to be easy to make a judgement as to their involvement today, but it is an investment in the whole of the lives of individuals. From today to the end of their lives, who can say what the outcome is going to be?

I am weekly encouraged by the level of support from the trustees here, and their commitment to education, and their belief that we have got, largely speaking, a very strong body of people committed to their governing bodies as foundation and other governors ... I remain optimistic.

There were strong echoes of Glastonbury in what the director for Athelney had to say:

God works in funny ways ... If you believe in God, God won't let the Church, as the body of Christ, die, will He? It may change, it may re-form, it may re-invent itself, and that's maybe what's happening ... I don't blame God about anything. Something may present itself as a challenge, but I regard challenges as opportunities, and I think this is an opportunity ... What we're moving into is a 'done with', 'in partnership with' arrangement, where priests and parishioners are taking on completely different roles.

The director for Lacock took strong issue with Grace:

I totally disagree. It's not my experience. I see a deeper and deeper understanding of what our schools are about, and a deeper commitment to enhancing the lives of our children, a real passion for making a difference. One of the reasons for that, I would accept, is the heritage that we continue. It's not so much through me, but two key people have had a massive impact in this diocese, [by developing] lay spirituality. So I would argue that each of our schools has a white hot core of faith, which is very strong and very vibrant. So no, I totally disagree that spiritual capital is being eroded. I see it as being enriched and enhanced and deepened. I find it really exciting, and I see there's real green shoots for the Church for the future. The cork is out of the bottle now. The clericalism is beginning to go, and Catholic Christian spirituality, mainly from our schools, is being allowed to develop.

On the other hand, Grace found an ally in Tewkesbury:

I think there's a lot of truth in that situation as described by Gerald Grace, and it has taxed me considerably over recent years. What we're trying to do in this diocese is to supply the opportunities for teachers at all levels to hear good quality theological discussion and debate ... to get people not only to be competent and ready to support the school with their prayers, but also to be able to understand their faith better, in order that they can articulate that with one another, and be able to continue some sort of lively discussion about what it is the Church believes, what they believe, and how the two differ or coincide. We feel that's an investment that the diocese has to make.

I think it's somewhat remiss of us that we've allowed our schools generally to rely on professional religious people to take responsibility for the ethos and spirituality of the school, which lets the lay members of staff off the hook, and the problem that arises from this: ... the concept of a single curriculum which is sacred all the way through found a great deal of opposition and misunderstanding from those very schools where the sisters, brothers, or friars had taken responsibility for the spiritual side of the line, and the secular teachers had just taught the secular curriculum, and it was hard to bring these two things together in these schools. Where the schools were set up to be diocesan schools rather than religious trusts, that problem didn't seem to arise to nearly the same degree. Because of that situation, some of the lay members of staff felt disempowered about what they were contributing to the spiritual life of the school. Now we're setting that right. It's early days to say ... I'm hoping we'll turn the tide, but I haven't got enough evidence to show that that's the case yet. I'm optimistic, yes. We've got an awful lot of things to fend off and [we've got] to continue fighting.

Support for Grace also came from Tintern, but the director here also raised the more general issue of work / life balance:

I think there will be more challenges to governors and to heads on commitment, on what the job looks like.

He thought Catholic primary schools had more of a future:

because I think the clergy see and support the primary schools because they see the fruits of their labours [in them] and there's that community feel. Where secondary schools are concerned, [they] don't always help themselves. They talk about ethos, and yet they're sometimes not even welcoming to the clergy. What they want the clergy for is capitation, and the relationships are quite different. Judgements by clergy are often made by the number of pupils in the churches, and if that's the yardstick there's no future for secondary schools, because a lot of our pupils aren't in the pews on a Sunday.

So in terms of the future of secondary schools, numbers on roll, admissions, all that needs to be looked at, but I think that the primary schools are still vibrant Catholic communities, and doing a lot to evangelize a number of parents. I'm not sure it's the same with secondary. It's different altogether.

What these comments reveal is unanimous confidence amongst the diocesan directors I have interviewed that, in the words of the fourteenth-century anchoress St Julian of Norwich, 'all will be well', despite the many challenges and difficulties that may lie ahead. This confidence is based squarely on their religious belief: 'The Lord will look after us;'... 'God won't let the Church ... die, will He?' Some, for example the directors in Athelney and Lacock, already discern evidence to support their view. Others, as in Glastonbury, either do not, or, if they do, did not share their thinking with me.

In contrast, there was a sharp division of view about Grace's thesis that the inherited spiritual capital of schools is being eroded. At one extreme, the director for Lacock 'totally disagree[d]'. At the other, his colleague in Tewkesbury thinks 'there is a lot of truth in that situation as described by Gerald Grace', though even here there was a careful differentiation between those schools that had been established by religious orders, whose members had 'taken responsibility for the spiritual side of the line', and the diocesan schools, where lay teachers had always taken the lead. And again, the director for Tewkesbury, perhaps arguing against himself, in admitting the problem, said 'Now we're setting that right.' In between the two there are gradations of view, but the thrust of the diocesan directors' comments is, overall, a rejection of Grace's thesis. Putting all the evidence together seems to indicate that the various sociological and legislative changes that I have described have had a substantial impact on the work of the Catholic schools whose governors have participated in my study. In support of this, I have repeatedly drawn attention to the way in which the evidence I have collected tends to support McLaughlin's concept of the dual school – a single institution conducting two separate activities within itself, the two activities being, in Arthur's words, 'one specifically Christian and the other secular'.[2] This, if true, appears to create a fundamental incongruity with the view of Catholic education promulgated by both The Sacred Congregation for Catholic Education and by the Catholic Bishops' Conference of England and Wales. It also appears to lend support to Grace's thesis that the inherited spiritual capital of Catholic schools is being diluted.

[2] Arthur, J., *The Ebbing Tide, The Policy and Principles of Catholic Education*, p. 227.

Appendix 1

Occupations of Respondent Governors

(Other than elected teacher / staff governors and ex officio heads)

Teachers	17	Product Manager	1
Accountants	5	Purchasing Manager	1
Higher Education	5	Retailer	1
Nurses	5	Teaching Assistant / Laundry	
Housewives	4	Operative	1
Barristers	3	Wine Merchant	1
Scientists	3		
Administrators	2		
Bankers	2		
Civil Servants	2		
Education Advisers	2		
Parish Priests	2		
Retired (no further details)	2		
Surveyors	2		
Teaching Assistants	2		
Artist	1		
Bursar	1		
Construction Manager	1		
Education Welfare Officer	1		
Electronic Engineer	1		
Health Care Assistant	1		
Inspector of Taxes	1		
Insurance Underwriter	1		
IT Consultant	1		
IT Sales	1		
LEA officer	1		
Marketing Director	1		

Appendix 2

Governors' Questionnaire

The first section of this questionnaire asks about your experience as a school governor.

1a. For how many years have you been a governor of this school? ☐

1b. What category of governor are you: CO-OPTED, ELECTED STAFF, ELECTED TEACHER, FOUNDATION, HEAD, LEA, MINOR AUTHORITY, OTHER (please specify) ——————————, DON'T KNOW? (Please circle the answer).

2. Have you in the past served as a foundation governor of another Catholic school? (please circle)

| YES | NO |

3. If the answer to Q2 is YES, for how many years? ☐

4. Are you a governor of another maintained school? (please circle)

| YES | NO |

5. If the answer to Q4 is YES, is it a CATHOLIC, CHURCH of ENGLAND, COMMUNITY, FOUNDATION or OTHER (please specify ——————————————) school? (Please circle the answer).

6. If the answer to Q4 is YES, what category of governor are you – CO-OPTED, ELECTED STAFF, ELECTED TEACHER, FOUNDATION, LEA, MINOR AUTHORITY, OTHER (please specify) ——————— DON'T KNOW? (Please circle the answer)

7. (If applicable) Who first asked you if you would like to be a foundation governor of your present school? (e.g. bishop, dean, governor, head, parish priest).

_____

8. Do you think your work is of value to the school? (please circle)

YES	NO	DON'T KNOW

9. Why do you think so? _____

_____

10. What interests you about your work as a governor?.

_____

_____

_____

_____

11. If you are invited to serve as a governor of this school again, will you agree? (please circle)

YES	NO	DON'T KNOW

12. What are your reasons for making this decision? _____

_____

_____

_____

The next section asks you about the support you get in your work as a governor

---

13. Does the Diocese provide training in:-
(please circle)

The appointment of teaching staff?	YES	NO	DON'T KNOW
The admission of pupils?	YES	NO	DON'T KNOW
Curriculum policy (other than RE)?	YES	NO	DON'T KNOW
Buildings matters?	YES	NO	DON'T KNOW
RE?	YES	NO	DON'T KNOW
Distinctive ethos of a Catholic school?	YES	NO	DON'T KNOW

14. If you answered YES to any part(s) of Q13, have you attended any Diocesan courses since you were last appointed/elected a governor of your present school?   (please circle)

YES	NO

15. If the answer to Q 14 is YES, which of the topics listed above was/were covered? _____
_____

16. Does the Diocese provide regular briefings for governors?
                                                    (please circle)

YES	NO

17. If the answer to Q16 is YES are these briefings
         (a) meetings?
         (b) newsletters or circulars?
         (c) both?
(please circle one letter (a) (b) or (c))

18. If the Diocese provides briefing meetings are these
         (a) termly?
         (b) annually?
         (c) other? (please specify) _____

19. How many have you attended in the last 12 months?
    (please circle)

0	1	2	3	4	4+

20. When you were last appointed / elected, did the Diocese arrange a commissioning service?   (please circle)

YES	NO	DON'T KNOW

21. If the answer to Q20 was YES did you attend it? (please circle)

YES	NO

22. Does the LEA provide training in   (please circle)

The appointment of teaching staff?	YES	NO	DON'T KNOW
The admission of pupils to Catholic schools?	YES	NO	DON'T KNOW
Curriculum policy?	YES	NO	DON'T KNOW
Buildings matters?	YES	NO	DON'T KNOW

23. If you have answered YES to any part(s) of Q22 have you attended any LEA courses since you were last appointed/elected a governor? (please circle)

YES	NO

24. If the answer to Q23 was YES, which of the topics listed above was/were covered? _____

_____

25. Does the LEA provide regular briefings for governors?
                  (please circle)

YES	NO	DON'T KNOW

26. If the answer to Q25 is YES, are these
    (a) meetings?
    (b) newsletters or circulars?
    (c) both?

27. If the LEA provides briefing meetings are these termly?
    (a)
    (b) annually?
    (c) other?(please specify) _____
    (please circle one letter (a) (b) or (c))

28. If LEA meetings are arranged, how many have you attended in the last 12 months ? (please circle one)

0	1	2	3	4	4+

29. Have you within the last 12 months read any articles about education in any of the following? (please circle)

Briefing	YES	NO
Catholic Herald	YES	NO
Catholic Times	YES	NO
Priests & People	YES	NO
Tablet	YES	NO
Universe	YES	NO

The next section asks about the work of your governing body

30. Has your school a Mission Statement ? (please circle)

YES	NO	DON'T KNOW

31. If the answer to Q30 is YES, how would you describe the governing body's involvement?
    (a) We approved a draft prepared by staff and submitted by the head.
    (b) A group of us worked on it with the head and the governing body approved the final draft.
    (c) The whole governing body was involved in drafting and agreeing it.
    (please circle one letter (a) (b) or (c))

32. How would you describe the governing body's involvement in the preparation of the school development/improvement plan?
    (a) We approved a draft prepared by the staff and submitted by the head.
    (b) A group of us worked on it with the head and the governing body approved the final draft.
    (c) The whole governing body was involved in drafting and agreeing it.
    (d) Don't know.
    (please circle one letter (a) (b) (c) or (d))

33. How much of the LEA's curriculum policy for subjects other than RE has your school adopted?   (please circle)

All of it	Most of it	About half	Not very much	None	Don't know

34. If the answer to Q 33 is NONE, how would you describe the
governing body's role in formulating your school's policy?
  (a) We approved a draft prepared by the staff and submitted the
      head.
  (b) A group of us worked on it with the staff and the governing
      body approved the final draft.
  (c) The whole governing body was involved in drafting and
      agreeing it.
  (please circle one letter (a) (b) or (c))

> **The next section asks questions about some problems which
> Catholic schools may face from time to time.**

35. It is Bishops' Conference policy that only practising Catholics be
appointed to headships, deputy headships and posts in RE
departments. If you were to be involved in appointments to any of
these, are there any circumstances in which you might be prepared
to consider appointing a non Catholic?

                                              (please circle)

| YES | NO | DON'T KNOW |

36. If the answer to Q35 is YES, please describe briefly the
circumstances

_____

_____

_____

_____

_____

37. Catholics who apply for posts as teachers in Catholic schools are
expected to be 'in good standing' with the Church. In practice, this
usually means they should not be in irregular matrimonial situations
or be practising homosexuals. Do you think these standards are still
relevant in contemporary society? (please circle)

| YES | NO | DON'T KNOW |

38. Please give your reasons for this _____

_____

_____

_____

_____

_____

39. If your school is or was to be oversubscribed by Catholic pupils, are there any circumstances in which you would be prepared to admit non Catholics in preference to Catholics?   (please circle)

| YES | NO | DON'T KNOW |

40. If the answer to Q39 is YES, please describe briefly in what circumstances:-

_____
_____
_____
_____
_____

Finally, some questions about yourself

41. Are you male or female?   Please circle.

42. Your age is   (please circle)

| 20–30 | 31–40 | 41–50 | 51–60 | 61–70 | 70+ |

43. If you have/had children, are/were they educated at:-
    (a) a Catholic primary school (maintained or independent)?
    (b)   (please circle)

| YES | NO |

(c) a Catholic secondary school (maintained or independent)?
    (d)   (please circle)

| YES | NO |

44. Do you take part in any other Church activity? e.g. Catenian, eucharistic minister, KSC, musician, reader? If so, please describe it briefly.

_____
_____
_____

45. What is your occupation? _____

46. At what stage did you complete your formal education?
    (please circle)
    (a) SCHOOL CERTIFICATE/CSE/GCE/GCSE;

    (b) HIGHER SCHOOL CERTIFICATE/'A' LEVEL;

    (c) FIRST DEGREE;

    (d) SECOND DEGREE

    (e) OTHER (please specify) _____

47. What is your ethnic background? (please circle)WHITE: ASIAN;
    ASIAN BRITISH; BLACK: BLACK BRITISH; CHINESE or
    OTHER RELATED GROUP; MIXED; OTHER.

48. Please use the space below to make any other comments about the
    rewards and / or frustrations of your work as a governor that may
    not have been covered in the questions.

49. As part of this project, I shall also be carrying out a small number of
    interviews, both by telephone and face-to-face, to investigate some
    issues in more depth. If selected, would you be willing to take part?

    Telephone interviews   (please circle)

YES	NO

    Face-to-face   (please circle)

YES	NO

    If you answered YES **please supply your name, telephone number
    and/or address:-**

Name _____

Telephone number _____

Address _____

Bibliography

Abbott, W.M. (ed.), *The Documents of Vatican II* (London-Dublin, Geoffrey Chapman, 1966).

Allies, M. H., *Thomas William Allies* (London, Burns & Oates, 1907).

Archives of the Archbishop of Westminster (1846), *Resolutions of the Vicars Apostolic*, 4th day, 24 April, p. 89 (unpublished).

Arthur, J., 'Catholic Responses to the Education Reform Act', in Francis, L. and Lankshear, D. (eds), *Christian Perspectives on Church schools: A Reader* (Leominster, Gracewing Fowler Wright Books, 1993).

Arthur, J., 'Policy perceptions of Headteachers and Governors in Catholic Schooling', in *Educational Studies*, vol. 19, no. 3, 1993, pp. 275–88.

——, *The Ebbing Tide, Policy and Principles of Catholic Education* (Leominster, Gracewing Fowler Wright Books, 1995).

Arthur, J. and Bailey, R., *Schools and Community: The communitarian agenda in education* (London, Falmer, 2000).

Arthur, J., Boylan, P., Grace, G., and Walsh, P., *Can there be a Catholic School Curriculum? Renewing the Debate* (London, Centre for Research and Development in Catholic Education, Institute of Education, 2007).

Auld, R., *William Tyndale Junior and Infants Schools Public Enquiry, A report to the Inner London Education Authority* (London, Inner London Education Authority, 1976).

Bagshawe, Bishop Edward Gilpin, *Ad Limina Report*, 1875 (Nottingham, Diocesan Archive transcribed by Canon A. P. Dolan, 2006).

Baker, K., *The Turbulent Years* (London, Faber and Faber 1993).

Ball, S. J., *Class Strategies and the Education Market: The Middle Classes and Social Advantage* (London, Routledge, 1993).

Barlow, Sir M. and Holland, R., *The Education Act 1918* (London, National Society's Depository, 1918).

Baron, G. and Howell, D. A., *The Government and Management of Schools* (London, Athlone Press, 1974).

Bauman, Z., *In Search of Politics* (Cambridge, Polity Press, 1999).

Beck, G. A. (ed.), *The English Catholics 1850–1950* (London, Burns Oates, 1950).

Beck, U., *The Reinvention of Politics* (Cambridge, Polity Press, 1997).

Bernstein, B., *The Structuring of Pedagogic Discourse* (London, Routledge, 1990).

——, *Pedagogy, Symbolic Control and Identity: theory, research and critique* (London, Taylor and Francis, 1996).

Bossy, J., *The English Catholic Community 1570–1850* (London, Darton, Longman & Todd, 1975).

Bourdieu, P., 'The Forms of Capital, in McPherson', J. (ed.), *Handbook of Theory and Research for the Sociology of Education* (New York, Greenwood Press, 1986).

——, *The Logic of Practice* (Oxford, Polity Press, 1990).

Bryce Report, Royal Commission on Secondary Education, London, HMSO, 1875, in facsimile in *British Parliamentary Papers* (Irish University Press, Shannon, Ireland, 1970, vols. 40–5).

Butler, R. A., *The Art of the Possible* (London, Hamish Hamilton, 1971).

Callaghan, J., Ruskin College Speech in *Education*, 22 October 1976.

Cashman, J., *The 1902 Act and Roman Catholic Schools: a study of a community's efforts to gain and preserve denominational education in its schools* (Keele, University of Keele, unpublished Ph.D. thesis, 1995).

Catholic Bishops' Conference of England and Wales, *Spiritual and Moral Development Across The Curriculum* (London, Catholic Education Service, 1995).

——, *The Common Good in Education* (London, Catholic Education Service, 1997).

——, *Governing a Catholic School* (London, Catholic Education Service, 1998).

——, *Catholic Directory 2009* (Manchester, Gabriel Communications, 2009).

Catholic Education Council, *The Education Act 1980 and Catholic Schools* (London, Catholic Education Council, 1980).

Catholic Education Service, *Evaluating the Distinctive Nature of a Catholic School* (London, Catholic Education Service, 1999).

Catholic Education Service for England and Wales, *Digest of 2009 Census Data for Schools and Colleges* (London, Catholic Education Service for England and Wales, 2010).

Central Advisory Council for Education (England), *Children and their Primary Schools* (London, HMSO, 1967). (The Plowden Report).

Chadwick, O., *The Victorian Church*, vols 1 and 2 (London, A & C Black, 1966 and 1970).

Champ, J., *William Bernard Ullathorne, A Different Kind of Monk* (Leominster, Gracewing, 2006).

Church Schools' Review Group, *The Way Ahead: Church of England Schools in the New Millennium* (London, Church House Publishing, 2001). (The Dearing Report).

Congregation for Catholic Education, *The Catholic School on the Threshold of the Third Millennium* (Vatican City, Libreria Editrice Vaticana, 1998).

Connell, L., 'Administration of Secondary Schools: Leeds v. Board of Education, 1905–11', in *Journal of Educational Administration and History*, vol. 5, no. 2, 1973.

Cook, C., *A short history of the Liberal Party 1900–1976* (London, Macmillan, 1976).

Courteney Murray, J., in *Bridging the Sacred and the Secular*, ed. Hooper, L. (Washington DC, Georgetown University Press, 1994).

Cox, C. B. and Dyson, A. E. (eds), *The Black Papers on Education* (London, Day-Poynter, 1971).

Creese, M. and Earley, P., *Improving Schools and Governing Bodies* (London, Routledge, 1999).

Cross Commission Report (1888), Final Report of the Commission appointed to inquire into the Elementary Education Acts, England and Wales, London, HMSO, in facsimile in *British Parliamentary Papers* (Irish University Press, Shannon, Ireland, 1970).

Daglish, N. D., 'A "difficult and somewhat thankless task": politics, religion and the Education Bill of 1908', in *Journal of Educational Administration and History*, vol. 31, no. 1, 1999.

Dean, C., Dyson, A., Gallannaugh, F., Howes, A. and Raffo, C., *School Governors and Disadvantage in England* (York, Joseph Rowntree Foundation, 2007).

Deem. R., Brehony, K. and Heath, S., *Active Citizenship and the Governing of Schools* (Buckingham, Open University Press, 1995).

Department for Education, *The Education Act 1993* (London, HMSO, 1993).

——, *Governing Bodies and Effective Schools* (London, Department for Education, 1995).

——, *A Guide to the Law for School Governors* (London, Department for Education, 2011).

Department for Education and Employment, *The Governors' Role in Raising Standards* (London, Department for Education and Employment, 1998).

——, *Roles of Governing Bodies and Headteachers* (London, Department for Education and Employment, 2000).

Department for Education and Skills, *Steering not rowing*, Conference report (London, Department of Education and Skills, 2002).

——, *The Education Act 2003* (London, HMSO, 2003).

Department of Education and Science, *Circular 10/65: The organisation of Secondary Education* (London, HMSO, 1965).

——, *A New Partnership for our Schools* (London, HMSO, 1977). (The Taylor Report).

——, (1980) *The Education Act 1980* (London, HMSO, 1980).

——, *Better Schools* (London, HMSO, 1985).

——, *The Education (No. 2) Act 1986* (London, HMSO, 1986).

——, *The Education Reform Act 1988* (London, HMSO, 1988).

Dickens, C., *A Christmas Carol* (Oxford, Oxford University Press, 2006).

——, *Bleak House* (Oxford, Oxford University Press, 1998).

——, *Oliver Twist* (Oxford, Oxford University Press, 1999).

Disraeli, B., *Sybil* (Oxford, Oxford University Press, 1998).

Donnelly, C., 'In pursuit of school ethos', in *British Journal of Educational Studies*, vol. 48, no. 2, 2000, pp. 134–54.

Eaton, M., Longmore, J. and Naylor, A., *Commitment and Diversity, Catholics and Education in a Changing World* (London, Cassell, 2000).

Engels, F., *The Condition of the Working Class in England* (Oxford, Oxford University Press, 1999).

Ensor, Sir R. C. K., *England 1870–1914* (Oxford, Oxford University Press, 1990).

Equality Act 2010 (London, HMSO, 2010).

Evenett, H. O., *The Catholic Schools of England and Wales* (Cambridge, Cambridge University Press, 1944).

Fisher, H. A. L., *An Unfinished Autobiography* (London, Oxford University Press, 1940).

Gärtner, N., 'Administering "*Operation* Pied Piper" – How the London County Council Prepared for the Evacuation of its Schoolchildren 1938–1939', in *Journal of Educational Administration and History*, vol. 42, no. 1, 2010.

Gaskell, E., *Mary Barton* (London, Penguin Books, 1996).

——, *North and South* (London, Penguin Books, 1995).

Giddens, A., *Modernity and Self-Identity* (Cambridge, Polity Press, 1991).

——, *Beyond Left and Right: The Future of Radical Politics* (Cambridge, Polity Press, 1994).

——, *Runaway World* (London, Profile Books, 1999).

Gillborn, D., *Education and institutional racism* (London, Institute of Education, 2002).

Gosden, P., 'Public Education in England 1839–1989', in *1839–1939, Public Education in England* (London, Department of Education and Science, Her Majesty's Inspectorate of Schools, 1990).

Grace, G., *Catholic Schools, Mission, Markets and Morality* (London, RoutledgeFalmer, 2002).

——, 'Urban Education; confronting the contradictions: an analysis with special reference to London', in *London Review of Education*, vol. 4, no. 2, 2006.

Guy, R. E., *The Synods in English* (Stratford-upon-Avon, St Gabriel's Press, 1886).

Halpin, D., 'Democracy, inclusive schooling and the politics of education', in *International Journal of Inclusive Education* 3.3, 1999, pp. 225–38.

Haviland, J., *Take care, Mr. Baker* (London, Fourth Estate, 1988).

Hickman, M. J., *Religion Class and Identity* (Aldershot, Avebury Press, 1995).

Hirst, P., 'Associational Democracy', in Held, D. (ed.), *Prospects for Democracy* (Stanford, Stanford University Press, 1993).

—— *Associative Democracy: New Forms of Economic and Social Governance* (Cambridge, Polity Press, 1994).

——, *From Statism to Pluralism* (London, UCL Press, 2000).

Holland, M. G., *The British Press and the Educational Controversy 1847–1865* (New York and London, Garland Publishing Inc., 1987).

Hornsby-Smith, M. P., *Catholic Education: The Unobtrusive Partner* (London, Sheed and Ward, 1978).

Howson, J. and Sprigade, A., *The State of the Labour Market for Senior Staff in Schools in England and Wales 2009–2010* (London, Education Data Surveys at TSL Education Ltd, 2010).

——, *26th Annual survey of senior staff appointments in schools across England and Wales 2009–2010* (London, Education Data Surveys / TSL, 2011).

Jenkins, R., *Gladstone* (London and Basingstoke, Macmillan, 1995).

Johnson, R., 'Thatcherism and English education: breaking the mould or continuing the pattern?', in *History of Education*, 18 (2), 1989, pp. 91–121.

Jowitt, A. and Perks, R., *Destination Bradford. A Century of Immigration* (Bradford, Bradford Libraries and Information Service, 1987).

Kandinsky, W., 'And, Some Remarks on Synthetic Art', in Lindsay, K. and Virgo, P. (eds), *Complete Writings on Art*, vol. 2 (1922–1943) (New York, Da Capo Press, 1982).

Kennedy, P., *The Catholic Church in England and Wales 1500–2000* (Keighley, PBK Publications, 2001).

Keys, W. and Fernandes, C., *A Survey of School Governing Bodies* (Slough, National Foundation for Educational Research, 1990).

Kitching, J., 'The Catholic Poor Schools 1800–1845', in *Journal of Educational Administration and History*, vols I, no. 2 and II, no. 1, 1969.

Kogan, M., Johnson, D., Packwood, T. and Whitaker, T., *School Governing Bodies* (London, Heinemann Educational Books, 1984).

Konstant, D. (ed.), *Signposts and Homecomings* (Slough, St Paul's Publications, 1981).

Lannon, D., *Catholic Education in the Salford Diocese* (Hull, University of Hull unpublished M.Phil. thesis, 2003).

Maclure, J. S., *Educational Documents England and Wales* (London, Chapman and Hall, 1965).

Magnus, P., *Gladstone* (London, John Murray, 1960).

Marsh, P. T., *Joseph Chamberlain, Entrepreneur in Politics* (New Haven and London, Yale University Press, 1994).

McClelland, V. A., *Cardinal Manning, His Public Life and Influence* (London, Oxford University Press, 1962).

McCormack, A., *Cardinal Vaughan* (London, Burns & Oates, 1966).

McLaughlin, T. H., *Parental Rights in Religious Upbringing and Religious Education within a Liberal Perspective* (London, University of London unpublished Ph.D. thesis, 1990).

——, 'The Educative Importance of Ethos', in *British Journal of Educational Studies*, vol. 53, no. 3, 2005, pp. 306–25.

Ministry of Education, *Command Paper Cmd 6523* (London, HMSO, 1944).

Morrish, L., *Education since 1800* (London, George Allen and Unwin, 1970).

Murphy, J., *Church, State and Schools in Britain, 1800–1970* (London, Routledge and Kegan Paul, 1971).

Murphy, J., *The Education Act 1870* (Newton Abbott, David and Charles, 1972).

Murphy, M., *Catholic Poor Schools in Tower Hamlets (London) 1765–1865 Part 1: Wapping and Commercial Road* (Roehampton, Roehampton Institute of Higher Education, 1991).

——, *Catholic Poor Schools in Tower Hamlets (London) 1765–1865 Part 3: Spitalfields and Neighbourhood* (Roehampton, Roehampton Institute of Higher Education, 1991).

——, *The Associated Catholic Charities of the Metropolis* (London, Michael Murphy, 1995).

Newcastle Commission Report (1861), 'Report into the State of Popular Education in England', London, HMSO, in facsimile in *British Parliamentary Papers*, vols 3, 4, 5 & 8 (Irish University Press, Shannon, Ireland, 1969).

Newman, J., *Modernising Governance: New Labour, Policy and Society* (London, Sage, 2001).

Norman, J., *The Big Society* (Buckingham, University of Buckingham Press, 2010).

O'Connor, M., *Plowden plus ten* (London, *The Guardian*, 4 January 1977).

Ofsted, *Improving Schools* (London, HMSO, 1994).

——, *Making It Better: Improving School Governance*, A Report from HM Chief Inspector of Schools (London, HMSO, 2001).

——, *Framework 2003 – Inspecting Schools* (London, HMSO, 2003).

——, *Every Child Matters: Framework for the inspection of schools in England from September 2005* (London, Ofsted, 2005).

O'Keeffe, B., 'Reordering Perspectives in Catholic Schools', in Hornsby-Smith, M. P. (ed.), *Catholics in England 1995–2000* (London, Cassell, 1999).

Pattison, R., 'The Birrell Education Bill of 1906', in *Journal of Education Administration and History*, vol. 5, no.1, 1973, pp. 34–41.

Pius XI, Pope, *Rappresentanti in Terra* (Rome, Libreria Editrice Vaticana, 1929).

Power, S., Edwards, A., Whitty, G. and Wigfall, V., *Education and the Middle Class* (Buckingham, Open University Press, 2003).

Pring, R. A., 'Implications of the Changing Values and Ethical Standards of Society', in Thacker, J., Pring, R. A. and Evans, D. (eds), *Personal, Social and Moral Education in a Changing World* (Windsor, NFER-Nelson, 1987).

——, *Philosophy of Education: Aims, Theory, Common Sense and Research* (London and New York, Continuum, 2004).

——, 'Faith Schools: Have they a place in the Comprehensive

System?', in Hewlett, M., Pring, R. A. and Tulloch, M. (eds), *Comprehensive Education: Evolution, achievement and new directions* (Northampton, University of Northampton, 2006).

R. v Trustees of the Roman Catholic Diocese of Southwark ex p. Kemmis-Betty 1990, in *The Universe*, 13 January 1991, p. 2.

R. v Trustees of the Roman Catholic Diocese of Westminster ex p. Mars in *Local Government Reports*, vol. 86, pp. 507–23 (Croydon, Charles Knight Publishing, 1987).

Reid, W. T., *Life of the Rt. Hon. W.E. Forster* (London, Chapman and Hall, 1888).

Report of The Commissioners for the inquiry into The State of Large Towns and Populous Districts, *Parliamentary Papers Session 1845*, vol. 18.1 (London, HMSO. 1845).

Roberts, S., *Catholic Childhoods: Catholic Elementary Education in York, 1850–1914* (York, Borthwick Institute of Historical Research, University of York, 2001).

Royal Commission on Local Government in England, *Research Studies 6. (School Management and Government)* (London, HMSO, 1968).

Royal Commission on Local Government, *Report* (London, HMSO, 1969).

Rutter, M., Maughan, B., Mortimore, P. and Ouston, J., *Fifteen Thousand Hours* (Shepton Mallet, Open Books Publishing Ltd, 1979).

Rynne, X., *The Third Session* (London, Faber and Faber, 1965).

Sacred Congregation for Catholic Education, *The Catholic School* (London, Catholic Truth Society, 1977).

——, *Lay Catholics in Schools: Witnesses to Faith* (London, Catholic Truth Society, 1982).

——, *The Religious Dimension of Education in a Catholic School* (London, Catholic Truth Society, 1988).

Scanlon, M., Earley, P. and Evans, J., *Improving the Effectiveness of School Governing Bodies* (London, DfEE, 1999).

Selby, D. E., 'Manning, Ullathorne and the School Board Question 1870–76', in *Journal of Educational Administration and History*, vol. V, no.1, 1973.

Selleck, R. J. W., *James Kay-Shuttleworth – Journey of an outsider* (Ilford, The Woburn Press, 1994).

Sharp, P., *School Governing Bodies in the English Educational System: An Historical Perspective* (Leeds, University of Leeds, 1995).

Siedlecka, J., *The Permanent Diaconate in the UK and Ireland – an overview* (London, The Independent Catholic News, 20 June 2005).

Smith, F., *The Life and Work of Sir James Kay-Shuttleworth* (London, John Murray, 1923).

Spencer, A. E. C. W., *Reconstruction of the 2009 Census of Catholic Schools in England and Wales. Introduction to the Series* (Taunton, Russell-Spencer, 2011).

Sperandio, J., 'Vision and Leadership in Educational Administration: Sir George White of Norwich (1840–1912)', in *Journal of Educational Administration and History*, vol. 38, no. 1, 2006.

Stephens, W. B., *Education in Britain 1750–1914* (Basingstoke and London, Macmillan Press Ltd, 1998).

Storr, C., 'The purpose of Catholic Schools', *The Tablet*, 28 October 2006.

Streatfield, D. and Jefferies, G., *The Reconstitution of School Governing Bodies* (Slough, National Foundation for Educational Research, 1989).

Sullivan, F. B., *Lord Butler: The 1944 Act in Retrospect* (Milton Keynes, The Open University Press, 1980).

Sullivan, J., *Catholic Schools in Contention* (Dublin, Lindisfarne Books, 2000).

——, *Catholic Education: Distinctive and Inclusive* (Dordrecht, Kluwer Academic Press, 2001).

Swartz, D., *Culture and Power: The Sociology of Pierre Bourdieu* (Chicago, University of Chicago Press, 1997).

Watson, J. S., *The Reign of George III* (Oxford, Oxford University Press, 1959).

White, J., *London in the Nineteenth Century* (London, Jonathan Cape, 2007).

Whitty, G., Power, S. and Halpin, D., *Devolution and Choice in Education, The School, the State and the Market* (Buckingham, Open University Press, 1998).

Wolf, A., 'Working Girls', in *Prospect*, issue 121, April 2006.

Woodham-Smith, C., *The Great Hunger* (London, Hamish Hamilton, 1962).

Woodward, Sir L., *The Age of Reform* (Oxford, Oxford University Press, 1962).

Index

Lightning Source UK Ltd.
Milton Keynes UK
UKOW020334151011

180319UK00001B/22/P